MARTIN SCORSESE

INTERVIEWS

CONVERSATIONS WITH FILMMAKERS SERIES

PETER BRUNETTE, GENERAL EDITOR

MARTIN
SCORSESE

INTERVIEWS

EDITED BY PETER BRUNETTE

UNIVERSITY PRESS OF MISSISSIPPI / JACKSON

http://www.upress.state.ms.us

Copyright © 1999 by University Press of Mississippi

Manufactured in the United States of America

02 01 00 99   4 3 2 1

The paper in this book meets the guidelines for permanence and durability of the Committee on Production Guidelines for Book Longevity of the Council on Library Resources.

Insert photographs courtesy Museum of Modern Art, Film Stills Archives

Library of Congress Cataloging-in-Publication Data

Scorsese, Martin.
    Martin Scorsese : interviews / edited by Peter Brunette.
        p.   cm. — (Conversations with filmmakers series)
    Filmography: p.
    Includes index.
    ISBN 1-57806-071-0 (cloth : alk. paper). — ISBN 1-57806-072-9 (pbk. : alk. paper)
        1. Scorsese, Martin—Interviews.   2. Motion picture producers and directors—United States—Interviews.   I. Brunette, Peter.
II. Title.   III. Series.
PN1998.3.S39A5   1999
791.43'0233'092—dc21   98-28414
                                                                                      CIP

British Library Cataloging-in-Publication Data available

CONTENTS

INTRODUCTION

MARTIN SCORSESE, THE ONE-TIME enfant terrible of American
cinema, now past fifty, is regarded by many film critics and film historians
as our greatest living director. From *Mean Streets* (1973), the deeply autobiographical film that first brought him substantial notice, to the recently
released *Kundun* (1998), Scorsese has successfully managed, like perhaps no
other American filmmaker, to make artistic, personal films within the Hollywood studio system. In the interviews that follow, in which his personal
intensity, presence, and obsession with craft are always fully felt, the classic themes of both Scorsese's life and his films are sounded early on. What
is most remarkable, though, is how little these themes change over the
course of the twenty-five year span that this collection covers.

In the earliest interviews, from the early 1970's, we learn about his super-
stitiousness (more than twenty years ago he said that "I'm convinced that
I have very little time left physically"), his psychotherapy, the asthma that
has plagued him since childhood, and his many neuroses — for example,
his fear of flying — about which he speaks openly. Over and over, obsessively, he talks about the isolation of his childhood, his avoidance of all
sports, and the way in which he turned to movies as a defense mechanism.
We hear, again and again, his delivery described as staccato, incredibly
fast, nervous. We learn of the failed marriage and depressing separation
from his first child, traumas that will frequently replicate themselves, with
each set of interviews registering another divorce and more personal dis-
ruption, as the years go on. The most fascinating of these interviews turn
almost into mini-psychoanalytic sessions, and interviewers invariably call

the unpretentious director "Marty" in their written pieces. In the early 1980's, we are witness to a personal nadir, perhaps, with Scorsese's confession to *Positif* interviewer Michael Henry of his flirtation with suicide. By the time we get to the interviews done in the 1990's, however, Scorsese comes off as a much-mellowed man (if still neurotic), full of knowledge of the Bible, of art, and of the classics of literature. He has even become a wise man, perhaps, after his own fashion, a man whose analysis of Reagan-era filmmaking, say, is trenchant and deep. Discussing his relation to literature with Anthony DeCurtis in 1990, Scorsese says, "I guess I'm still cowed a little by the tyranny of art with a capital A. And there has always been the tyranny of the word over the image: anything that's written has got to be better. Most people feel it's more genuine if you express yourself in words than in pictures. And I think that's a problem in our society." In 1993, he lovingly and fascinatingly describes his attempt to convey the sensuality (of the clothes, the flowers) of the world of Edith Wharton's *The Age of Innocence,* a far cry from the mean streets of New York's Little Italy. And, as perhaps befits a man now in deep middle-age, ethical questions seem to become more important than ever.

We also see the intense loyalty to a small cadre of friends and fellow workers whom Scorsese turns to over and over again for each film, which is itself, of course, a very European practice that accords perfectly with this worshipper of European filmmaking. Depending on whom he is married to at the time, we see how intimately his wives are involved in his work— a fact which may partially explain why he has been divorced so often but which is more likely a sign of his attempt to make his loved ones part of what is, undoubtedly, his deepest passion. Inseparable is his unremitting drive to realize his personal vision, and it is surprising to see references to such pet projects as *New York, New York* and *The Last Temptation of Christ* (both deeply disappointing failures for Scorsese) mentioned so early, and so often, in the initial interviews collected in this book. By the time he turns forty, buoyed by the immense critical success of *Raging Bull,* he sensibly (though not very convincingly) says that he wants to "simplify" and begins to ask whether life is not in fact more important than work, after freely admitting that the latter had always taken precedence over any relationship. It is a balancing act, as the interviews clearly show, between ultimately irreconcilable opposites, and one that is never really resolved.

There is also the accent on the Catholic beliefs of his childhood, which apparently led him seriously to consider becoming a priest when a teenager. As the years go on, his religious references become, if anything, much more pronounced. And as with many working-class Italians, in this country as well as in Italy, Catholicism is also inextricably mixed with the Mafia. The authenticity of his life—somehow, it's taken for granted that a life lived in Little Italy, among gangsters, is more "authentic" than the impossible-to-imagine (for Scorsese at least), life in suburbia—is an important theme right from the start, and clearly lends a sense of authenticity to his films as well.

He speaks powerfully of the terrible ethnic hatreds that ruled the streets as he was growing up, and seems to enjoy startling his middle-class interviewers and, by extension, we who read his words. As he told Guy Flatley, a staff writer for the New York Times, in 1975, "Some people are shocked that these guys are running around, buying and selling hot stuff. But *I'm* not shocked—I'll buy tooth paste from them for 19 cents instead of 50 cents. Why not? It's not as if they're dealing in heroin. And don't forget, even numbers runners are hardworking guys."

So much of the texture of Scorsese's films comes from this autobiographical aspect, and this is as true of *GoodFellas* (1990) as it is of *Mean Streets* (1973). What also links these two films is Scorsese's insistence that both of them are meant to be *documentaries* of a sort, as well as dramas, artifacts that speak of what a certain type of person said, what they thought, the way they dressed and moved. Similarly, in 1993 he speaks of his adaptation of Edith Wharton's novel, *The Age of Innocence,* as "anthropology." In this film, the challenge, in Scorsese's words, was "re-creating a world even more specific in detail than *The Last Temptation of Christ.*" Again, in the 1996 interview in *Sight & Sound,* he specifies the ways in which *Casino,* his film on Las Vegas in the 1970's, was, as much as anything else, conceived as a documentary on that time and place.

We also see his early obsession with the cinema, especially for the more obscure films and the least typical, a passion that goes far beyond a mere profession or job. This will last his whole career, of course, and will find him putting obscure cinematic references in the unlikeliest of places. For example, we learn that there's a Godard reference in *Taxi Driver* and, even more astonishing, a reference to the cancer-ridden priest in Bresson's ascetic *Diary of a Country Priest* (1950) in Travis Bickle's choice of food. He says later that making *New York, New York* was such a "nightmare" experience that it signalled the end of his love affair with cinema, but it was an affair, as we see in subsequent articles, that was to be easily rekindled. In a 1987 interview, Scorsese talks for the first time about his interest in film preservation and his efforts against computer colorization, interests that continue to the present day.

Related to this is the full-blown, profoundly artistic commitment to film technique. Scorsese may in fact be one of the most technically self-aware directors who ever lived, and this comes out clearly in several of the interviews, especially those with Gavin Smith of *Film Comment,* who is obviously equally fascinated with technique. Scorsese has been committed to storyboarding all of his films since the beginning, which seems to indicate the primacy of the visual in his films, yet he has also been obsessed with such things as the precise nuances of the music he uses in every film. In his 1990 interview with Smith, Scorsese is dazzling in his description of the purpose of nearly every song on the soundtrack of *Good-Fellas,* as he is in 1996, speaking to Ian Christie about the music in *Casino.* In his discussion of *The Age of Innocence* with Smith in 1993, he displays an awareness of technique in every single shot and every single camera movement, all of which are always clearly *chosen,* that is nothing less than astounding. Despite his interest in formal elements, however, he stresses from the very first that all his films start with an acute focus on character above all. For example, in 1976, he says, speaking of the immortal character Travis Bickle from *Taxi Driver,* that "in order to bring about social change, you have to start by understanding individual characters.... The best way is to start with a character and then put him through scenes, through conflicts, that illustrate your themes.... I always start with a person, not a statement."

Again and again, it becomes clear that, as he said in 1976, the "thematic idea running through" his movies is "the outsider struggling for recognition." What's more, he freely admits that this outsider is, first and foremost, *him,* and that all his principal characters represent some kind of working out of his own personal problems and hangups and quirks. He says that he works from his dreams, and that if he did not feel as angry as Travis does in *Taxi Driver,* he wouldn't have had to make the film. *New York, New York,* we learn, despite its stylized nature, and the fact that it was set in the postwar period, was also overtly based on "myself, our relationships, our marriages." With *The King of Comedy,* the autobiographical element works in two directions. Scorsese says that Rupert Pupkin's continual rejection has its basis in the early rejections that the director had to endure as well, and that his personality stems from Scorsese's desire "to succeed at all costs," but now that he and De Niro have become better known, he says, he can also identify with the Jerry Lewis character who is plagued by people like Pupkin who want something from him. The offbeat *After Hours,* set in the New York milieu Scorsese knows so well, is also, he reveals, about another outsider, and he admits that he made the film out of the frustration he felt when Paramount cancelled his pet project, the adaptation of *The Last Temptation of Christ.*

We also learn of his improvisatory method of dealing with actors, an approach that has not altered much since the beginning of his career. Its high point is probably the famous scene in *Taxi Driver,* when De Niro stands in front of the mirror practicing his aggression, and later, the scene in *GoodFellas* when Joe Pesci goes crazy in the bar. It becomes clear in these interviews that Scorsese has a kind of intuitive relationship with his actors, especially with De Niro, and he becomes very cautious when discussing the actor's method. In fact, it becomes obvious that it is this very penchant for improvisation that created such a clash with the super-stylized sets of *New York, New York,* and that caused that film to fail so miserably. Whether it works or not, this interest in improvisation squares with the generally intuitive approach to filmmaking that Scorsese prefers, one that has stood him in such good stead in so many brilliant films. He told Richard Corliss in 1988 that "I don't enjoy shooting movies. There's too many people around, too many things to go wrong, too many personalities, and you have to be very... rational. I don't like being rational. I don't like being held back."

Included here is also a noticeable accent on collaboration, and Scorsese is always exceptionally generous in sharing credit for his successes (and blaming himself for his failures). In one interview, in fact, he makes the astonishingly modest claim that the success of *Taxi Driver* is largely due to it screenwriter, Paul Schrader, and that *Raging Bull* owes its excellence primarily to actor Robert De Niro.

The theme of his ongoing difficulties as an "auteurist" director working in the commercial world of Hollywood is sounded early as well. Even in the mid-1970's, Scorsese realizes clearly that blockbuster, crowdpleasing successes like *Jaws* and *Rocky* can only make it harder for him to continue to make his unvarnished, hyper-realistic films that show things, true things, that people would perhaps rather not see. Ironically, in "Martin Scorsese's Gamble," published in 1976, he was hoping that *New York, New York*—a film that would turn out to be his most complete, unmitigated commercial failure—would allow a way around this. It is there that he puts the question in the most direct way possible: "The question of commercialism is a source of worry. Must one make a choice, must it be a matter of either setting your sights on winning an Academy Award and becoming a millionaire, or making only the movies you want to make and starving to death?" In that same year, during the filming of *Taxi Driver,* we discover that Scorsese argued bitterly with executives from Columbia, who wanted the film to be fast and cheap, over a specific shot of Cybill Shepherd and Robert De Niro that he wanted to set against crowds passing by outside, but which would have cost more money that way. "That night, I went through a lot of crises and made a lot of phone calls. I said to a friend, 'That's it. If they don't like the way I'm gonna make the picture, then I won't make the picture.' That's when you realize that you really have to love something enough to kill it." By 1978, after *The Last Waltz,* his modest but successful documentary on the last tour of The Band, he says, with good reason, that he wants to get away from all big budget projects. But of course this will change, and the remark mostly reflects the disappointment of the moment. After *Raging Bull* came out in 1980, he was convinced that this would be the last film he would ever make in America. This thought was, naturally, tremendously anxiety-producing, because he felt he was incapable of making anything but an American film.

The biggest frustration of his entire career, though, was clearly the struggle to get *The Last Temptation of Christ* made. After the project had been cancelled the first time around, Scorsese expressed his bitterness in the 1986 interview with *American Film*. There he said, "hopefully, I can still get *The Last Temptation of Christ* made someday, but it won't be in this country, and it won't be financed by this country. At all. Forget it. That film has nothing to do with the American industry. I mean, I love Spielberg pictures. You have those wonderful little kids. But I don't think everyone should have to make them." (In the event, *The Last Temptation* was made in 1988 by an American studio, Universal, but with a minuscule budget.) In the meantime, he made the commercially successful *The Color of Money*, starring Paul Newman and Tom Cruise, as an exercise in "pure technique," as he told an interviewer in 1987. He also offers a bitter assessment of the "corruption" of the present-day audience in that same interview: "Look how corrupt they've gotten, with films like *Top Gun* and *Rocky*. They *have* been corrupted; it's a pity.... They're being shortchanged, the audience. They're going for easy emotions, and it's a pity. I really feel that." When he finally did get to make *The Last Temptation* in 1988, the film was greeted by a howl of protest from the religious right. In 1989 he says that what frightens him is that films like *Rocky*, with their happy endings, have forced out the more realistic films that he wants to make. "On the worst side, they're sentimental. Lies. That's the problem. And where I fit in there, I don't know.... It's very hard for me to do the uplifting, transcendental sentimentalism of most films, because it's just not true. And it's not because I'm this great prophet of truth—it's just like embarrassing to do it on the set. How would you stage the scene? What would you tell the actors?" Nevertheless, by 1992, a more mature Scorsese seems to have made his psychological peace with Hollywood, even if the financial problems continue, when he says "the artists coming out of America in film come from Hollywood. The Hollywood film. And I'm proud to be associated with Hollywood because of that.... I'm still a Hollywood director, and I'm always proud to be considered that by the rest of the world."

Another highly charged question that is put to him from the earliest interviews is the question of violence, and he is remarkably honest and straightforward in his answers. In 1976, he says that "violence has always been a pretty scary thing for me, but I'm fascinated by it, especially by the aimlessness of it. It's always erupting when you don't expect it." In a different interview that same year he said that the violence "has got to be plain, straight, and fast, and awkward, awkward and stupid-looking, just the way it would happen in real life." When asked why people always bleed from the neck in his movies, Scorsese scandalously responds: "To me, I like the idea of spurting blood, it's ... really like a purification, you know, the fountains of blood ... but it's realistic, all realistic. That's my own head, you know... I like the idea of getting shot." Clearly, these are not films for the squeamish.

By the time of the 1992 interview published in *South Atlantic Quarterly,* though, Scorsese is clearly much more reflective on the subject. Comparing the infamous ending of *Taxi Driver* with Sam Peckinpah's ultra-violent *The Wild Bunch,* Scorsese says that "you can't stop people from getting an exhilaration from violence, because that's human." Yet he insists that the audience's exhilaration is produced by more than the violence: "[It] is also in the creation of that scene in the editing, in the camera moves, in the use of music and the use of sound effects, and in the movement within the frame of the characters. So it's like ... *art*—good art, bad art, or indifferent, whatever the hell you want to say it is, it's still art. And that's where the exhilaration comes in." He does admit to a certain queasiness as to how the end of *Taxi Driver* has been taken, and continues the analogy: "As much as I love the shoot-'em-out at the end of *The Wild Bunch,* I wouldn't put it on for fun. If you put it on for fun, that's something else. That's a whole other morbid area."

Counterbalancing what might be for some this unwholesome fascination with violence is the extent to which films like *Taxi Driver, Casino, The King of Comedy,* and a host of others ultimately move beyond this conflicted sphere to become perspicacious sociopolitical commentaries on American life and institutions. In one interview, for example, we refreshingly learn that in Scorsese's mind, *Mean Streets* was clearly intended to be a *political* document as much as anything else, a direct conflation of the methods of the Mafia with the methods of an all-powerful government newly extricated from the horrors of Vietnam.

One of the great pleasures of reading this collection of interviews straight through, I think, is precisely the wonderful sense the reader gets of the evolution of a deeply emotional, intuitive young man into a thoughtful, wise one who nevertheless manages to bring his passion with him, intact, through the years.

Conforming to the policy of the University Press of Mississippi in regard to its interview series, the interviews collected in this book have not been edited in any significant way. While this may result in some repetition in Scorsese's remarks, it does offer more integrity for the scholarly reader. More importantly, these repetitions, marks of the director's private demons and obsessions, are themselves never less than revealing.

CHRONOLOGY

1942	Born November 17, 1942 in Flushing, New York, to Catherine and Charles Scorsese.
1964	Graduates from New York University as a film major.
1972	Makes *Boxcar Bertha* for B-movie producer Roger Corman.
1973	The release of *Mean Streets,* starring Harvey Keitel and Robert De Niro, Scorsese's first important film.
1974	*Alice Doesn't Live Here Anymore,* for which its lead, Ellen Burstyn, wins an Academy Award for Best Actress.
1976	*Taxi Driver* is released.
1977	The release of the ill-fated musical, *New York, New York.*
1978	*The Last Waltz,* Scorsese's documentary on the final concert tour of The Band.
1980	*Raging Bull,* which wins a Best Acting Oscar for Robert De Niro and an Oscar for Editing for Thelma Schoonmaker.
1981	John Hinckley tries to assassinate President Ronald Reagan in order to impress Jodie Foster, whom he has become obsessed with from watching *Taxi Driver.*
1983	*The King of Comedy* appears, starring Robert De Niro, once again, and Jerry Lewis.

1985   *After Hours,* a darkly comic tale, is released.

1986   *The Color of Money,* starring Paul Newman and Tom Cruise, opens. It is Scorsese's most overtly commercial movie.

1988   With the release of *The Last Temptation of Christ,* Scorsese brings the wrath of the religious right down on his head.

1990   *GoodFellas,* his second film about the Mafia, appears.

1991   Scorsese's remake of the classic *Cape Fear* is released.

1993   The appearance of *The Age of Innocence,* an adaptation of Edith Wharton's novel set in turn-of-the-century New York society.

1995   *Casino,* Scorsese's second return to Mafia themes, is released.

1997   Scorsese receives the American Film Institute's Life Achievement Award.

1998   *Kundun,* Scorsese's film biography of the Dalai Lama, appears, but is not commercially successful.

FILMOGRAPHY

1963
WHAT'S A NICE GIRL LIKE YOU DOING IN A PLACE LIKE THIS?
Director/writer: **Scorsese**
Music: Richard H. Coll
Cast: Zeph Michaelis, Mimi Stark, Sarah Braveman, Fred Sica, Robert Uricola
16mm, B&W
9 minutes

1964
IT'S NOT JUST YOU, MURRAY
Director: **Scorsese**
Screenplay: **Scorsese** and Mardik Martin
Cinematography: Richard H. Coll
Production Design: Lancelot Braithwaite
Music: Richard H. Coll
Editing: Eli F. Bleich
Cast: Ira Rubin, Sam DeFazio, Andrea Martin, Catherine Scorsese, Robert Uricola, Bernard Weisberger, Victor Magnotta, Richard Sweeton, John Bivona
16mm, B&W; blown-up to 35mm
15 minutes

1967
THE BIG SHAVE
Director/writer: **Scorsese**

Cinematography: Ares Demertzis
Special Effects: Eli F. Bleich
Cast: Peter Bernuth
16mm, color
6 minutes

1969
WHO'S THAT KNOCKING ON MY DOOR?
Director/writer: **Scorsese**
Producers: Joseph Weill, Betzi and Haig Manoogian
Cinematography: Michael Wadleigh (Wadley), Richard H. Coll, Max Fisher
Art Direction: Victor Magnotta
Editing: Thelma Schoonmaker
Cast: Zina Bethune (the young girl), Harvey Keitel (J. R.), Lennard Kuras
(Joey), Michael Scala (Sally Gaga), Harry Northrup (Harry), Bill Minkin (Iggy),
Phil Carlson (the guide), Wendy Russell (Gaga's small friend), Robert Uricola
(the armed young man), Susan Wood (Susan), Marissa Joffrey (Rosie),
Catherine Scorsese (J. R.'s mother), Victor Magnotta and Paul DeBionde
(waiters), **Scorsese** (gangster)
(First version, 1965, BRING ON THE DANCING GIRLS; second version, 1967,
I CALL FIRST; in 1970, also released under the title J. R.)
35mm, color
90 minutes

1972
BOXCAR BERTHA
American International Pictures
Producer: Roger Corman
Director: **Scorsese**
Screenplay: Joyce H. Corrington and John William Corrington, based on
characters from *Sister of the Road* by Boxcar Bertha Thompson as told to
Dr. Ben L. Reitman
Cinematography: John Stephens (Gayne Rescher, uncredited)
Production Design: David Nichols
Music: Gib Builbeau, Thad Maxwell
Editing: Buzz Feitshans (**Scorsese**, uncredited)
Cast: Barbara Hershey (Bertha), David Carradine (Bill Shelley), Barry Primus
(Rake Brown), Bernie Casey (Von Morton), John Carradine (H. Buckram

Sartoris), Victor Argo and David Osterhout (the McIvers), Grahame Pratt
(Emeric Pressburger), "Chicken" Holleman (Michael Powell), Harry Northrup
(Harvey Hall), Ann Morell (Tillie), Marianne Dole (Mrs. Mailer), Joe Reynolds
(Joe), Gayne Rescher and **Scorsese** (brothel clients)
35mm, color
93 minutes

1973
MEAN STREETS
Warner Brothers
Executive Producer: E. Lee Perry
Producer: Jonathan T. Taplin
Director: **Scorsese**
Screenplay: **Scorsese** and Mardik Martin, from a story by **Scorsese**
Cinematography: Kent Wakeford
Editing: Sid Levin
Cast: Robert De Niro (Johnny Boy), Harvey Keitel (Charlie), David Proval
(Tony), Amy Robinson (Teresa), Richard Romanus (Michael), Cesare
Danova (Giovanni), Victor Argo (Mario), George Memmoli (Joey Catucci),
Lenny Scaletta (Jimmy), Jeannie Bell (Diane), David Carradine (drunk),
Robert Carradine (young assassin), Lois Walden (Jewish girl), Harry
Northrup (Vietnam veteran), Dino Seragusa (old man), D'Mitch Davis
(black cop), Peter Fain (George), Julie Andelman (girl at party), Robert
Wilder (Benton), Ken Sinclair (Sammy), Catherine Scorsese (woman on
landing), **Scorsese** (Shorty, the killer in the car)
35mm, color
110 minutes

1974
ALICE DOESN'T LIVE HERE ANYMORE
Warner Brothers
Producers: David Susskind and Audrey Maas
Director: **Scorsese**
Screenplay: Robert Getchell
Cinematography: Kent Wakeford
Production Design: Toby Carr Rafelson
Editing: Marcia Lucas
Music: Richard LaSalle

Cast: Ellen Burstyn (Alice Hyatt), Kris Kristofferson (David), Harvey Keitel (Ben), Alfred Lutter (Tommy), Jodie Foster (Audrey), Billy Green Bush (Donald), Lane Bradbury (Rita), Diane Ladd (Flo), Lelia Goldoni (Bea), Vic Tayback (Mel), Valerie Curtin (Vera), Murray Moston (Jacobs), Harry Northup (Joe and Jim's bartender), Mia Bendixsen (Alice aged 8), Ola Moore (old woman), Martin Brinton (Lenny), Dean Casper (Chicken), Henry M. Kendrick (shop assistant), **Scorsese** and Larry Cohen (diners at Mel and Ruby's), Mardik Martin (customer in club during audition)
35mm, color
III minutes

1974
ITALIANAMERICAN (documentary)
National Communications Foundation
Producers: Elaine Attias, Saul Rubin
Director: **Scorsese**
Written by: Lawrence D. Cohen, Mardik Martin, **Scorsese**
Cinematography: Alec Hirschfeld
Editing: Bert Lovitt
35mm, color
48 minutes

1976
TAXI DRIVER
Columbia
Producers: Michael and Julia Phillips
Director: **Scorsese**
Screenplay: Paul Schrader
Cinematography: Michael Chapman
Art Direction: Charles Rosen
Editing: Marcia Lucas, Tom Rolf, Melvin Shapiro
Music: Bernard Herrmann
Cast: Robert De Niro (Travis Bickle), Cybill Shepherd (Betsy), Jodie Foster (Iris), Harvey Keitel (Sport), Peter Boyle (Wizard), Albert Brooks (Tom), Leonard Harris (Charles Palantine), **Scorsese** (passenger watching silhouette)
35mm, color
II2 minutes

1977
NEW YORK, NEW YORK
United Artists
Producers: Irwin Winkler and Robert Chartoff
Director: **Scorsese**
Screenplay: Earl Mac Rauch, Mardik Martin, from a story by Rauch
Cinematography: Laszlo Kovacs
Production Design: Boris Leven
Editing: Irving Lerner, Marcia Lucas, Tom Rolf, B. Lovitt
Original Songs: John Kander and Fred Ebb
Saxophone Solos and Consultant: Georgie Auld
Musical Supervisor: Ralph Burns
Choreography: Ron Field
Costumes: Theadora van Runkle
Cast: Liza Minnelli (Francine Evans), Robert De Niro (Jimmy Doyle), Lionel
Stander (Tony Harwell), Barry Primus (Paul Wilson), Mary Kay Place (Bernice), Georgie Auld (Frankie Harte), George Memmoli (Nicky), Dick Miller
(Palm Club owner)
35mm, color
137 minutes

1978
THE LAST WALTZ
United Artists
Producer: Robbie Robertson
Executive Producer: Jonathan Taplin
Director/Interviewer: **Scorsese**
Cinematography: Michael Chapman, Laszlo Kovacs, Vilmos Zsigmond,
David Myers, Bobby Byrne, Michael Watkins, Hiro Narita
Production Design: Boris Leven
Editing: Yeu-Bun Yee, Jan Roblee
Concert Producer: Bill Graham
Music Editing: Ken Wannberg
Treatment and Creative Consulting: Mardik Martin
Performers in Order of Appearance: Ronnie Hawkins, Dr. John, Neil Young,
The Staples, Neil Diamond, Joni Mitchell, Paul Butterfield, Muddy Waters, Eric
Clapton, Emmylou Harris, Van Morrison, Bob Dylan, Ringo Starr, Ron Wood

The Band: Rick Danko (bass, violin, vocal), Levon Helm (drums, mandolin, vocal), Garth Hudson (organ, accordion, saxophone, synthesizers), Richard Manuel (piano, keyboards, drums, vocal), Robbie Robertson (lead guitar, vocal)
35mm, color
119 minutes

1978
AMERICAN BOY: A PROFILE OF STEVEN PRINCE (documentary)
Producers: Bert Lovitt, Jim Wheat, Ken Wheat
Director: **Scorsese**
Cinematography: Michael Chapman
Editing: Amy Jones, Bert Lovitt
Original Music: Neil Young
Cast (in order of appearance): Julia Cameron, Mardik Martin, Kathi McGinnis, George Memmoli, Steven Prince, **Scorsese**
35mm, Color
55 minutes

1980
RAGING BULL
United Artists
Producers: Robert Chartoff and Irwin Winkler
Director: **Scorsese**
Screenplay: Paul Schrader and Mardik Martin, based upon *Raging Bull* by Jake La Motta, with Joseph Carter and Peter Savage
Cinematography: Michael Chapman
Production Design: Gene Rudolph
Editing: Thelma Schoonmaker
Music: Pietro Mascagni
Cast: Robert De Niro (Jake La Motta), Joe Pesci (Joey), Cathy Moriarity (Vickie), Frank Vincent (Salvy), Nicholas Colosanto (Tommy Como), Mario Gallo (Mario), Frank Adonis (Patsy), Joseph Bono (Guido), Frank Topham (Toppy), **Scorsese** (man in dressing room)
35mm, B & W
128 minutes

1982
THE KING OF COMEDY
Twentieth-Century Fox
Producer: Arnon Milchan (Embassy International Pictures)
Director: **Scorsese**
Cinematography: Fred Schuler
Production Design: Boris Leven
Editing: Thelma Schoonmaker
Music: Robbie Robertson
Cast: Robert De Niro (Rupert Pupkin), Jerry Lewis (Jerry Langford), Sandra Bernhard (Masha), Diahnne Abbott (Rita), Shelley Hack (Cathy Long), Catherine Scorsese (Rupert's mother), Cathy Scorsese (Dolores)
35mm, Color
109 minutes

1985
AFTER HOURS
Warner Brothers
Producers: Amy Robinson, Griffin Dunne, Robert F. Colesberry (Geffen Company)
Director: **Scorsese**
Screenplay: Joseph Minton
Cinematography: Michael Ballhaus
Production Design: Jeffrey Townsend
Editing: Thelma Schoonmaker
Music: Howard Shore
Cast: Griffin Dunne (Paul Hackett), Rosanna Arquette (Marcy), Verna Bloom (June), Teri Garr (Julie), John Heard (Tom), Linda Fiorentino (Kiki)
35mm, Color
97 minutes

1986
THE COLOR OF MONEY
Touchstone Pictures
Producers: Irving Axelrad and Barbara De Fina
Director: **Scorsese**

Screenplay: Richard Price, based on the novel by Walter Tevis
Cinematography: Michael Ballhaus
Production Design: Boris Leven
Editing: Thelma Schoonmaker
Music: Robbie Robertson
Cast: Paul Newman (Eddie), Tom Cruise (Vincent), Mary Elizabeth Mas-
trantonio (Carmen), Helen Shaver (Janelle), John Turturro (Julien), Forest
Whitaker (Amos)
35mm, Color
117 minutes

1988
THE LAST TEMPTATION OF CHRIST
Universal Pictures
Producers: Barbara De Fina and Harry J. Ufland
Director: **Scorsese**
Screenplay: Paul Schrader, based on the novel by Nikos Kazantzakis; Jay
Cocks (2 scenes, uncredited); **Scorsese** (2 scenes, uncredited)
Cinematography: Michael Ballhaus
Production Design: John Beard
Costumes: Jean-Pierre Delifer
Editing: Thelma Schoonmaker
Music: Peter Gabriel
Cast: Willem Dafoe (Jesus), Harvey Keitel (Judas), Verna Bloom (Mary,
Mother of Jesus), Barbara Hershey (Mary Magdalene), Gary Basaraba (the
Apostle Andrew), Victor Argo (the Apostle Peter), Michael Been (the
Apostle John), Paul Herman (the Apostle Phillip), John Lurie (the Apostle
James), Leo Burmester (the Apostle Nathaniel), Andre Gregory (John the
Baptist), Peggy Gormley (Martha), Randy Danson (Mary), Harry Dean
Stanton (Saul/Paul)
35mm, Color
164 minutes

1989
NEW YORK STORIES (SEGMENT ONE, "LIFE LESSONS")
Touchstone Pictures
Producer: Barbara De Fina

Director: **Scorsese;** other segments directed by Woody Allen ("Oedipus Wrecks") and Francis Coppola ("Life without Zoe")
Screenplay: Richard Price
Cinematography: Nestor Almendros
Production Design: Kristi Zea
Costumes: John A. Dunn
Editing: Thelma Schoonmaker
Music: Carmine Coppola, August Darnell
Cast: Nick Nolte (Lionel Dobie), Rosanna Arquette (Paulette), Richard Price (Artist at Opening), **Scorsese** (Man Having Picture Taken with Lionel Dobie)
35mm, Color
120 minutes (entire film)

1990
GOODFELLAS
Warner Brothers
Producers: Barbara De Fina, Bruce S. Pustin, Irwin Winkler
Director: **Scorsese**
Screenplay: Nicholas Pileggi and **Scorsese**, from Pileggi's novel *Wiseguy*
Cinematography: Michael Ballhaus
Production Design: Kristi Zea
Costumes: Richard Bruno
Editing: Thelma Schoonmaker
Cast: Ray Liotta (Henry Hill), Robert De Niro (James Conway), Joe Pesci (Tommy De Vito), Lorraine Bracco (Karen Hill), Paul Sorvino (Paul Cicero), Frank Sivero (Frankie Carbone), Tony Darrow (Sonny Bunz), Catherine Scorsese (Tommy's mother)
35mm, Color
146 minutes

1991
CAPE FEAR
Tribeca Productions, Cappa Films, Amblin Entertainment, Universal Pictures
Producers: Barbara De Fina, Kathleen Kennedy, Frank Marshall, Steven Spielberg (uncredited)
Director: **Scorsese**

Screenplay: Wesley Strick, based on the novel by John D. MacDonald and the 1962 screenplay by James R. Webb
Cinematography: Freddie Francis
Production Design: Henry Bumstead
Costumes: Rita Ryack
Editing: Thelma Schoonmaker
Music: Elmer Bernstein, adapted and arranged from the music for the 1962 *Cape Fear* by Bernard Herrmann
Cast: Robert De Niro (Max Cady), Nick Nolte (Sam Bowden), Jessica Lange (Leigh Bowden), Juliette Lewis (Danielle Bowden), Joe Don Baker (Claude Kersek), Robert Mitchum (Lieutenant Elgart), Gregory Peck (Lee Heller), Martin Balsam (judge), Illeana Douglas (Lori Davis), Fred Thompson (Tom Broadbent)
35mm, Color
128 minutes

1993
THE AGE OF INNOCENCE
Columbia Pictures
Producers: Barbara De Fina, Bruce S. Pustin, Joseph P. Reidy
Director: **Scorsese**
Screenplay: Jay Cocks and **Scorsese,** from the novel by Edith Wharton
Cinematography: Michael Ballhaus
Production Design: Dante Ferretti
Costumes: Gabriella Pescucci
Editing: Thelma Schoonmaker
Music: Elmer Bernstein
Cast: Daniel Day-Lewis (Newland Archer), Michelle Pfeiffer (Ellen Olenska), Winona Ryder (May Welland), Richard E. Grant (Larry Lefferts), Alec McCowen (Sillerton Jackson), Geraldine Chaplin (Mrs. Welland), Mary Beth Hurt (Regina Beaufort), Stuart Wilson (Julius Beaufort), Joanne Woodward (narrator), **Scorsese** (photographer)
35mm, Color
139 minutes

1995
CASINO
De Fina-Cappa, Syalis D.A. & Legende Enterprises, Universal Pictures
Producers: Barbara De Fina, Joseph P. Reidy

Director: **Scorsese**
Screenplay: Nicholas Pileggi and **Scorsese,** based on Pileggi's book *Casino: Love and Honor in Las Vegas*
Cinematography: Robert Richardson
Production Design: Dante Ferretti
Costumes: John A. Dunn, Rita Ryack
Editing: Thelma Schoonmaker
Cast: Robert De Niro (Sam "Ace" Rothstein), Sharon Stone (Ginger McKenna), Joe Pesci (Nicky Santoro), James Woods (Lester Diamond), Don Rickles (Billy Sherbert), Alan King (Andy Stone), Kevin Pollak (Phillip Green), Dick Smothers (Senator)
35mm, Color
177 minutes

1998
KUNDUN
Walt Disney Productions, Refuge Productions, De Fina-Cappa, Touchstone Pictures
Producers: Barbara De Fina, Laura Fattori, Scott Harris, Melissa Mathison
Director: **Scorsese**
Screenplay: Melissa Mathison
Cinematography: Roger Deakins
Production Design: Dante Ferretti
Costumes: Dante Ferretti
Editing: Thelma Schoonmaker
Music: Philip Glass
Cast: Tenzin Thuthob Tsarong (Dalai Lama, adult), Gyurme Tethong (Dalai Lama, aged 10), Tulku Jamyang Kunga Tenzin (Dalai Lama, aged 5), Tenzin Yeshi Paichang (Dalai Lama, aged 2), Tencho Gyalpo (Dalai Lama's mother), Tsewang Migyur Khangsar (Dalai Lama's father), Geshi Yeshi Gyatso (Lama of Sera), Sonam Phuntsok (Reting Rimpoche), Lobsang Samten (Master of the Kitchen), Gyatso Lukhang (Lord Chamberlain), Jigme Tsarong (Taktra Rimpoche), Tenzin Trinley (Ling Rimpoche), Robert Lin (Chairman Mao)
35mm, Color
134 minutes

MARTIN SCORSESE

INTERVIEWS

He Has Often Walked *Mean Streets*

GUY FLATLEY/1973

MARTIN SCORSESE SAID GOODBYE TO God a long time ago. But you'd have a devil of a time selling that story to the stewardesses on the plane that recently carried him here from his home in Hollywood.

"Every time I get on an airplane," Scorsese admits, "I know I'm not really an atheist. 'Oh God, dear God,' I say the minute the plane takes off, 'I'm sorry for all my sins, please don't let this plane crash.' And I keep pray- ing—*out loud*—until the plane lands."

Now that the plane has landed and God is dead again, the short, intense Italian-American is free to sit in the placid safety of his Pierre suite and pur- sue the one subject which, for him, truly smacks of divinity. That subject is movies—from Griffith's *Broken Blossoms* to Rossellini's *Stromboli* to Fuller's *I Shot Jesse James* to Scorsese's *Alice Doesn't Live Here Anymore*.

Scorsese's *who*? *Alice Doesn't Live Here Anymore* is the 31-year-old director's new movie, one which will star Ellen Burstyn as a would-be nightclub singer who makes a wild and woolly adjustment to widowhood. In fact, Scorsese has scurried to New York for the sole purpose of scouting up suitable suit- ors for the freshly liberated lady. One of Alice's more ardent admirers—a gentle-seeming bachelor who turns out to be a married maniac—has already been cast, however. That sickee will be played by Harvey Keitel, who scored in Scorsese's 1969 film, *Who's That Knocking at My Door?*, and in *Mean Streets*.

Mean Streets, of course, is the Scorsese sleeper which shook up the critics when it unspooled at the recent New York Film Festival and which is now serving the customers at Cinema I a gut-raw, yet strangely operatic, slice of life among the small-time thugs and spiritual misfits of New York's Little Italy.

Cinema for the squeamish it isn't. Cars screech, guns blast, women wail, men vomit, fists pound with speed and fury. And we sense the futility, we know that all those dumb, pathetic figures parading defiantly across the screen are doomed by the violence in and around them. We know exactly how far Charlie, a young and dangerously softhearted hood, will get in his frantic effort to protect Johnny Boy, his mush-brained buddy, from vengeful assassins.

Yet, in the end, we are jolted when—together with Charlie's epileptic girlfriend Teresa—they are bloodily ambushed trying to escape across the Brooklyn Bridge. (The half-pint, dark-eyed Sicilian who pulls the trigger is played by Scorsese himself—a bit of self-casting which may have proved meaningful to Dr. Robert Kahn, Scorsese's California analyst, whose therapeutic talents are gratefully acknowledged in the film's closing credits.)

Mean Streets may not be pretty, but—according to its maker—it is true to ghetto life. The character of Charlie, with his priest-spawned feelings of guilt, is based partly on Scorsese himself and partly on a close friend who still lives in Little Italy. The wild and vulnerable Johnny Boy, too, is real—though, like Scorsese, he has fled far, far from his native turf. Were it not for Scorsese's insatiable appetite for movies, however, it is conceivable that he would be dwelling today down on Elizabeth Street, where his parents were born and still live and where he himself grew up—a frail, asthmatic boy doing his best to keep pace with one of Little Italy's more rambunctious gangs.

Unlike Charlie in *Mean Streets,* Scorsese managed to remain on the straight side of the law. "We weren't *that* kind of gang. There was a lot of horsing around, but we seldom got into real fights. We were more into the social thing, hanging out in bars, picking up girls. By the time my friends and I were 12 or 13, we were drinking an awful lot of hard liquor."

What about hard drugs? "Never. We didn't even smoke pot. We thought it was as bad to use drugs as it was to sell them. I still feel that way, although

I do try a little grass now and then. But I can't really smoke, because of my asthma. But never the hard stuff. That was the major point of accuracy in *The Godfather*. The mafia looks down on pimps and drugs."

One or two critics looked down on *Mean Streets,* calling it a low-budget copy of Francis Ford Coppola's monumental look at the mafia. "Mardik Martin and I wrote the screenplay for *Mean Streets* seven years ago, so we could hardly have been influenced by *The Godfather.* We weren't trying to do the same sort of thing at all. Francis Coppola made an epic Hollywood picture, an old-fashioned movie—in the good sense—like *Gone With the Wind,* only better."

Nor were those Corleone kids noticeably churned-up by memories of their Catholic boyhoods. Scorsese, on the other hand—like the scrupulous protagonist of *Mean Streets*—did not take church dogma and liturgy lightly. "My friends used to say, 'Jeeze, Marty, do you really *believe* all that stuff the priests tell you?' Well, I did believe it, every word of it. I wouldn't touch meat on Friday, and I believed I would go to hell if I missed Mass on Sunday. As a matter of fact, I went into the seminary after grade school, but they threw me out at the end of my first year for roughhousing during prayers. They thought I was a thug."

Scorsese was crushed, but he managed to thug and chug his way through Cardinal Hayes High School in the Bronx, still cherishing the dream of one day becoming a priest, a dream he continued to dream at NYU—until the day he stumbled upon the film department. "I was bitten, and the whole vocation thing shifted."

It shifted so drastically that Scorsese was soon turning out stunning student films and, eventually, he taught a course in filmmaking at NYU. During the sixties, he also worked as a news editor at CBS, shot commercials and served as supervising editor on *Woodstock*. Finally, in 1968, he wrote and directed his first feature, *Who's That Knocking at My Door?* Like *Mean Streets,* Scorsese's maiden movie probed the psyche of a sensitive young Italian-American drifter, an emotional cripple whose relationships were poisoned by prejudice.

"It's the ghetto that creates prejudice," Scorsese says. "I can remember when I was 5 and my brother was 12, we were walking down the street one day and suddenly we saw a big crowd of people. They were standing around a man who had fallen, and his head was bleeding. My brother took a look at him, and then he turned to me and said, 'Oh, he's only a Jew.' And that is one of my earliest memories.

"We hated the Irish, too, because of the Fifth Precinct. It was unheard of for any of us to call a cop, unless it was to give him some graft. Cops were always Irish, always drinking, and always had their hands out. We used to bribe them so we could play stickball in the street. It's still that way—believe me, Serpico only skimmed the surface."

Is it possible that *Mean Streets* overstresses the seamy side of life in Little Italy? There must be some decent, hardworking people living there. "Sure—the majority of the people in Little Italy are decent, hardworking people. My parents are over 65 and they're *still* decent, hardworking people. My mother worked in the garment center for over 30 years, and because there was some switch in management, she's no longer eligible for retirement benefits. Now she's going around to job interviews.

"But there is also this milieu of young turks. Some people are shocked that these guys are running around, buying and selling hot stuff. But *I'm* not shocked—I'll buy tooth paste from them for 19 cents instead of 50 cents. Why not? It's not as if they're dealing in heroin. And don't forget, even numbers runners are hardworking guys."

Scorsese never sold hot tooth paste and he never ran numbers. What he did was he went to NYU, found himself a nice girl who was part Irish and part Jewish, and he settled down to a life of domestic bliss. But the bliss was brief and his former wife now lives in New Jersey with her second husband, and with Scorsese's 8-year-old daughter Catherine.

"In a way, I guess my marriage was a form of rebellion. Up to that time, I had been dating a Sicilian girl and, to this day, that girl is very close to my parents. I got married in Saint Patrick's Cathedral in 1965, and I left the church not long after that. There were problems about mortal sin, certain sexual things. But what *really* did it was sitting in a church in Los Angeles and hearing a priest call the Vietnam war a holy war."

Scorsese's own sense of rage over Vietnam was eloquently reflected in *Street Scenes 1970*, his documentary about antiwar protesters. Yet he feels that *Mean Streets* is by far his most political film. "*Mean Streets* shows that organized crime is similar to big government. They're both machines. In the Sicilian culture, we learned never to expect much from the government, having been trod upon by one government or another for some 2,000 years. That is why the *family* is the unit we always look to for strength.

"Still, that does not mean that I should sit back without making a protest. There has been more underhanded stuff done in Washington than we'll ever be able to fathom. It's almost been worth two terms of Nixon to find out just how things work. Peter Boyle caught on to *Mean Streets*. We were at a party in Hollywood recently, both of us drinking a lot, and he came up and grabbed me by the arm and said, 'Hey, you really slipped it in under them, didn't you? No sermon, nothing. You just showed them that our whole way of life in this country has been leading to one place and one place only—Watergate.' "

But there is more to life than politics and movies, which is where pretty Sandra Weintraub comes in. "Sandy will be working very closely with me on *Alice Doesn't Live Here Anymore*. She's actually like an associate producer—she starts at the very beginning of a film, discussing dialogue with me and making suggestions for casting. It was Sandy who suggested David Carradine—whom I had directed last year in *Boxcar Bertha*—for the small role of the man who gets murdered in the bar in *Mean Streets*. People say I'm giving Sandy a job because she's my girlfriend but the fact is she *understands* film—she even did some of the editing on *Mean Streets*—and when you find somebody like that, you should hang on to her."

Sounds like a match made in movie heaven. Is there any chance they'll come down to earth long enough to tie the knot? "I'm not sure. What's the difference, anyway? If you're with a girl for two or three years, you *are* married. Of course, it might be different if we wanted children. Sometimes I think it would be nice to have kids, but not in this business. This is such an ego-oriented profession; you deal with yourself first."

In truth, Scorsese's ego does not obscure the love he feels for his daughter; he is obviously troubled by their separation. "She lives with her mother and stepfather, she goes to a good private school, and she is happy. The best I can do is pay for her education, and now—since *Mean Streets*—that's easier to do. I've seen her more this past year than before . . . but it's a whole new thing for her, getting used to me. My wife and I broke up when Catherine was 3 or 4. We've got to get to know each other. It would be good to have her with me for a month or so.

"Catherine has been into film since she was 5, when I took her into a cutting room and let her operate the movieola," Scorsese says with fatherly pride. "She knows all about freeze frames, and she even knows films by their directors. 'I want to see a Dick Fleischer film,' she'll say. Her favorite movie right now is *The Poseidon Adventure*. When she told me that, I said, 'What? You're no daughter of *mine*!'

"She came to see *Mean Streets* at the Film Festival. Her stepfather brought her, and I had to get a telephone book for her to sit on. It was a funny thing—she was delighted with the festival itself, the atmosphere of Lincoln Center and all that, but the movie seemed to bewilder her. I don't think she could follow the story, with everything happening so quickly. Afterward, she was tongue-tied, sort of embarrassed."

Scorsese himself seems momentarily tongue-tied. "You know," he say finally, "the only thing she could think to say was, 'How did you ever get all that *blood* to work?'"

Dialogue on Film: Martin Scorsese

THE AMERICAN FILM INSTITUTE/1975

JAMES POWERS: *O.K. ladies and gentlemen, in violation of all fire laws, I welcome you to this crowded seminar. You've just finished seeing Mr. Scorsese's work and I won't intrude myself any further between you and him. Questions anybody?*

QUESTION: *Why did you choose to move the camera so much in* Alice Doesn't Live Here Anymore?

MARTIN SCORSESE: There are a lot of reasons for that. First, and it's really an intellectual reason I'm giving you now—it doesn't mean anything to you, watching the picture, it's just something for me, that's all. The intellectual reason is that I was trying to capture a number of characters who were really very much in a state of confusion and never really settling. So the camera is always kind of shifting around, moving around, slightly sliding. Whenever it seems to stop, it starts all over on the other side again. When it does stop, they are usually in scenes of stability, like in the bathroom scene between Ellen Burstyn and Diane Ladd. And in the scene where she has just made love to Kris Kristofferson—the two of them talking—it's basically a medium shot on her with Kris in the frame, a medium shot of her with Kris in the foreground or a medium shot of him with her in the foreground, so the two are together in the frame. The camera only moves twice in that scene—when she gets up to demonstrate what she used to do as a kid, the camera moves this way (motioning) and

---

Reprinted by permission of The American Film Institute.

when she comes back to sit on his lap, the camera moves in, just the way she's moving in, on him.

Q: *In other words, you move the camera essentially because the character moves the camera?*
M S: Oh, no, no. It has nothing to do—sometimes the camera moves because the person moves, so you move it. But other than that, in this case, the camera moved when she got up to move. I could have just panned but it was an actual track. It has a different meaning for me. The other thing is I like a moving camera.

Q: *You didn't move the camera much in* The Big Shave *either. Why was that?*
M S: *The Big Shave*—you couldn't move too much in that room. That was all clips like a TV commercial. In *Mean Streets,* it was the same thing, the guys talking at the table, the sliding, sinister feeling to it. In *Boxcar Bertha,* when Barry Primus was trying to pull a fast one with the cards so he's kind of smiling sleazily, the camera's kind of sleazy, sliding against the edge of the table. That's where it really started, in *Boxcar.* What I was looking for was to give a kind of psychologically unstable feeling to the audience with those characters at those moments. You just don't feel quite settled watching those scenes. That sequence in *Alice* where Ben breaks into the room— now, if you notice, that sequence begins with Alice talking to her young boy, Tommy, and he says, "Are you coming home late again tonight?" That scene could have been shot simple two-shot, close-up to close-up, but I did it hand-held and went around this way and in that sense it was a premonition of violence because the camera is kind of violent, seemingly for no reason. But if you go back and look at it—and the whole picture is like that—I mean, we did it that way. Sometimes I was in rooms where I couldn't avoid it; I had to use a hand-held camera. The room was the size of this couch so I had to move the camera by hand, whereas many times I had planned it to be moved by dolly. Like in the scene in *Alice* where they go pick up the kids in the police station, the whole thing was laid out in dolly, all in one take. It is in one take now, only it's hand-held. People think I did it hand-held to give it documentary, quote, unquote, feeling, the old phony black-and-white realism, because in the late '40s, it was all grainy black-and-white and it gave you the impression of something being realistic. But in this case that was definitely not the reason. The reason was

because I had a welfare worker and I had to get rid of the kid. We couldn't dolly to the point where now we get the measurements here, focus, now you move over here, get the measurements here, they have to hit each mark. This way, we did it hand-held with a 16mm lens on an Arri BL and everything was in focus and I could shoot the scene fast and get the hell out of there. That's a pain in the neck. I would have liked to have done it with a dolly. This scene was all laid out nicely.

Q : *Did you rehearse* Alice*? How did you rehearse it?*
M S : *Alice* was rehearsed. *Alice* has more rehearsal and improvisation than *Mean Streets* had. The reason was—Ellen asked me to do the picture for her. She got the script through David Susskind and Francis Coppola told her to, you know, she was looking for young filmmakers and Francis said, "Take a look at *Mean Streets*." *Mean Streets* hadn't opened yet and Warner Brothers had just bought it. She looked at it and liked it. Sandy Weintraub read the script for me and she said, "This is one of the few scripts that have any interesting characters in them so you'd better take a look at it." Because we were getting hit with scripts that dealt with similar worlds to *Mean Streets*. The reason I'm going all the way back is because it's very complicated—you can't just say how much rehearsal we had on that picture because it's really a crazy thing. Anyway, the point is that what happened with *Alice* was that we started working when I met Ellen. I wanted to see if Ellen had the same ideas I had about the script. And she did and I had similar ideas to what she had. John Calley wanted us to, you know—Ellen was an Academy Award nominee for *The Exorcist* and *Mean Streets* was going to open. They had no idea how good or bad it was going to do financially but we got incredible reviews at the time. So they said, "Let's put the two of them together and if they agree on certain things, fine." And that's what happened. We agreed to do that kind of a film. You could call it, I don't know what. It's a picture about emotions and feelings and relationships and people in chaos. Which is something very personal to me and to Ellen at the time. We felt like charting all that and showing the differences and showing people making terrible mistakes ruining their lives and then realizing it and trying to push back when everything is crumbling—without getting into soap opera. We opened ourselves up to a lot of experimentation.

Robert Getchell, who wrote the script, we talked to him and he said, "Yeah, I realize the beginning with the husband is not quite right and the last whole sequence where she meets the farmer is not quite right." I said, "O.K. let's take a chance at rewriting that." So we started to rewrite that stuff and we still weren't satisfied. I started doing improvisations in New York with Ellen and some other actors in certain scenes. Then, from the improvisations, myself and Sandy Weintraub and Larry Cohen—Larry Cohen was the production executive and actually in the long run wound up producing the picture—we got together and we started writing up scenes and ideas based on the improvisations that Ellen and I did. Those scenes were then shifted over to Robert Getchell—we let him take a rest because he had been doing a year of rewrites on the thing under Susskind—and he looked at it and agreed with most of the things we wanted to do. He added some stuff, he wrote whole new scenes, he came back with new ideas. Certain scenes I still didn't care for and I said, "We're going to try working on these scenes. These scenes are good, keep these. I'm still not sure about this." So what happened eventually was that whenever we did improvise something, we improvised it usually during the rehearsal period, two weeks prior to shooting. The other improvisations were in New York while we were casting because we needed to get the script in shape. And then, two weeks before we started shooting in Tucson, we improvised a little more and then we sent that back to Bob and Bob gave us a few extra lines. Sometimes, you see, his dialogue was important because of colloquialisms and things which I didn't know in the Southwest. He gave us that sort of thing and we took the best of what he could give us, we gave it our best, and very often you'll find a scene like Ellen and Kris Kristofferson in the kitchen, which started out as a kind of scene where in the original script it has her saying, "Oh, I remember sitting under the trees thinking about Alice Faye," and we had already done that, you know. So what could be new? It's a scene that really reveals each person to the other. Ellen got up and said, "I used to do this when I was working with my brother, my first business in show business." She actually did it and that's what's in the picture. I said, "That's great." Then Kris gave us his lines. The only written stuff in the scene is at the end where he says, "Are you sure what you want to do? Do you want to go home? Do you want to sing? You can't have everything."

Q: *So those were improvised before shooting and transcribed and rewritten?*
MS: Oh, yes. Transcribed and rewritten. For a scene like that, though, we improvised it and kept on improvising it and what really happened was

that we had it written down the morning of the shooting. Which I didn't care for very much but we did it anyway and therefore I shot a 15 minute scene. This 15 minute scene was eventually cut down to about three minutes. But again, that's another reason for shooting it simply — medium shot, medium shot, two-shot. Same thing with the bathroom scene.

Q : *The thing that's interesting, though, is that you're really right on the edge all the time between going over to soap opera and yet you don't and it works. Did you evolve any rehearsal techniques or anything to get the actors to that point?*
M S : Well, we were really dealing with our own feelings and our own emotions. A lot of peoples' lives are soap operas; mine is anyway. Basically I think if you're in touch with your own feelings — it was almost like analysis for all of us. It's crazy. It was a madhouse but it was fun. That was the good thing about it because when somebody would come up with a good idea, it was really good. We'd write it down, improvise, terrific. It was a matter of trying to feel what you were feeling at the moment. We kind of — and that's one of the faults, I feel — we got caught up more with what was happening to us. Maybe it isn't a fault; I don't know. But we got caught up more with what was happening to us at the moment, in our own feelings, on the set, in that damned Tucson. I'm a New Yorker and I'm in the desert. Cactus. I got crazy with cactus alone. So I've got all those feelings wound up in me and that's what came out. Because I was feeling like that at the moment. It was unlike *Mean Streets* because *Mean Streets* was a picture that went straight down the line.

Q : *I got a feeling of improvisation in* Mean Streets *also.*
M S : Yes, there's some improvisation there. Of course, the scene where Bob De Niro and Harvey Keitel are in the back room arguing over money was totally improvised.

Q : *How do you then choose your actors? Particularly for* Mean Streets, *because they were extraordinary actors with the capacity also to improvise and still maintain character. You had some really good characters. Did you have the characters before the actors or how did you work that?*
M S : Mardik Martin and I wrote *Mean Streets* in 1966. Wrote the outline. I wrote the outline first and then brought it to Mardik, who used to write all my shorts with me at NYU. Mardik and I sat down and Mardik worked out

the structure for me and I worked out the characters and the incidents. Then we took the script around for years and we could never get it done. That was the end of that so we put it away. Well, eventually, when we did get it done, I had those characters down. It was originally written for Harvey Keitel to play the lead of Charlie, mainly because when we wrote the first version of *Mean Streets,* I had just completed a film called *Who's That Knocking at My Door?* I should say, the first version of that film, because it took me three years to finish it. So what happened was that, after the first version of *Who's That Knocking at My Door?*, which was a disaster, I sat down and said, "Now I'm going to write something that, everything I couldn't get in in *Who's That Knocking?,* I'm going to get in here." It turned out to be *Mean Streets.* Besides it being almost autobiographical, it was easier, in a sense, to make than *Alice.* Because I had a grasp of the people; I knew the people. De Niro knew the people. He knew the guys from downtown, he lived on 14th Street. Keitel knew them because he knew them from *Who's That Knocking?* and he came from Brooklyn. Richard Romanus, the guy who played Michael, we found him at the Jon Voight workshop here in L.A. but actually, he was a New Yorker. And David Proval is also a New Yorker from Brooklyn but we found him in the Jon Voight workshop also. Amy Robinson is a New Yorker. We found all of these guys and the film kind of lent itself to improvisation. There are only, maybe, three or four scenes that are really improvised. But we also improvised during rehearsal again. Taped and then written from the tape.

Q : *There are several moments in* Mean Streets *where it's not voiceover in the usual sense but where you almost get inside the character's head in terms of what he's thinking. Was that really in the script or did that come later?*
M S : We had more of that. We had more in the script and I chopped it out.

Q : *It worked almost to the point where it was unnoticeable.*
M S : Yes, that's what I tried to get to. Because what happened was, the first version of the script was steeped very much in the religious conflict. See, the whole idea was to make a story of a modern saint, you know, a saint in his own society but his society happens to be gangsters. It should be interesting to see how a guy does the right thing, that's the old phrase they use, "The right thing," in that world. Somebody does something

wrong, you've got to break his head or you shoot him. It's as simple as that. He became a character who refused to acknowledge that and eventually did the worst thing he could do which was to put everything off, put all the confrontations off, until everything explodes. It's the worst thing you can do. It's the same way in the movie business. You've got to go into the room with the producer first thing and say, "Hey, I think this thing sucks. I won't do it." That's what you've got to do. Otherwise you can put it off and put it off until, finally, they cut your picture down or whatever—they fire you or you walk off and it's a disaster. It's a matter of knowing where your heads are at right away. But this character wants to avoid unpleasantness at all costs. You notice he's always separating people when they fight. "Come on, we're all friends," he says. The voiceover was the whole business of his own relationship with God, his own way of looking at things. And also his guilt. This is a minor thing—it's not even in the film—but it's in the film if you're really Catholic and you look at it closely. He would go to confession but he wanted to deal with things in his own way so he would never really—there's an old heretical sect that felt they were not worthy of anything. They would go to confession but would not go to communion because they felt they were not worthy. That's where he says, "I'm not worthy to drink your blood or to eat your flesh." It's a whole guilt thing. No matter where he goes, he's lost.

Q: *How do you work with an actress in breaking down inhibitions in order to shoot a nude scene? Particularly, say, in* Mean Streets?
M S : Well, that was her first nude scene. It wasn't mine. To get *Who's That Knocking?* distributed, I had to have a nude scene in it. I happened to be in Amsterdam at the time. This was the third version of it, in 1968. We were in Amsterdam and I couldn't come to America so I had Harvey Keitel fly over to Amsterdam and we got a bunch of girls and did this crazy nude scene which was incredible. We had a lot of fun with it and the type of picture that *Who's That Knocking?* was—it's a pity you didn't see it because it's the type of picture that was done over such a long period of time that there's no transition between scenes. You have no idea where people are. The only thread of it is the characterization. It was very heavily influenced by all the New Wave movies and all the jump cuts and that kind of stuff. Mainly the jump cuts because we had no time to shoot establishing shots. *Mean Streets* has no establishing shots, practically. We never had an estab-

lishing shot of the guy going into his uncle's restaurant uptown. It's very important that you understand that the restaurant is uptown, the one with the red walls, in the East 60s. Not downtown. But we just didn't have time to shoot it because we shot the picture in 27 days. But the nude scene—we were nervous the first time in Amsterdam doing that nude scene—

Q : *So you became an old hand at it?*
M S :   Well, that was 1968 and this was 1971. We were shooting it in a small room at the Hilton hotel in L.A.—no, the Biltmore hotel in L.A.—and I just got everybody out who was not needed except the cameraman and the assistant cameraman and the soundman, that's it. And the script lady. We made it very comfortable. We were very nervous at first. We didn't have enough time to shoot it. Most of the scene is lost. We had to drop most of the scene because of that. There's a part where he attacks her and they roll around on the bed—that was part of the warm-up but I used it anyway. It's just a matter of keeping it private. It can't be a circus. Because I get embarrassed. I don't want people running in and out.

Q : *Did you say that the scene in the bathroom between the two women was improvised? I was really impressed by the relationships between the women, particularly those two. The evolution of their friendship was really real and good, I thought. But what I didn't understand—that's why I was wondering if it was in the script—was the other waitress. She became very vaudevillian after awhile and I didn't quite understand what you were doing.*
M S :   Because of the stylism? There's a lot of things in *Alice.* I tried one stylistic thing. I mean, by the end when they embrace and there's applause, where's the applause coming from? Do you think it's coming from the people? Maybe it is. Maybe it's coming from the other side of the camera. That's the idea. The idea was to try to shift styles in the picture so that the last scene which was really not the last scene—the last scene in reality is her and the boy, the way it should be—is really a shift in style. You begin the stylistic changes in that Mel and Ruby's sequence, when the girl couldn't—we had so much fun with her changing plates and I kept shooting it and I liked it. Try something, you know. Maybe it's a little undisciplined but what the hell, we'll try it. The first cut of *Alice* was three hours and 16 minutes. There's so much character stuff thrown out, it's a real pity. It's a pity because we couldn't see it in the script and cut it out in the script. That's the main thing: If you can cut it in the script, cut it.

Don't shoot it. Because if you shoot it and it's character stuff, you start losing your character stuff. The husband, Billy Green Bush, he's a great actor
and it's a pity the guy's only up there for a few minutes and he comes off
as some sort of slug, some sort of animal. In reality, we have another ten
minutes of film on him. O.K. he's nasty, he was angry but he had reasons
for it. He was tired, he didn't like his job, he was upset. We had a little
more dialogue in the bedroom scene, where she starts to cry. We had all
that stuff. But we couldn't use it. The picture really began with them getting in the car. We discovered that everything else is really a long
prologue. Everything was to get them in the car faster.

Q: *Couldn't you have used more of that prologue instead of the little girl scene
in the beginning where it was all red?*
MS: I like the red prologue. I had a chance to use a Hollywood set. I mean,
how else are you going to do a flashback? How do you want to do a flashback? That's the whole point. Goddam script opened, said, "Flashback, 1948.
Monterey, California." The dialogue's exactly the same as it was in the script.
Here's a little girl and the farm and the whole thing. And I say, "How am I
going to do this?" The production guys at Warners said, "Well, you know,
you could shoot it in black-and-white." I said, "Yeah, that'd work. Everybody would know it was a flashback." They said, "You could shoot it with
a fog filter." I said, "That'll work, too. It's a flashback." They said, "You
could put up a title and then you shoot it straight." I said, "That'd work,
too, but there's got to be another way." If the character is really hung up
on movies a lot, I felt then that she would sort of remember — half fantasy
and half remembrance — if it's 1948, then the flashback should look like it
was shot as a movie in 1948. Which means that all the exterior scenes are
really indoors. That's what I tried to do. I got a little crazy with the site and
the redness and all that stuff. I had fun with the fog. You know, you've got
fog machines, use a fog machine. See what happens. Got a crane — use a
crane. It's fun. Also I figured it's a very strange opening for a picture so what
the hell. And, if you notice, it's square screen — it's 1.33. The first scene is
Tobacco Road. It's copied exactly.

Q: *Were you thinking about* The Wizard of Oz?
MS: Yeah, *The Wizard of Oz. Duel in the Sun,* for the redness of the sky. All
in all, William Cameron Menzies. A little of *East of Eden* because the house
reminded me of *East of Eden.*

Q: *A little of* Gone With the Wind, *too.*

MS: Oh, a lot of *Gone With the Wind.* Again, William Cameron Menzies. Absolutely. Because, for me, William Cameron Menzies was always the magic of movies. As a kid, seeing those films, I saw *Duel in the Sun* on its first release—I think I was six years old—and I've never forgotten it. It's a very important picture for me. So when you have a chance to do something like that, you do it. It cost $85,000 for that one day of shooting—to build—not counting the crew. My first feature, *Who's That Knocking?* cost $35,000. And they kept saying, "Martin, are you sure you don't want that scene? Don't worry about the cost because if it doesn't work, we can drop the scene." Anyway...

Q: *Was the music written in too?* Alice*'s music?*

MS: Written in?

Q: *Well, the specific songs?*

MS: The only songs that were written in were the medley because she had to switch songs on certain words—"Where Or When?" to "When Your Lover Has Gone" to "Gone With the Wind." So those were actually written in. "Where Or When?" we used in the beginning because I liked the idea of "Where Or When?" because it has to do with sort of *déja vu,* which is what the movie is about really, being in the same place before, only with new people, making the same mistakes—

Q: *The rock music?*

MS: The rock music, I put that in. The script indicated rock music coming down the street. I said, "How many pictures have opened with the camera going down the street? And they go into a window? This one's got to be just a little different." Originally I was going to use "Spaceman" by Harry Nilsson. I knew I had to pick the songs that that kid would listen to—Harry Nilsson, Mott the Hoople, if I could have gotten David Bowie I would have liked that, Leon Russell, "Roll Away the Stone," which we never really used, except the opening I think we were dollying into the U-Tote-Em. The other was "Daniel" by Elton John. This is all sort of teenie-bopper stuff in a way which is enjoyable music but it's not *Mean Streets,* it's not "Live Cream." At the end of *Mean Streets,* we use "Live Cream, Volume Two." There's a whole sequence where the car is crashing and it's really incredible, vibrating music. Also the old rock and roll in *Mean Streets* and, of course, the Italian music and Jesus, tons of other stuff.

Q : *I like the way you integrated the music into* Mean Streets *especially. I was wondering at what point you thought of the music?*
M S : The music was always in the original script.

Q : *I got that impression because the rhythm of the film was—*
M S : "Be My Baby" was the song. You can't beat that. I mean, that's 1963 or 1962 in New York. That's the Ronettes. We used to hear that late at night. There was always a social club stuck in the back of some building and that song was always playing, echoing in the streets. That sound—the Crystals, the Ronettes, Martha and the Vandellas, all the female singing groups of that time—that's what it was. Right before the Beatles.

Q : *Did that influence the way you shot it or was that in mind?*
M S : That was in mind. All that stuff.

Q : *I wanted to ask you about the editing of* Alice Doesn't Live Here Anymore. *I thought it was particularly nice. Were you with the editing all the way through?*
M S : Yes.

Q : *How close were you to it?*
M S : Well, I edited all my own pictures prior to *Alice*. On *Alice,* I worked with an editor, Marcia Lucas, a friend of mine, George's wife. I felt I wanted to work with an editor. For the first time, working with an editor, I wanted an editor who would not take the picture, somebody with whom I could work because I cut some of the scenes myself. But you somehow find yourself on a different level of production now where you don't have very much time to edit your own pictures any more because you're always moving on to something else. Like when I was editing *Alice,* I did *Italian-American* at the same time. I put a guy named Bert Lovett in charge of that. And I was doing preproduction on another picture which was ridiculous to do and I found that out a little too late. So I trusted Marcia, trusted her judgment. For example, the great gray gorilla story that the kid tells in the car, which is an improvisation, a story the kid used to tell to me—I used to strangle the kid, that's how I directed him. But that scene was edited by Marcia totally. It was a two-shot, close-up, close-up. I didn't touch it. She got into the feeling of the acting. The feeling really came from the acting—my energy into them, their energy into me, and it just went into the cutting. The scene between Kris and Ellen in the kitchen, I made the first cut. The

violent scene, with Harvey Keitel coming through the door, I made the first cut. But then Marcia recut, under my supervision, the whole picture.

Q : *It was beautiful editing all the way through. I particularly liked the scene where you had the two ladies together, lying there in the sun, and then you came to the long shot of that loneliness, there by themselves in the desert with the wind blowing.*

M S : That's funny because the first cut on that was done by our assistant editor. I didn't know that. Marcia wanted to give the guy a chance and he did it. I thought she had done it and I said, "It's pretty good. All it needs is a little tightening and a dissolve out to the wide shot at the end." Which was what was planned originally.

Q : *What was it like working with Sid Levin on* Mean Streets?
M S : Sid didn't cut it; I cut it. Sid came in and showed me and made an initial cut into the last section where they're singing "O Marienello" at the end, which is the traditional song that ends all the Italian festivals in the street. When you see the guy with the hand through the window and you see everybody in the street and the uncle is watching TV, he made an initial cut on that for the first few bars of music for me because I had gotten stuck. At that point, I couldn't cut it. It was five months' editing and I was really freaked. The rest of it I cut. Brian De Palma came in and helped and Sandy Weintraub helped me. But, see, I can't take credit on a picture because I'm in the Directors Guild of America and I can't take credit as editor.

Q : *Why not?*
M S : It's a ruling. *Boxcar Bertha,* same thing. A guy named Buzz Feitshans has got the credit. He never even saw the cut. He was down on location with us but he never even saw the cut. He got credit as editor and I cut that. On this picture, I couldn't take any chances. I had to use somebody else.

Q : *Could you talk a little bit about how you financed* Mean Streets *and how it came together? It was done independently, right? And then you sold it to Warner Brothers?*
M S : Yeah, O.K., I'll tell you. The first place I brought *Mean Streets* to was the AFI in New York. At that time, they were just starting a feature program. I went over and gave them about a 50-page outline. It was ridiculous. The

girl was nothing and it had no character but it had all the basic elements. They told me they couldn't do it. They said, "We should be doing this kind of thing but we can't do it." Then I took it to Joe Brenner, who's a sex film distributor who distributed *Who's That Knocking?* with the sex scene in it. I was trying anything. I said, "I'll shoot it in 16, anything." He said, "No." So we put it away. One of my old professors at NYU told me, "Hey, nobody wants to see films about Italian-Americans anyway so forget about it." This was about a year before *The Godfather* was written as a book. Mardik and I wrote this thing with the *Godfather* image and all that in 1966, 1967. What happened was that we put it away for a long time. In 1968, I thought I had some access to some money and I got it out and rewrote it again. Another rejection. So I put it away, totally. Then I came to Hollywood to edit *Medicine Ball Caravan,* because I had edited *Woodstock* with T. Schoonmaker under Mike Wadleigh. Freddie Weintraub needed somebody to salvage *Medicine Ball Caravan* because they had a nine-hour cut—it was in three gauges—35mm Techniscope, 16mm and 8mm. It was nine hours long and nobody knew what was happening. It had no continuity, nothing. He brought me out here and said, "Try and see what you can do." I thought I was going to be here two weeks and I've been here ever since. But what eventually happened was, the first week I got out here, *Who's That Knocking?* had opened in L.A. under the title J.R. It kept changing titles because the theater distributor didn't like the title *Who's That Knocking?* It played at the Vagabond and he showed it as J.R. It got good reviews and Roger Corman went to see it. I met Roger the first week I was out here and he said, "Would you like to do the sequel to *Bloody Mama*? It's got guns, it's got costumes." I said, "Yeah, I'll do it." He said, "I'll see you in six months with the script." I said, "Oh." I figured in New York for nine years I'd been going through the same shit, everybody saying, "Six months... Nine months... We'll be right back... Be back next week..." You never get a phone call back so I forgot about it.

The next thing I know, I go to work on *Medicine Ball Caravan,* which almost killed me, physically, because it was a monstrous job and we did so many technical effects. I mean, you can only do so much when there's no content. A month later, after I finished *Medicine Ball Caravan,* I was helping Cassavetes do some *Minnie and Moskowitz* sound effects because John had seen *Who's That Knocking?* years ago in New York and loved it. Sure enough, it was nine months later and I figured Roger Corman was never going to call. So he called. He had a script. I read the script, liked it, went ahead and made *Boxcar Bertha*. Now *Boxcar Bertha* was finished seven months later and at that time I was scheduled to do one more picture for Roger Corman, *I Escaped From Devil's Island*. We were going to shoot in Costa Rica. Next thing I know, I showed a two and a half hour rough cut of *Boxcar Bertha* to a bunch of friends—Carradine and all the people in the picture and Corman and Cassavetes. Cassavetes took me aside the next day and spoke to me for three hours. He said, "Don't do any more exploitation pictures. Do something that you really—do something better." He was never a fan of exploitation pictures. I like exploitation pictures. But he was just never a fan of that kind of stuff. He never liked it. I said, "The only thing I have is this *Season of the Witch*." *Mean Streets* was called *Season of the Witch* at that time. So he said, "Rewrite it."

Sandy and I got together and she read it. I said, "What do you think?" She said, "Well, you put more into description that what you told me about the neighborhood." In other words, there were stories that I used to tell her in *Mean Streets* about the mook scene and about the firecrackers and all that which were never in the original script. She said, "Why don't you put those scenes in the picture?" I said, "That's a good idea." I did that and chopped out a little more of the religious stuff because there was a lot of religious stuff in it and trimmed it down a little and we started bringing it around. I brought it to Francis; he said he was going to read it but never did. He couldn't read it. He was in the middle of *The Godfather,* going crazy. We brought it to a lot of people. Roger Corman was the first I brought it to. His readers loved it. I said, "Can we do it?" Roger said, "Marty, I understand we got a script from you and everybody here says it's one of the best scripts we've received. However, I'd like to ask you one thing." He said, "I haven't read it. Has it got gangsters?" I said, "Yes, it's got gangsters." He said, "Has it got guns?" I said, "Yes, it's got guns." He said, "Has it got violence? Has it got sex?" I said, "Yes." He said, "My brother just made a picture called *Cool Breeze,* which is the first time that my brother Gene is making money. It's making a lot of money." He said, "Now, if you're willing to swing a little, I can give you $150,000 and you can shoot it all with a non-union student crew in New York. The only thing is, I'd like the picture to be black." I said, "Roger..."—goes to show you how much I wanted to make the picture—I said, "I'll think about it." I walked out knowing that I couldn't do it. That same week a good friend of mine, his name is Jay

Cocks, his wife was out here doing *Old Times,* a Harold Pinter play, with Faye Dunaway—his wife is Verna Bloom—and she was out here alone and wanted to have dinner with me. She said, "This young guy just came into town, his name is Jonathan Taplin; he used to be road manager for Bob Dylan and The Band and he wants to get into movies. He's 26 years old. I said, "Fine, we'll go for dinner." At dinner he says, "What scripts do you have?" I think: I'll just scare this guy away, so I say, "I've got this script called *Season of the Witch.* You wanna see it?" He says, "Yeah, I'll see it." Then he said, "During the week I'd like to see all your other films." So I think, "If the script doesn't scare him away, the films will." Because all I had at the time was *Who's That Knocking?* and three shorts. What happened was that he read the script and called me up and told me that he liked the script, which I couldn't believe. I said, "Oh, really? Well, wait'll you see the pictures." He saw *Who's That Knocking?* and he saw *It's Not Just You, Murray,* and he saw another movie and he saw *The Big Shave.* He called up and said, "I like your pictures." This was all in the space of one week. I said, "O.K. Sunday night we're having a preview of *Boxcar Bertha* at the Pantages. Sam Arkoff hates it. Roger Corman likes it but everybody at AIP hates the picture." I said, "Come to the preview with us." And I figure we'll blow it right there. If the audience doesn't like it, we're dead.

So we go to the preview at the Pantages and it was the best preview they'd had since *Wild Angels.* Arkoff was outside and he told me, "It's almost good now." He smiled. He wouldn't give it all to me but he liked it. Afterward, Jon and Sandy and I and some other people went to Chianti, the restaurant where this whole thing started, and we had a few drinks and he said, "If Roger can get me a letter saying he'll distribute the film, I can get you money to make it in Cleveland." Now Jonathan Taplin, his middle name is Trumball, he's related to the guy who painted George Washington crossing the Delaware—it's kind of odd, a person like this doing a picture like *Mean Streets.* So I said, "O.K. fine." We went to Roger. Roger said, "O.K. you've got the letter." We walked out and I was stunned. I said, "We've got the letter, which means we can probably get the money." He said, "Yeah." He went to Cleveland and he called me back a few days later and he said, "Terrific news. They got the letter and they want to go ahead." I said, "How much are you going for?" He said, "$300,000." I said, "Terrific."

Then what happened next is a little shady—not shady in the sense of the dealings—a little shady in my own mind because I'm not sure exactly what happened. He got the money from a guy named E. Lee Perry, who's got executive producer credit on the picture—a young guy, he was about 24 years old at the time and had just inherited a lot of money—we got the money from him and for about three weeks we were going strong. To make money, I was editing a picture for Roger that was directed by Vernon Zimmerman called *The Unholy Rollers* and I was also editing *Elvis on Tour* at the same time.

I was doing two pictures at once and we were also doing rewrites on the script, building up the girl's character, doing all kinds of things. Then he called one day and said, "The money fell through." I said, well, that's it. By that time, *Boxcar Bertha* had opened and a lot of guys knew me but they still felt it was a B picture, an exploitation picture, and they wouldn't have anything to do with me. They were offering me things like black exploitation pictures and they wanted to get me into that kind of stuff. I said, "Gee, I don't know." I was ready to do it but even then, some of those I couldn't get. They wouldn't give them to me. first they offered them to me, then they saw *Boxcar,* then they said, "No, I don't know if it's right." Anyway, I don't know how it happened but this guy Perry came back into town and we had dinner with him. It was him and his wife and Taplin and his girl friend and me and Sandy. It was very relaxed because I knew that the guy wasn't giving us any money so I didn't have to worry. We just told a lot of funny stories and had a good time and the next thing I know we've got the money back. What had happened was that the kid's family had called up Jon's family and said, "Your son is trying to swindle our son." That kind of thing, you know. But we got the money. I only found out last week in New York how much we really got and that was $175,000. That was it. The rest of the money came from a deferment from CFI labs. CFI rates the scripts they get and they rated ours a 90 or something like that and they gave us complete facilities—screening, processing, developing, opticals, answer print, everything—to be paid back a year after the picture was finished. So then I said, "The only guys who can make this picture that I know"—because Jon had never made a picture—"who can make this picture quickly and make it look like it was done for more money than it was made for are the guys that made *Boxcar Bertha*—Paul Rapp, who worked for Roger Corman for a bunch of years, Peter Fain and a bunch of guys." He went to see Paul Rapp and Paul budgeted the picture and he called me up one day and said, "In order to shoot this picture for

$300,000, you're going to have to shoot it in Los Angeles." I said, "I can't shoot this picture in Los Angeles," He said, "Then don't make the picture." I said, "Well, what do you mean, shoot it in Los Angeles? What are we going to do?" He said, "Go to New York, shoot some background stuff for four days and then come back here and we'll do all the interiors here. We can't crash the cars in New York. We can't pay the Teamsters so we'll have to find a place here at night." I said, "O.K. I can write it into the script that they go to Brooklyn." Which is what they end up doing, they go to Brooklyn. I shot the car crash in downtown L.A. at night. All the other exteriors are New York. Even the beach is New York because the water looks different at Staten Island than it does out here. It's true. We shot that in New York and all the interiors are L.A. except for the hallways. The hallway stuff is very important because we couldn't find a hallway to double. We shot those literally where the film takes place. In fact, we were working out of the lady's house who was the mother of the boy Robert De Niro was portraying. We worked out of her house and we worked out of my mother's house. But we only shot six days in New York. We kept stretching it to get more of the New York feeling. That also limited our shooting because the best I could do was put the people in the middle of the buildings and let the buildings do all the talking. Atmosphere-wise, you know. When De Niro's shooting his gun off the roof, the roof is New York because you see the Empire State Building, but the window is Los Angeles. When David Carradine gets shot in the bar, the guy falling in the street is actually in New York—that was a double—we shot that first. We blocked out his face just right so that he falls and hits the car, that sort of thing. The rest of the scene was shot in Los Angeles. The guys who were the doubles were all old friends of ours. His name was Larry the Box; he was a safecracker.

Q : *Did you screen the stuff you shot in New York before you shot stuff to match out here?*
M S : No, we had no time to look at anything. We had no time to look at rushes. I looked at rushes maybe on a Saturday and that was about it. The thing was done like a jigsaw puzzle. Like the scene where Bobby's up on the roof and he does this business (motioning), and all that. I set up the shot and then I had to go set up another scene so I said, "Bobby, make sure you know exactly where you are so we'll get it." The guys who shot the stuff in New York were a guy named Alec Hirschfeld, who's Jerry Hirschfeld's

son, a cameraman, and many of them were students—Mitch Block and a bunch of guys. Dale Bell, who was the associate producer on *Woodstock*, set it up for us. We only shot six days in New York. The festival stuff was shot in October before we even started doing preproduction. At one point, Jon Voight was going to be in the picture. The night in New York that we discovered he wasn't going to be in it, I went right back to Harvey Keitel and Harvey did it that day. The stuff you see of Harvey walking through the feast was done right at the spur of the moment, when I said that he was going to be the lead. I got him a coat down at Barney's and we went. That was that. But there were a lot of crazy things like that on the picture. The blowing up of the mailbox was done in San Pedro by the second unit. Again, I drew the pictures for them and said, "Get me this." I went to the location and looked at it the night before. I said, "Line it up over here." I came back and told Bobby what I wanted, told the second unit cameraman what I wanted. David Osterhout, who plays one of the McIver brothers in *Boxcar Bertha,* was also my second unit director there too. He shot it that way while I was shooting another scene because I couldn't take the ride to San Pedro. It was too far. It would have taken me away for too long.

Q : *So it was done on time and on the money?*
M S : It was done in 27 days. We had to finish when we finished and that was that. But money, no, we went over a little. I kept adding scenes. I added the backroom scene, the long improvisation. I added a scene in front of the gun shop in New York. I added the scene where they steal the bread in front of his uncle's shop. All that stuff. I added a lot of stuff like that. I kept pushing the limits of the budget and drove everybody crazy. But that was the only thing we could do because the more we got down there, the more fun we had and the more we realized the atmosphere we wanted to get. A lot of my old friends are in the film, a lot of guys who are now just hanging around, are there in the picture as extras. Where we really went over budget was in the music. The music killed us.

Q : *Paying for rights?*
M S : Yes. The Rolling Stones came to $15,000. Each. First it was $7,500 each, then they doubled it.

Q : *Did you have time to rehearse on* Mean Streets*?*
M S : Yes, I had ten days rehearsal.

Q : *What about improvisation?*

M S :   Oh, the improvisation took place in rehearsal. We taped it, wrote it down. We worked out of the Gramercy Park Hotel.

Q : *In your opinion, what influence did those limitations have on the final product of* Mean Streets?

M S :   The limitation is that the picture is sloppy, if you ask me.

Q : *Do you storyboard?*

M S :   Every picture is on a storyboard so we know what we're doing in terms of camera. We know exactly where we're going. We can line up our shots totally. If we light all one way, we do all the shots from that angle. Then we switch around and do the other side. It's really like a jigsaw puzzle, the whole thing. That's what Paul Rapp and those guys are great at. In the morning I'd lay out all my storyboards and they'd juggle all the pictures, put them over here—but that doesn't mean you're shooting in sequence in scenes, you know. That means you're shooting your scenes out of sequence. Not only in one scene but you're shooting three lines that are in the middle first. It's very hard for the actors but it worked. It was the only way we could get the picture done on time. There are things in there where I would have liked to have held a two-shot but I had to cut, cut, cut, cut, cut. You know, it's a pain in the ass.

Q : *How do you account for the fact that* Mean Streets *received almost unanimous critical acclaim and, as far as I know, it was not very successful at the box office. Could you talk a little about that?*

M S :   The picture opened at the New York Film Festival—was very successful in New York, still is, it plays in New York now—it was a combination of inexperience and circumstances. The inexperience came from the fact that Jon Taplin, my producer, said that because the picture got great reviews and we did such good business in New York the first couple of weeks, he wanted to open the film in 25 cities. Just like *The Last Picture Show* and *Five Easy Pieces.* He went to Bert Schneider and talked to him and he said, "Do it because there's nothing opening in October except *The Way We Were* and that isn't going to make a cent." Famous last words. I convinced Jon to only open it in San Francisco, L.A., Washington, Chicago, and, I think, Boston. He said, "O.K. let's try it that way first." Because I thought it was a good idea, too, but everybody was saying to be careful because *Five Easy Pieces* and *The Last Picture Show* were Americana — not just because *Mean Streets* was totally urban — but the other films had more of a universal appeal in terms of the whole country. That's probably why they did very well. Leo Greenfield, who's the head of distribution for Warner Brothers, felt that we were wrong. We asked John Calley and he said, "O.K. do it." Naturally, they're not going to prove themselves wrong. They opened the picture in Los Angeles at the Plaza Theater in Westwood and Leo said, "It's a lousy theater. You don't want to open there but we're going to have to open there. Do you want to open there?" We said, "Yeah."

See, we thought the New York Film Festival meant something out here. It doesn't mean a thing. Nobody even knew about the picture. We had nice, big full-page ads. Also, the ads were no good. We had no idea how to sell the picture. I had no idea how we were going to sell that kind of picture. How are you going to sell it? As *The Gang That Couldn't Shoot Straight*? That was our first concept — guys running around with shorts on with guns and hats because Johnny Boy takes off his pants at one point. It would have looked like a comedy. It is funny but it wasn't meant to be. The combination of not knowing how to sell the picture, the combination of opening in New York — and Leo Greenfield said to let it play in New York and he was probably right — we should have let it play in New York till 1974 and then opened it here in 1974.

Next thing I know, we opened in L.A., got nice reviews, did two weeks' business and that was that. Every place else, the same thing. At the same time, *The Exorcist* was coming in. That was $14 million and it was a company whose whole life depended on *The Exorcist* at that time because *Mame* they were a little shaky about. Naturally, they're not going to worry about a picture they paid $750,000 for and they didn't make anyway. They're not going to cover that and why should they? As they say, "Why throw good money after bad?" In fact, they want us to buy back the foreign rights and we're in the process of doing that now. I'm trying to get them to rerelease it in L.A. but they want to wait. At least they should show the damn picture in Los Angeles, you know. Because the only people that have seen it are in the Bel-Air circuits and the Beverly Hills circuits, in peoples' houses. That's the only place they screen it.

In a sense, it's not all their fault and it's probably our fault. It's inexperience and it's a damned hard picture to sell. How do you sell a picture like that? I remember we had two ads—one with a gun in it and one with a dead body in it. Don Rugoff said to me in New York, "The ads that don't sell are the ads that have guns and dead bodies." Those were our two alternative ads. What do I do? I said, "Don, we just made two ads and those are our ads." Then they tried a run in New York and they made it look like *Blackboard Jungle* and *The Amboy Dukes* which was O.K. with me. At that point I said, "O.K. run it off as a junior Mafia picture. I don't give a damn. Change the title. Do something but the point is, I want people to see it." I mean, it's got quite a following in New York. In the neighborhood now, West side and East side, if there's any trouble they always say, "Well, it's *Mean Streets* time, gentlemen." It's really made its imprint there.

But the point is that, if a picture is $14 million, you're going to have to go after that picture. What are you going to do? If you were hasty enough to open too soon, it's too late, kids. They loved the film, Calley and Ted Ashley. Ted Ashley lived in that area for awhile. Calley did, too. In fact, when they looked at the film, they would say, "I used to live in that building right on the corner there." That kind of stuff. So it's a pity. Chalk it up to experience.

Q : *Do you see any alternatives to that situation?*
M S : The alternative is learning. What do you do? I'm not a distributor. I'm not an exhibitor. And I'm not an advertiser.

Q : *I mean, even to the distribution situation, do you see any alternatives?*
M S : I don't see any. I have enough trouble making the picture. The best distribution is the distribution we're getting now with the *Alice* picture. It's because they had several months to prepare. They had months to prepare the damned picture.

Q : *How are they distributing it?*
M S : They are distributing *Alice* very well in New York, at the Sutton theater. It opens here today at the Regent in Westwood. Then, I think, today, tomorrow and Friday it opens in 60 cities, including Canada. Like in Chicago, they're opening in four cities on the map of the Chicago, there's two here and two here (making a square), and they're all in the suburbs. So it'll be a suburb picture, which is good. Get the housewives to go first and that sort of thing.

Q: *What was the budget on* Alice?

M S: *Alice* started out as $1.6 million. I don't know what it ended up as. I was ill for a few months and it may have gone over. I went over five days' shooting. I had a seven-week schedule and I made it eight. There were some extra scenes I added. Ellen had to go the the Academy Award ceremony. It wasn't her fault but she was naturally nervous. We had to shoot simple scenes the first day before she went and we had to shoot very simple scenes the second day and the third day, we shot the bathroom scene and it just wasn't quite what we wanted. Diane and Ellen and myself all felt that way so we reshot the bathroom scene, which was a whole day of shooting. She was still a little edgy but it's a hard thing. She had to fly out to L.A., go to the Academy Awards, come back and shoot a picture. It was really murder and she's in practically every scene. It isn't like, O.K. we can shoot other scenes, it was hard. Then I added three or four more scenes to the picture and that was that. We wound up shooting five extra days. But I think that's pretty average, depending on what happens in a picture. It seemed to me, I don't know, the editing went on a little longer than it should have because I was ill. I don't know what the price is now on the picture.

Q: *You got no flak?*

M S: None at all. They left me alone completely.

Q: *Did you shoot any in L.A.?*

M S: Nothing was shot in L.A. except the opening sequence which was the last set to be built on the Gower Street Columbia lot. Now they're tennis courts.

Q: *Is that an advantage, to not shoot in Los Angeles?*

M S: I don't know. Tucson is a movie town. You can do anything you want there, it's good. It's a good town to shoot in, if you can take Tucson. I'm not putting down Tucson but I'm a New Yorker, and—you know—the desert and everything, the snakes, the cactus...

Q: *Was everything shot there?*

M S: Everything was shot there. We were right in the middle of the gas crisis. We had to do crazy routes when she was driving because we didn't have enough gas to bring all the trucks to Phoenix. We had to make Tucson double for Phoenix. We couldn't shoot in Phoenix and double that for Tucson, understand? We had to have her make a mistake and go to Tucson. It was a lot of crazy things. People keep asking, logically, "Why does she wind up in Tucson on her way to Monterey?" And I say, "Well, it's the gas shortage." It had nothing to do with the picture; it had to do with us and the production.

Q : *It was totally shot out of continuity, you say?*
M S : Oh, no, we shot in continuity.

R E S P O N S E : *I thought you said the bathroom scene was the third day —*
M S : Well, towards the end, during the last two weeks of shooting, we shot some stuff out of continuity. Kris Kristofferson had to leave and things like that.

Q : *How did you cast the young boy?*
M S : Marion Dougherty Associates in New York went through about 300 kids and I would read a few of them and didn't care for too many of them. Then Sandy Weintraub told me there was one kid I had to see. She had asked him what he wanted to be when he grows up and he said, "A stand-up comic." I met the kid in my hotel room and he was kind of quiet and shy. I looked at Sandy and said, "What, are you kidding me?" She said, "Believe me. Maybe he's a little nervous in here. Get him together with Ellen; it should be something crazy that happens." Sure enough, he came into the room and I would tell Ellen to throw little improvs in every now and then to throw the kids off. Usually, when we were improvising with the kids, they would either freeze and look down or go right back to the script. But this kid, you couldn't shut him up. With this kid, she had to hang on. She kept looking at me. We kept giving each other looks and writing down things. "Fine, see you later, Alfred. Fine, thank you." I said, "That's it, thank God." We had to use a New York kid because of the welfare laws. We'd have never gotten the film shot. For Audrey I used Jodie Foster. My God, two days shooting she's in the picture. If I had had a few more days with her we could have had some real fine improvisations. But the kid is a real pro—it was like doing another television commercial for her—she came in—bang, bang, bang. She was great.

Q : *All of her stuff was done in two days?*

M S : Two days, all of her stuff in two days. And, man, I know we could have gotten better — it's good now — we could have gotten more. Damn situation with the welfare workers. That woman came over to me and said, "Stop." I said, "What do you mean, 'stop?'" She said, "Stop. The kid has to go to school." I said, "O.K." So we stopped. Our shots became like student film time. Two-shot, thank you, bang. It was catch what you can and I had to do a lot of hand-held stuff, which I was telling you about before. Because of the welfare workers, I had to do that whole sequence hand-held. People think you're going for, quote, realism. Realism stinks in that kind of situation. It doesn't work. The worst thing with the welfare worker was the thing with the little girl in the beginning of the film. We'd built that set for $85,000 and the whole key to the scene was where she says, "Blow it out your ass." That line. And "Jesus Christ," she says. We have the kid walking down the road, she's eight years old, and she says her lines.

The welfare worker comes over and says, "She can't say those lines." I said, "Lady, we just built this whole set. What do you mean, 'She can't say those lines?'" She said, "It's nothing to get upset about." I said, "Nothing to get upset about! We didn't build this set overnight. They've been build-ing it for months. I've been fighting the studio to get this set. It's the last day of shooting. You mean we can't use the goddamn kid to say the line?" She said, "Well, I don't care what you've done, you can't use the kid to say the line." She got furious and walked off. So we had the kid say other things. But, luckily, we had taken one take where the kid actually said it and that's what we used.

Fat George from *Mean Streets,* George Memmali, came over on the set that day — the guy who does the mook scene — he came over and I said, "George, this is crazy." He said, "I'll take care of this lady." He walked over and he started talking to her and doing all sorts of things. It didn't matter. We wound up looping it anyway.

Q : *So you don't get in trouble after the fact, having her say it once?*

M S : No, we've got it on film. I don't know how that works. This was my first studio film. I don't know what happens. I made all the wrong phone calls. I got in trouble because I called over some guy's head to get a pencil. "You're supposed to call Harry for the pencils!"

Q : *Did you enjoy working with the kid?*

M S : It's hard, it is hard, really. I really love the kid, he's great. He's now been in several films since then. His latest film is called *Love and Death,* he plays the young Woody Allen.

Q : *He hadn't acted before?*

M S : No, he never did—a couple of commercials.

Q : *Do you think AIP and Roger Corman are still a viable way to go, a good place to use as a stepping stone for working with the majors? Early on, there were a lot of people who came out of there, like Coppola and Bogdanovich, and then it seems to me that there was a long lag. Now people find that once they've made a picture there, it's so much easier to continue to make those kinds of pictures.*

M S : Sure, I was going to make either *I Escaped From Devil's Island* or *The Arena,* about the gladiators in ancient Rome. I'm dying to make a picture about ancient Rome. I said, "Gee, I can do a comedy and have some fun." But luckily, we didn't do it. I can only tell you from my experience. My experience was the university, because I didn't have enough money to buy even an 8mm camera. I used to draw all my pictures. My first movies were all drawn, like storyboards, when I was a kid. Steve Spielberg used to have his own 8mm camera, used to do a lot of his own 8mm stuff. I couldn't do that. Eventually, I borrowed my friend Joey's camera, one of the characters in *Mean Streets,* and I shot some 8mm stuff.

The university was the place that got me the money, got me the chance to make the pictures. Then from there, Corman, really. I was killing myself in New York. Death. Pure death in New York. If it wasn't for Mike Wadleigh in New York, it would have been ridiculous. Mike was a student with me at the same time. That's when we started cutting the music films and we had some fun with that. But we would have died. I mean, guys I knew are dead now. Really.

Q : *Do you prefer to direct things that you've written? Could you talk about some of the advantages and problems involved?*

M S : In my case, it was always a matter of knowing your limitations. Knowing that I cannot photograph a movie. I'm not interested in photographing a movie. I did some photographing when I was a student and it was fun but I'm really not interested in that. I might eventually do some documentaries like I did on my parents this year. That's something different, though. My first film was written entirely by me, *What's a Nice Girl Like You Doing in a Place Like This?* Then *Murray* was written with Mardik Martin. *The Big Shave* was written by me. Then *Who's That Knocking?* was written completely by me. That's when I realized my limitations. Mardik and I got together on *Mean Streets*. I prefer working with somebody a great deal but at this stage of the game, I don't think it's worth even taking "story by" or co-writing credit.

I really don't need it. I'm never going to get a job to write *Sister Carrie*. I'm not known as a writer but, eventually, what happens is that you come out as a writer anyway. Look at *Alice*. What I've been describing about *Alice,* a lot of it was written in a sense by Ellen but Getchell did the whole thing. Yet Ellen did a lot of it, I did a lot of it, Larry Cohen, Sandy, the actors got together. Somehow it comes out to be something I want to do, one way or the other. That's very important. Really, my biggest problem right now is finding writers to work with. Especially guys who will not bother you, guys who understand the way I work, which is that things really change a lot. I've been in some situations where writers sit on the set and watch you. That I can't have, unless you need the guy there for certain colloquialisms or whatever. Getchell was never down in Tucson. Larry Cohen would call him up and say, "We've got a problem with this line. Can you give us a better one?" Or maybe we'd send some stuff to him and he'd send it back rewritten. But it was because *Alice* was not really prepared in script form, going in.

We had to go because Warner Brothers sort of said, "You go now or you don't go at all." They weren't tyrants about it but Susskind said, "Listen, the whole idea is to get the picture started in production so make sure you've got the script." We came up with some sort of script and we knew that we were eventually going to rewrite as we went along. I really don't want to do that again. I mean, my films will be rewritten as we go along anyway. But right now I want to go with a solid script from beginning to end. I like working with other writers. Sometimes I'm lazy, I can't write by myself. Other times I just don't know whether—I don't know—it's all character and feeling. That's where it comes from.

Q : *You say you draw a storyboard on everything?*
M S : Yes, practically everything.

Q : *You don't ever just improvise with the camera or make changes with your actors?*

M S : Oh, sure, you do that. But at least you have your board there. You know where you're coming from. This shot goes from here and drives to here and the camera moves like this and the camera is going to tilt down. And they say, "You can't tilt down, you'll be in the lights." I ask, "What's the best thing?" They say, "We can track down but we'll have to switch to the crab dolly and we're on the Elemack." I say, "How long will it take to switch to the crab dolly?" "Ten minutes." "Do we have the ten minutes?" I ask my production manager. He says, "I wouldn't advise it." I say, "O.K. skip the tilt."

There are so many different things that happen. It's impossible. You've got to be able to move fast. But, no, I found in *Alice* that I did a lot of the drawings but I'm finding that the more I do a picture, the more I find that I'm not storyboarding it that much anymore. I storyboard certain scenes and then the rest of the picture is overhead diagrams and little drawings in the script. Camera moves, arrows and things like that.

Q : *What are you working on now?*

M S : I'm probably going to do a picture called *Taxi Driver* next, written by Paul Schrader. That's to be done in New York and here, I guess.

Q : *With Robert De Niro?*

M S : De Niro is supposed to be in it and Michael and Julia Phillips are producing and Columbia is supposed to make it. Then I'm going to do a musical, a '40s musical, *New York, New York,* which is going to be all here in L.A. on studio sets. It's about the decline of the big bands and a couple, a saxophonist and a girl singer in a band, who try to make a go of it but they have no money and they break up and then they get back together after they make it.

Q : *Which character were you in* Mean Streets?

M S : I was Charlie, the lead character, but there were other elements of a friend of mine because I never had enough money—I couldn't sign for those loans. All that was the other guy. The conflicts within Charlie were within me, my own feelings.

Q : *I know that some people see* Mean Streets *and they are confused about what happened at the ending. What exactly happened? Did you make a decision whether he actually sold them out or not?*

M S : Sold who out? Charlie sold them out? No, he never did that. Charlie just waited too long so that everything blows up in his face. He acts very irrationally by taking them out of town. It's the worst thing he could do. He takes his friend's car and he takes the girl which is the worst thing he could have done. He should have kept her out of it totally. But he let everybody pressure him. "All right, all right, all right." Disaster. He's a character headed full on toward disaster. See, it's the idea of success — in fact, when I first wrote it, it was like an allegory for what was happening to me trying to make movies. Mardik and I were working together, writing scripts about ourselves at that time, trying to get things going. At that time, the sex films were coming out. We were going to do a film called *This Film Could Save Your Marriage* because in every one of those films that was a catch-phrase. We were going to do everything, anything we could get our hands on and we never got anywhere. We just did shorts and documentaries. It was frustrating. The picture was for me, I hate to use the word "allegory," but that's what it was for me. I drew from personal experiences about a guy trying to make it.

Q : *And not making it?*

M S : Yeah. He learns something else, though. What that is is a kind of enlightenment of some sort. He realizes something about himself which Johnny Boy knows from the very beginning. Especially when he sees him with his cousin and they have that fight in the street and he says, "Hey, you didn't do anything for me." Because he knows that Charlie is doing everything for himself, even when he's helping other people.

It's like the Pharisees, the guys who used to give money to the poor and blow trumpets so everybody could turn around and watch them give money to the poor. Christ said that they had already received their own reward because they had received their reward on earth. Something like that. We had tons of that in there, that kind of thing.

Q : *But wasn't there a moment when he changed the route on the ride out of the city or something like that?*

M S : That's because we had to make it match to L.A.

Q : *Right. That's why, anyway—*

M S : Oh yeah, when he said, "Where are you going?"

Q : *Yes and he switched the road and the guys found them.*

M S : That's what happens when you shoot things in 27 days. What do you do?

Q : *Did you have any problems when you were shooting the movie about your parents? I thought it was just wonderful and a very appealing thing, to do a movie about your parents. What was their reaction?*

M S : The film came about through a series called *The Storm of Strangers,* being done by the National Endowment for the Humanities. This guy called me up and asked me if I wanted to do a picture on the Italian section. They were doing one on the Greeks, the Jews, Armenians, blah, blah, blah. It's going to be for bicentennial TV, 1976. They all have to be a half-hour long. So I said, "No," because we were in the middle of shooting *Alice.* A day later, I called back and said, "Wait a minute, I think I would do it if you want to do it my way." Which was to go to my mother's house, my mother's apartment on the lower East side, and to shoot while we were having dinner and I would ask my parents questions about my grandparents. He said yes. What he had in mind was, of course, a still of the people getting off the boat and the camera zooming in and the voice saying, "So the Italian got off the boat," and that sort of stuff. I wanted to do it a little differently.

They first got a little nervous. We set it up when I was in Cannes. I set it up with Dale Bell, the same crew that shot most of the New York stuff in *Mean Streets.* I called them from London and when I got there on Saturday, they had it all set up for me. Mardik Martin, in the meantime, had written up all the questions because my parents know him well. He used to go to our home to eat. What you see first in that film is the warm-up. I tried to get them to warm-up but what happened was that they didn't need it, obviously. I don't know if anybody has seen it here, except for you. But the point is that they really got into it and we wound up with a picture that was really much more than about immigration.

The picture is about 48 minutes long and now I think they're going to make a truncated version for TV, a 30-minute version, which I'm not too happy about. People want it for commercial distribution and the government is sort of bureaucratically holding back so we have to be very careful. Hopefully, it will get released. But my parents didn't give me any trouble, no. My father didn't go see the picture at Lincoln Center at the New York Film Festival because he had a hard time watching *Mean Streets,* you know, because he went through all the palpitations of it's your movie up there and 2,000 people are seeing it for the first time. He got the same feeling. Now with *Italianamerican,* the fact that he's on screen and he hadn't seen it and he imagined seeing it for the first time in front of 2,000 people—he felt he'd come off terrible so he saw it privately. That was O.K. My mother went instead. I couldn't be there, my mother took over anyway. She threw kisses to everybody, signed autographs. That was like a blueprint for the third part of *Mean Streets,* which is going to be about Charlie when he gets married, settles down, has a couple kids and lives on Staten Island. That's a picture to be done years from now but Mardik and I are working on that now.

Q : *I was curious about the ending in* Alice. *Why did you have the mother and the boy alone, especially since the guy that she was going to marry was coming along also?*

M S : The most important relationship in the film was her and the boy. Kris Kristofferson was just another one of the guys. O.K. so we do a little crazy thing with the audience applauding or whoever's applauding but it was just to settle things there and then to go on with the real ending of the picture, which was her and the kid. Once they begin to understand a little more about themselves as people, then she may have a chance at having a better relationship with a man. And so does Kris. The whole idea of the picture is that they start making the same mistakes as they did with their ex-spouses, without realizing it. Even when they fight, they're not fighting about issues, they're fighting about emotions. They don't know what they're telling each other. Nobody comes out and calls the other person. They never come out and say, "You did this and that's why, because you have this kind of hang-up in the past." They never say that. They don't know. They just don't know. But they do know that they want to get together. The most telling line in the picture is when, in the last sequence, he says, "I think I understand you." He says, "I think there's gotta be another way." She can't even say, "Yes." She just nods. That's the whole picture.

Q: *How did you choose him? I don't think he'd done anything since* Pat Garrett and Billy the Kid.

MS: That's right. I loved him in that. I loved the picture. I saw the rough cut of the picture, the long rough cut, and it was beautiful. I even liked the final version, which has got some problems. Kristofferson I liked but actually it was a suggestion from a friend of mine, Jay Cocks. I didn't like the idea. That was months before we cast him and finally we were really stuck for a guy to play David and Ellen Burstyn called up and said, "What about Kristofferson?" I said, "Now that's what we need." I didn't think he would do it but he wanted to do it because it was only two weeks' work. See, it interferes with his concert dates, that's why. I thought it was a great idea. Also I thought it would be something for him to play it a little differently, where he has to hit a kid and he's got to be a little more uptight. I had more on Kris in the picture, too. We cut more of him, too, damn it. More character stuff, that's unfortunate. It's difficult when you try to make a picture and every character has to be a full, rounded person. She's completely rounded, so's the little boy. But then you really have to round out the actress playing Bea. She's only in a few scenes but you have to make her as real as possible. Then there's Ben Eberhardt by Harvey Keitel, you have to make him as real as possible. Kris Kristofferson, the husband played by Billy Green Bush, Flo, Mel, Vera, all these people. It's nice when you have six hours, like in *Scenes from a Marriage,* when you can get different aspects of these people. But it was a little too ambitious to try to come up with a film in which you had four or five different relationships going on with maybe eight characters and all of their relationships were going to be fully rounded and the characters were all going to be three-dimensional. In the three hours and 16 minute version it was, but it was boring. It was tiring.

Q: *Let me ask you one more thing about Kristofferson's character, because I really like him but from the very first time you saw him, he seemed so secure. He looked like there he was and he seemed to be very different from all the other characters. He seemed to have more color.*

MS: He's been living on his own for awhile. I mean, how secure can you be that when your wife tells you she's leaving, you say, "I'll open the door for you?"

Q: *No, I mean from her point of view.*

M S : She's hooked. That's the point. We wanted to get across the idea that she sees the guy and she sort of just stumbles. "I love him, I love him." He looks at her and says, "Not bad." That kind of stuff. I wanted to get that right away. That's when he says, "Oh, I'll cut off the beard." She says, "Oh no. You want some more coffee?" She won't tell him that she'll go out with him but she won't let him go. It's little things like that all the way through the picture. It's a thin line between losing your dramatic impact and having a very realistic situation. The more realistic things become in a movie, sometimes the less dramatic it is. That was the problem we had here.

Q: *Do you ever find yourself in a situation where you have a particular vision of what you want to get from an actor and it doesn't seem to happen, they don't seem to get it, and you keep trying? I'm interested in some of your techniques in getting it out.*

M S : We try different things. I don't know what the method is or any of that stuff. I was only at the Actors Studio once, with Bobby De Niro, to watch him, and that was only a year and a half ago. I've never read any books on acting. I took an acting course once at NYU for a semester which is nothing. I really never got into any technique. What I find is that I really have to get to know the person, the actor, get to know them as a human being and have to really like them. I like the people I'm working with. And then, if they like me, there's a certain kind of mutual trust that happens. I let them try a lot of things. There are certain things that I know I don't want and certain things that I know I do want which I usually get.

Q: *This is in the rehearsal period?*

M S : In rehearsal, yes. But I tell you, even in shooting sometimes you say, "Hey, that's too much. Cool it down a little because you're emoting all over the place. Let's do it much softer." Most of my directions are really less. "Less, please, less." Or when I want a guy to get mad, like Harvey Keitel, smashing through the window, I didn't have to tell him anything. Nothing. Harvey did that. He knows. He was feeling that. I didn't have to tell him anything. There was one thing I wanted to say about that—well, I forgot what I was going to say but really, there's no magic. It's just getting to know the other person. In *Alice,* there's a lot of that. Bea, Lelia Goldoni, is in reality Ellen Burstyn's best friend so that scene where they say goodbye is all from reality. That's important. That's why I like that scene. Diane Ladd had the same relationship with Ellen over a period of ten years as you see in the picture. So I played on what they know. You know what I mean? I played on what they know.

Q : *Were they cast on Ellen Burstyn's suggestion?*
M S : Yes, they were suggested by her. But Lelia Goldoni came into the room—and there was David Susskind and myself, Sandy and Audrey Maas and Nessa Hyams, who at that time was casting director for Warner Brothers—it's a delicate thing when you say suggestion because anybody can give you a list of people. But you've got to see them and feel that they're right for you. So Lelia came in and all these other actresses were coming in and performing, doing a number, and they were all very smooth and very good. We were just talking, an interview, but when you walk into a room and there are six people sitting there, the poor actress or actor has to come in . . . so this lady Lelia came in, sat down. We said, "Hello, hello." She looked around and she said, "Well, if you expect me to start talking, forget it." I said, "This girl's great." She had beautiful eyes. I liked the idea that she had been in Cassavetes' *Shadows.* I thought it would be fun because it was a small part and it would be nice. Diane Ladd was originally suggested by Verna Bloom and Jay Cocks, again. At the same time, Ellen suggested her. I also looked at lots of other people and I just chose—I liked Diane Ladd the best.

Q : *How do you prepare the script when you first think about rehearsing it? Do you have any procedure you go through?*
M S : Not really. My rehearsal period was mainly between Ellen and the boy. We started with the first scene between her and the boy and went through that. Read it first, talk about new ideas for lines, talk about attitudes, new attitudes, that sort of thing, trying different things. Then I would call in another actor down in Tucson. We had Lelia down there for two days and we would rehearse her scenes. Some of those scenes, like the scene with the dress, was an improvisation. We came up with that, with the two of them. We talked about character. With Lelia, we went way back into her character, what kind of girl she was, whether she played around with men on the side. Ellen didn't, we felt, whereas Lelia did, we felt. You know, different kind of women.

Q: *How about before you rehearse, the stuff that you had to bring in to give the actors to get where they've got to be to make the story work?*

MS: Well, if the actor comes in, he knows what he's doing. If an actor comes in the room and he says, "I don't know. I just don't know what this character's all about," what's he doing in the picture? He's got to have an idea of his own, what the character is about. If his idea coincides with mine, fine, then we're going to make the picture. If his idea is totally opposite mine, then how are we going to make the picture?

Q: *I'm interested in the process of how you come up with your idea of what the picture is about.*

MS: It just hits me. I can identify with Alice, her problems. I can identify with Ben Eberhardt and his problems. I can identify with the kid. I can identify with Kris. I can definitely identify with the husband, not in this version but in the old version. So I know. There are certain feelings. If you don't get a feeling from the script, then you can't. I guess the old professionals could do it but I don't know if I could. I've got to know where the characters are going. I've got to have a feeling for them. It's really just instinct.

Q: *I noticed that most of your characters in both* Mean Streets *and* Alice *are from the Actors Studio. Do you have a preference for people who have been trained under this method?*

MS: Harvey was never in the Actors Studio. Do you know when they put him in the Actors Studio? They put him in the Actors Studio when he got his reviews in *Mean Streets*. He worked for years, he was an observer for years, he acted in front of them, he did things—I don't know, I think the Studio is great—the point is that I've known Harvey since 1965 and for years he would always be preparing a scene for the Actors Studio. He'd always fail. They never let him in. When they saw him in the movie, they let him in. You know, that's bullshit. And Bobby De Niro to a certain extent. I don't even know if he was in. I think he was an observer too. Now he's in, I guess. It turned out in *Alice* that most of the people were from the Actors Studio—Goldoni and Diane Ladd and Ellen, Vic Tayback and Harvey now. Billy Green Bush used to be in the Studio and he went somewhere else. It just turned out that way. As I say, *Mean Streets*, Richard Romanus and David Proval were from Jon Voight's workshop. Correct me if I'm wrong, I don't think they had anything to do with the Studio.

DAVID PROVAL: We used to go there sometimes on Tuesday nights.

MS: But were you a member?

DP: Observer.

MS: Observer? See, that's what I mean. There's a thing about a member. You've got to be—

Q: *But you get the same stimulus—*

MS: Do you act in it, though?

Q: *You can, yes.*

MS: Then why weren't they accepted? I don't understand why Harvey wasn't accepted.

Q: *It depends on the scene. Maybe he got nervous and blew it.*

Q: *In Alice, was that the written ending, the last shot, the last scene in the film? Was that the last scene in the script?*

MS: There was a scene before the cafe scene—Toby Rafaelson had the idea—she said, "Maybe you should think about switching those two scenes around. The cafe scene first and then her and the kid." I said, "You're absolutely right because it's a matter of her main relationship in the film being with the kid."

Q: *Was the sign, "Monterey," written in?*

MS: The sign, "Monterey," was there. It was like God put it there. I said, "Oh then, we can't change it, can we?" And that was that. I don't care whether it gets people confused or not. Screw it, you know. We could have very easily framed it down but I said, "Well, it's just one of those crazy things." It was a place called Monterey Village. Somebody said, "Isn't that funny?" I said, "Yes." That was that. Sometimes things happen like that.

Q: *What's a mook?*

MS: A mook. That scene actually occurred. Does anybody from New York remember the Fillmore East? There's a bar across from the Fillmore East— at the time the Fillmore East was called the Lower East Commodore, that's where I saw most of my movies when I was a kid—and they used to have a place right across the street from it called Foxy's Corner, on Sixth Street and Second Avenue. One night some of the neighborhood guys went in with the Johnny Boy character and his older brother and they got into a fight. They were trying to settle an argument. That's exactly, literally, what happened in the film. In fact, it was written for a bar like Foxy's Corner but then we found this pool hall on Hollywood Boulevard and we wanted to do it there because I thought everybody running around throwing pool cues at each other would be funny.

The guy said to Johnny Boy's older brother—everything was settled, everything was fine—and he said, "The bartender called you a mook." He said, "Called me a mook?" And he got crazy. In the middle of his craziness, he was just about to throw a table up in the air and he said, "What's a mook?" The guy said, "I don't know." Finally he threw the table up in the air and they started killing each other. Then they all made friends again. As they were walking out, the Johnny Boy character says, "Hey, friends, huh?" And he says, "Get your hands off me, you mother-fucker." Bang! they're into it again. So it was a very funny story.

But "mook," I later found out in San Francisco, is a slang for "mocha" or "bigmouth" among the Neapolitan people. See, we were Sicilians and there was always some sort of rivalry. There was rivalry between the Neapolitans and Sicilians and Calabrese. There was rivalry between all three against the ones that lived on the East side and the West side. Whether you were a Sicilian on the West side or the East side, they all hated each other. Even down to buildings. They got into rivalries between buildings. It was always crazy that way.

Q: *Did I just read this into it or were you deliberately, consciously using every element you could in* Mean Streets *to give us, the audience, the same feeling that these kids had growing up in that crazy world? I mean, I got really crazy in that film and I felt for the first time ever that I really understood New Yorkers. Before I never quite understood when they'd say, "You don't know what it's like, you grow up in the gutter and you street fight and you know how—"*

M S: Any place you go now, you can get shot for no reason. You get mugged. A car goes up the curb and hits you. It's the same thing out here but there's something extra-violent about New York. It's not only downtown but all over. Growing up in that neighborhood, we used to go to school in the morning, carrying a little briefcase, going to Saint Patrick's school around the corner and we lived a block away from the Bowery and there were always the drunks, the guys in the Bowery beating each other up with bottles. There was blood all over the street and you'd just step by. I mean, that's normal.

Q : *Were you using elements like the music and the harshness and the camera to make us all tense?*
M S : Oh, sure, yeah. But that was my own energy, though. I didn't say, "Now we're really going to drive them crazy." I had the camera move at a certain point because I felt that that was the way it should go. The music was very important because you can go by and hear the march from "Aida" and as you walk by another room you can hear "Handyman," and then in another place you hear Eric Clapton and then in another place you hear an old Italian folk song, and you keep going and there's Chinese music. Especially in the summertime, it was incredible. I don't know if anybody here ever lived in tenements in the summer but in one building it was all one house, all the doors open, everybody would go in each other's houses, everybody would eat whatever everybody else had and there were always fights in the streets. They were always beating up Puerto Ricans and blacks. That was it. Nothing else to do.

Q : *What about the West side?*
M S : Oh, the West side always had a little more class. They had more class. They had the artists moving in. There was always Greenwich Village on the West side.

Q : *Not around 36th Street.*
M S : No, no, you're right. Not around 36th Street. I'm talking about downtown. I always think of the West side as the Village. The Village area is always a little more tolerant of other groups. That's why *Mean Streets* is set on the East side in the Italian-American ghetto. That area is really very, very closed off, very secretive and sinister in a sense. That doesn't mean if you're living there now, a nice lady or a young kid or a student, that they won't take care of you. Because, as long as they know you're not pushing cocaine or something, they'll take care of you. If you're pushing cocaine, they want a piece of it. But it goes that way. It just goes that way.

Q : *Do you think that most women will identify with the character that Ellen Burstyn plays?*

M S : I don't know. I was just concerned that it ring as true as possible. So was Ellen. I know that she had a lot of things in it that she felt and I felt a lot of things about it. Getchell did too. It seems to me that a lot of women are relating to it. As a little girl, when she says that line, when she says she wants to be like Alice Faye—the point is that there's a spark in that kid and after 27 years that spark has been beaten down by circumstances. Not necessarily by the husband alone—that's where I feel the failure is— because the husband comes off one-dimensional, but by life, existence, where she says, "Soccoro sucks."

You know. That spark is destroyed in her in a sense. If her husband hadn't been killed, she would never have left him. See, that's the character. It's a very important point. I thought at first that it was very melodramatic to have the guy killed but that happens in life. A guy gets killed in a car crash or he has a heart attack in the middle of the street. It happens in New York all the time. She would not have moved unless the hand of God came down and said, "Bang. This is it. Make your decision. What are you going to do?" That little spark that was left in her from the beginning of the film starts to grow again and she makes up her mind to go out. In going out, she begins to realize that after 13 years of marriage to this guy, she's on the road. My gosh, she meets a guy, he's kind of attractive, she wants to get laid. The whole thing. Then it becomes a matter of her responsibility to herself as a human being.

Q : *Did you find in your first long cut that if the beginning went too long before the accident that it seemed too much like the hand of God?*

M S : No. In fact, my original plan for the picture was to make it look like an Ozzie and Harriet film, in the sense that you think you're going to be with this family for a long time and then suddenly, the guy dies. And it worked. But it seemed repetitious, and, you know, we really didn't need him except for character development. The way I shot it, I should have cut it in the script and not in the editing room.

Q : *The two-shot of the women sunbathing in* Alice—*was that something you visualized beforehand?*

M S : Yeah. What happened was that there was a scene written in the script with the two of them talking, taking a cigarette break in the back of Mel and Ruby's. Not outside, inside. I said, "Jesus Christ, if I have to stay in this place one more day" — I was going crazy in there. So I said, "Let's rehearse this scene outside by the garbage pail and have them have a smoke." In the rehearsal we took two chairs and Diane and I said, "Hey, what about sunbathing?" Terrific. They sat there and I had a little view-finder. I rarely use a viewfinder but I looked down and suddenly I saw something like that, you know, the two faces and that was the idea. We saved the real big close-ups for that scene. The rest of the film we shot pretty much in the old American tradition. I wanted it to be very much in the old American style which is medium-shot, medium-shot, two-shot, wide-shot.

Q : *It's the most distinctive shot in the whole film.*
M S : If you look at all the close-ups, that's the closest we get in all the picture.

Q : *What about your own personal growth as a filmmaker? Areas where you think you're weak or new things you'd like to try.*
M S : Well, it's all there. It's there in *Alice*; the weaknesses are there. And in *Mean Streets*. Structure, camera. It depends on what you're going to do with the camera. Certain films may call for less camera movement than others. I felt that *Alice* needed a lot of it. Structuring the script is very important so that I can meander now and then and not hurt it too much. I like meandering — it's very often thrown at me as a criticism — but to me it means character. For me, it means atmosphere. That's what I like to do. I like to be able to meander, as they say, within a structure. *Mean Streets* could have been much shorter by dropping the firecracker scene and the mook scene but I think it would have been less of a picture. It would have been much faster and it probably would have appealed to a wider audience but it was my picture and I wanted it to go that way. *Boxcar Bertha,* on the other hand, is a different picture altogether. Without doing *Boxcar,* you could have never done *Mean Streets* because the same crew made *Boxcar* that made *Mean Streets*. We shot *Boxcar* in 24 days in Arkansas. We learned how to make a picture. That was that.

Martin Scorsese's Gamble

GUY FLATLEY/1976

IT'S MARTIN SCORSESE'S 33RD birthday, and he's being honored with a party in his gloomily elegant home-away-from-Hollywood
home, the ornate, claustrophobic Cecil Beaton Suite at the St. Regis. It's not
a surprise party, yet he appears absurdly unfestive when he finally answers
the buzzer.

"Happy birthday, Marty. Am I early?"

"No," mumbles the tiny, dark-bearded, chalky-faced sufferer standing
bathrobed and bewildered in the doorway. "Everyone else is late."

Or possibly he has forgotten to invite everyone else to his party, since
Martin Scorsese has fallen into a distinct stupor of late, his frail, asthmatic
body sapped of its customary energy, his Italianate emotions spent directing *Taxi Driver,* a bizarre, brutally downbeat movie that will either
enthrone him as the boldest, most fiercely imaginative maverick among
the new breed of American film makers or pigeonhole him, perhaps per-
manently, as a poor commercial risk. Or both.

In recent months, producers have become shrewdly sensitive to the
public's insatiable appetite for escapist epics, for jumbo-budgeted, mini-
minded movies that rock no boats and make no statements bulkier than
"Beware of the Shark!" It was *Jaws,* after all—and not *Nashville* or *Smile* or
The Day of the Locust—that bit its way into box-office history. Clearly,
moviegoers are more in a mood for glossy garbage than tortuous truth; it's

nostalgia, preferably laced with violence and sex, they clamor for; it's all-star holocaust that has them standing in line, not unrelenting realism.

It's no accident that the upcoming Hollywood menu boasts such meaty morsels as a souped-up *Superman,* two remakes of *King Kong,* a dozen or so disastro-dramas, including *The Day the World Ended* and *The Night the Japanese Attacked Los Angeles,* a pair of slaughter-in-the stadium pictures labeled *Black Sunday* and *Two-Minute Warning,* and sequels to *Mandingo, The Sting, Airport 1975, The Exorcist,* and *Jaws.* Not to mention Raquel Welch as *Sheena, Queen of the Jungle.*

So what movie mogul with all his marbles would go out of his way to pour a million bucks or so down the drain on a feverish portrait of a skinny, shifty-eyed, psychopathic Vietnam veteran who sets out to purify New York of its politicians and pimps and perverts in one orgasmic blood-bath, a story soaked in the sewage of sin-city and crusted with the vermin of Times Square after midnight, a putrefying close-up of urban depravity and governmental greed, with no jokes and no jaws? That may be the very question that David Begelman, president of Columbia Pictures, is asking himself today, the day of *Taxi Driver's* New York premiere.

A tougher question to answer is what motivated Scorsese to make the movie in the first place. What kind of man deliberately jeopardizes a budding career by filming a story whose single ray of light is the platonic love affair between a pill-popping, pistol-packing taxi driver and a fouled-up, freaked-out 12-year-old hippie prostitute, a trash-strewn idyll climaxed by a stomach-turning shoot-out in an East Village tenement? What despairing view of society, what weirdly masochistic streak, prompted Scorsese to toy with a theme that could spell professional suicide? Is it conceivable that his obsessively cinematic perception blinded him to the realities of the Hollywood marketplace, that he truly believed Paul Schrader's unsparing screenplay contained the ingredients of a box-office biggie?

Or is there some method to his seeming madness? A rundown of Scorsese's cinematic output suggests a surprising pattern, a shrewdly daring scheme to shift artistic gear from film to film, to alternate the grim and the glamorous, the harrowing and the happy, in an apparent effort to convince Hollywood that he is a jack-of-all-trades, a master of both the extravagant and the austere. It has even been hinted that *Alice Doesn't Live Here Anymore,* a robustly commercial, rough-but-romantic comedy about a gutsy widow who survives numerous hard knocks to find eventual bliss with her sweet sewer-mouthed son and a sexy, supremely supportive new husband, was an act of atonement for Scorsese's earlier, shamefully uncommercial *Mean Streets.*

Alice turned out to be a sleeper, and Scorsese awoke one morning to find himself a bankable talent, the only kind Hollywood takes to its heart. Were it not for *Alice,* though, he might have remained as idle as the talented Terrence Malick, whose brilliant *Badlands* — like *Mean Streets* — won raves at the 1973 New York Film Festival before mushrooming into a box-office bomb. The pressure to be commercial in the assembly-line atmosphere of Hollywood is more intense than ever, and this pressure has undoubtedly taken a toll on Scorsese; it may even have been the decisive factor in his signing up with United Artists to make a lavishly budgeted musical called *New York, New York,* which will star Liza Minnelli and Robert De Niro — the demented *Taxi Driver* — as a 40s band singer and her sax-playing sweetheart and will be shot entirely in Hollywood on studio sets.

Dreams of box-office glory, however, could scarcely have inspired the project Scorsese hopes to tackle after *New York, New York* — a movie about Mother Cabrini, a woman envisioned by Scorsese as an unsaintly saint who "hustled in the streets and clawed her way through society."

"It's true that some films will involve me more than others," says Scorsese, considering the question of artistic compromise, of sustaining a career by juggling artistic and commercial triumphs. "It's also true that I might never have made *Taxi Driver* were it not for the success of *Alice.* The question of commercialism is a source of worry. Must one make a choice, must it be a matter of either setting your sights on winning an Academy Award and becoming a millionaire, or making only the movies you want to make and starving to death?"

Time will tell whether it will be necessary for Scorsese to starve to death, just as it will tell if he can adapt his raw, improvisational style to the lighter, more delicate demands of the musical, *New York, New York.* "I wanted to make a big, commercial Hollywood movie, and still get my theme across. We'll start off with aerial shots of New York, the way they did in all of those movies in the 40s, but everything else will be shot in the studio. Even the cars won't be real cars. But the people will be real, the couple will be real. Basically, the movie will be about two people who are in love but can't make a go of it together, and the failure of their relationship will be handled realistically.

"It's really too early to talk about me in terms of style, but I suppose you could say my movies are similar to me, to the way I am as a person, and my rhythm and pacing reflect the way I think and talk and move."

It may be too early to talk about Scorsese's style; still, there are significant elements that do carry over from film to film. The scalding intensity with which he illuminates his dark subjects, his gift for coaxing actors to be simultaneously natural and flamboyant, his unexpected trick of mixing earthy comedy with florid, nearly operatic melodrama, his willingness to probe his own troubled psyche in the course of shaping his art, and— most important—his passion for exploring character, all brand Scorsese as a director of stature.

Yet his visual technique does not knock your eye out with fancy framing and exotic pictorial designs. There are no preening, *Barry Lyndon*-like compositions, no cinematic paintings-for-the-ages. Nobody looks at a scene from a Scorsese movie and gasps, "This should be hanging in a museum." His scenes throb with crude life, his camera seems nervous, almost hysterical, jumping here, darting there, as if there may not be enough to capture the beauty, or ugliness, of the moment.

You don't remember events from a Scorsese movie so much as you remember faces. Alice, tough and tired and hanging on a thread of hope, singing "Where or When" to a barroom full of empty tables; a drunken punk in *Mean Streets,* turning suddenly from a urinal and facing an assassin's gun; Flo, a brassy but vulnerable waitress in *Alice,* shrugging away a customer's insult but registering a lifetime of hurt in her eyes; Teresa, the epileptic in *Mean Streets,* writhing on the floor of a tenement hallway, aware that she has been abandoned by both her boyfriend and her cousin; Travis Bickle, potential assassin in *Taxi Driver,* standing before a mirror and fantasizing menace with a freshly purchased pistol.

To achieve his sometimes repulsively real results, Scorsese employs a technique of controlled permissiveness with his actors. During rehearsals, he encourages improvisation, however wild, and welcomes suggestions for changes in dialogue and even in the over-all shaping of a scene. If these sessions prove fruitful, the changes are checked with the screenwriter, incorporated into the script and then shot precisely as rewritten.

"One of Marty's best qualities as a director is the way he deals with actors," says Harvey Keitel, the Jewish actor who played the Scorsese-like Italian hero of *Who's That Knocking at My Door?*—a 1969 embryo edition of

Mean Streets—and then again in *Mean Streets* itself, before going on to act a vicious, woman-punching weirdo in *Alice* and a scummy pimp in *Taxi Driver.* "Marty lets actors bring their own humanity—their eccentricities, their humor, their compassion—to a role. With Marty you have freedom, and you know something always pops up. Marty loves people."

People. The dominant characteristic of all of Scorsese's films, and the trait which sets him honorably apart from the majority of his moviemaking peers in this time of gimmickry and exploitation, is his preoccupation with people, with the things we can discover about them and the things which remain a mystery. And the people to whom he is most fanatically drawn are the misfits, the losers and the loners. His zeal for documenting the struggle of the alienated individual against an oppressive society undoubtedly stems from his own youth, in New York's Little Italy, from the spiritual suffocation so harshly mirrored in *Mean Streets,* with its semi-autobiographical rendering of an aimless Italian-American drifting from mass to Mafia to barroom and back again, a potentially whole man torn apart by religious guilt and hand-me-down bigotry.

The past—his raw-grained, fantasy-clutching childhood—might in fact yield a clue to what makes Marty run against the Hollywood current. And where he runs from here. "Marty never gave me much trouble," recalled Charles Scorsese, an immigrant clothes presser in the garment district who once, briefly, tried to settle his wife and two sons in Queens but was forced by financial woes to return to the tenement on Elizabeth Street in Little Italy, to the modest but inviting apartment where he lives today. "Oh, Marty and his friends used to drink my liquor and fill up the empty bottles with water and Karo syrup, but they were good boys. Marty was sickly, though, and couldn't keep up with the other boys, and that's how the thing with the movies got started. My son is smart, smart in the way of books, but not as smart as me in some other ways."

Some other ways may include the ways of religion and marriage. When he was a child, Marty wouldn't touch meat on Friday and he earnestly believed that skipping mass on Sunday might send him straight to hell. He entered a seminary immediately after grade school but claims he was tossed out after a year because the priests thought him a thug. Today he's no thug but he is an agnostic, having fled the church not long after his marriage in St. Patrick's Cathedral to a nice Jewish-Irish girl, one who now lives in New Jersey with her new husband and Marty's 11-year-old daughter, Catherine.

Still, smart or not, Charles Scorsese's wayward son is obviously a source of pride to his father, and anyone who has seen Marty's *Italian-American,* the hilarious, deeply moving documentary shown at the 1974 New York Film Festival, is aware of the enormous love he feels for his parents. Nevertheless, he dwells on Fifth Avenue, not Elizabeth Street, when he's in town these days.

Slumped in a plush chair in the Cecil Beaton Suite one evening not long before his Nov. 17 birthday, Marty unleashed a sigh mixed heavily with relief and exhaustion. The frustrations of shooting a movie amid the summer heat and filth and costly thunderstorms and front-office pressure were at an end, and *Taxi Driver* was ready for the editing room. Bone-weary and besieged by asthma, pleurisy and a case of the jitters that had him phoning his analyst for the first time in months, he coughed, sniffed, gobbled pills, drank herbal tea, sprayed his throat and spoke softly, incessantly — like a gentle machine-gunner — of movies past, present, and future.

"The first thing I remember seeing in a movie house was a trailer. 'Coming next week,' it said, and there was Roy Rogers sitting on a horse. 'That's Trigger,' my dad said. 'Do you know what Trigger is?' 'Yeah,' I said, 'it's something on a gun.' 'No,' he said, 'it's a horse. Wanna come back next week and see?' 'Yes,' I said. I was so excited."

Growing up in Little Italy had more than its share of excitement, not all of it good. "It's the ghetto that creates prejudice. I can remember when I was 5 and my brother was 12, we were walking down the street one day and suddenly we saw a big crowd of people. They were standing around a man who had fallen, and his head was bleeding. My brother took a look at him, and then he turned to me and said, 'Oh, he's only a Jew.' And that is one of my earliest memories."

Marty acknowledges that his marriage to a Jewish girl was a form of rebellion, and the other woman with whom he once shared a chunk of his life — and his dreams of Hollywood fame and fortune — was also Jewish. Sandy Weintraub met Marty through her father, Fred Weintraub — a producer who had given Marty a crucial job as editor on *Woodstock* — and until quite recently she functioned as his occasional editor, unofficial assistant producer and official roommate.

Not only was Sandy handy in the editing room; she also had a knack for nursing Marty back to health when he was seriously ill, as she did a little over a year ago, soothing his jangled nerves, devising diets, even concocting a special herbal tea. (Today, there is a new live-in Nightingale on the scene—Julia Cameron, a seductive journalist who came to interview Marty and stayed for dinner, and breakfast. Just a few weeks after Marty's 33rd birthday party—in a ceremony written by the betrothed couple and performed in the bride's home town of Libertyville, Ill.—Julia became Mrs. Martin Scorsese.)

Marty's health has always presented a problem, causing him acute physical and mental stress. "Not being able to play games when I was a kid, I developed defenses. I'd say, 'I hate sports, I'm going to go to the movies, or stay home and do my story board.' I drew my own stories, like comic books, and I do that with my movies now. I draw all the scenes, the camera angles and everything, first. I developed a great hatred of sports when I was a boy, a hatred which I have to this day. Tennis? I can't see people running around batting balls and breaking their ankles. Swimming? You have to be out of your mind to put your head under water."

Marty's passion for movies was even more pronounced than his contempt for sports, so nobody was the least bit astonished to see him zoom from Cardinal Hayes High School in the Bronx to the New York University Film School in Washington Square. And his time in the Village was an education in more ways than one. "When I went to the university, I met girls who were blond. As a kid, I had literally only known dark-haired girls. But the girls at N.Y.U. were blond, sweet-looking, intelligent, wore pleated skirts and spoke proper English. And they were very rich. A non-Latin type would have cast a dark-haired actress as the girl Travis idolizes in *Taxi Driver,* but I wanted Cybill Shepherd."

Marty learned to prefer blondes at N.Y.U., but mostly he learned the fundamentals of film-making, and what he learned he later taught. In 1968, he became an instructor at N.Y.U.'s film school, a job he held for two years before going on to filming television commercials, editing the news for CBS-TV, covering Hubert Humphrey's ho-hum Presidential campaign in 1972, and, at long last, Hollywood, where he edited a rock 'n' roll documentary called *Medicine Ball Caravan.*

His next big step was falling into the fast company of Roger Corman, filmdom's most benevolent businessman and undisputed king of the B's, who had taken a shine to *Who's That Knocking at My Door?* and offered Marty the chance to direct *Boxcar Bertha,* a sequel to Corman's potboiler *Bloody Mama* and Marty lost no time in climbing aboard. Nor did he waste any time in cranking out the product. "Roger's films make money because of the speed and the economy with which they are shot," Marty said. "You learn what's essential to a scene, and how to get it quickly shot. Roger came down to Arkansas, marched onto the set, made an angry face, stirred up the crew and got them to work a little harder. We shot *Boxcar Bertha* in 24 days for $650,000, and it made a profit. I got $5,000."

Boxcar Bertha had a few nice touches, but it was basically a blood-and-gore exploitation flick, brimming over with violence. "Violence has always been a pretty scary thing for me, but I'm fascinated by it, especially by the aimlessness of it. It's always erupting when you don't expect it, particularly in a city like New York. You're sitting in a restaurant, eating, and suddenly a car crashes through the window and you're dead. That's happened several times in New York. When we were scouting locations for *Taxi Driver* up by Lincoln Center one day, the ballet had just let out and a number of women were crossing to catch a bus. Suddenly a big guy walked over to a very old lady and punched her in the mouth, and a young lady began screaming and crying. The guy just turned around and walked away. Senseless violence. Yet if you got into that guy's head—into his character—who knows?"

Marty gets into the head of the psychopathic Travis, but there is surprisingly little violence, or sex, in *Taxi Driver,* with the notable exception of the climactic shoot-out—a horrifying, yet inevitable, sequence which was threatened by the M.P.A.A. with an X rating until Marty agreed to "desaturate the color," to literally tone down the deep, vivid red of the spurting blood. But, for the most part, *Taxi Driver* methodically avoids sensationalism, ignoring the ripe possibilities of a script crammed full of sleazy hustlers and minimizing the shock content of a potentially lurid scene in which the psychotic cabbie naively takes the rich-bitch tease into an Eighth Avenue porno movie house.

"When Travis falls in love with a woman, he can't admit he wants to make love to her. That's forbidden. What he feels for her is like a masturbating fantasy of the Blessed Virgin. The movie deals with sexual repression, so there's a lot of talk but no sex, no lovemaking, no nudity. If the audience saw nudity, it would work like a release valve, and the tension that's been building up would be dissolved. The valve in *Taxi Driver* is not released until Travis finally lets loose and starts shooting."

Travis is not the only sickee on the loose in *Taxi Driver*. Crazy is the correct word for the creep who commands the startled Travis to pull over to the curb, keep the meter running, and peek with him into the window of an apartment where his white wife makes love to a black man. The role is played by Marty himself and he manages to be even more convincingly repulsive than he was in the bit part of the amoral assassin at the end of *Mean Streets*.

Not that Marty intends to be next year's Robert De Niro. He must be about his business. "I don't have much time. I'm desperate. I gather as much information about myself and other people as I can, but I need time to put things together in my brain. I want to communicate on the basic human level—sad, funny, violent, peaceful. I don't want to do movies unless they further me not only as a film maker but as a person, unless I can say what I want to say with them. Sometimes I look at one of my scenes and I say, 'My God, look at that! a thousand things went wrong.' But then an emotion comes through, and I'm happy. That's where I am. On the other hand, I need the money—I have to eat, too—and I also have a compulsive drive to keep working."

Specifically, Marty had a compulsive drive to work on *Taxi Driver*. "I *had* to make that movie. Not so much because of the social statement it makes, but because of its *feeling* about things, including things I don't like to admit about myself. It's like when you're in therapy and the doctor takes a videotape of a session and then shows it to you. 'Notice how you reacted to that question?' he asks. 'See how defensive you are?' Well, I'm not into videotaping my life, but in a way I am trying to put certain things about myself on canvas.

"I know this guy Travis. I've had the feelings he has, and those feelings have to be explored, taken out and examined. I know the feeling of rejection that Travis feels, of not being able to make relationships survive. I know the killing feeling, the feeling of really being angry."

But doesn't *Taxi Driver* make a broader social statement? Doesn't it say that our country—with its poverty and filth, its Watergate and its Vietnam—breeds drifting creatures like Travis, people who can gain recognition only through acts of violence? Surely, the fact that he is a Vietnam veteran is not coincidental? "That's all in the movie, and I agree that changes should be made in the American social structure. But in order to bring about social change, you have to start by understanding individual characters. You begin by going into a microcosm. The best way is to start with a character and then put him through scenes, through conflicts, that illustrate your theme. Then the character grows, in a positive or negative way. I always start with a person, not a statement.

"Some people have said that *Alice* is a movie about women's liberation, but I think that's the wrong emphasis. It's about *human* liberation. Alice happens to be a woman who says to a man, 'This is what I need, and you give it to me or we can't live together.' You could say that *Mean Streets* is saying how hard it is to live on the Lower East Side, and you could say that *Taxi Driver* is about how hard it is to be a Vietnam veteran. But those are not the main themes.

"I look for a thematic idea running through my movies, and I see that it's the outsider struggling for recognition. Charlie, in *Mean Streets,* is an outsider and so are Teresa and Johnny Boy. Johnny Boy was going to blow up the whole system. And Alice is an outsider and, above all, Travis Bickle, the taxi driver, is an outsider. And I realize that all my life I've been an outsider and, above all, being lonely but never realizing it. Oh, I have lots of friends, lots of people around me, but I'm still on the outside.

"It's only beginning to dawn on me . . . it hit me about two nights ago, remembering, how lonely I was as a kid. My parents worked, and I came home from school at 3 and sat at the kitchen table making up stories on my drawing board, or watching TV or escaping to the movies. Not being able to be physical on the same level as the other kids, not being able to play ball or to fight. So I went off in the other direction, as chronicler of the group, trying to be a nice guy to have around."

It's Martin Scorsese's 33rd birthday. He's changed from his bathrobe to a spiffy blue suit and he smiles a wan, nice-guy smile as his mother slices cake and the Cecil Beaton Suite swells with the off-key sound of friends, old and new, singing "Happy Birthday, Dear Marty." Before long, though, he is sagging into a bedroom chair, isolated from the revelers in the next room. The outsider. His boyish body is motionless, his eyes pleading—like those of a child martyr on a long-ago holy picture. Earlier in the day, he had sat, tense and perspiring, proud and frightened, through the rough cut of *Taxi Driver,* and one can only try to guess his present, jumbled thoughts.

Will he soon be judged a cinematic genius, the daring young man who led the spineless movie industry out of the jaws of spiritual disaster? Will some repentant mogul rush forward with the money to help Marty realize his dream of making "a not very reverent, but a very human" movie about Mother Cabrini? Will United Artists take one look at *Taxi Driver*'s box-office receipts and say nix, nix to *New York, New York*?

As Marty's father would say, "Wanna come back next week and see?"

Martin Scorsese Tells All: Blood and Guts Turn Me On!

RICHARD GOLDSTEIN AND

MARK JACOBSON/1976

AFTER *MEAN STREETS*, MARTY Scorsese was New York's most evocative cinematic voice. He was Kid Ethnic, the skinny boy who tried to get respect in Little Italy by being sensitive instead of tough. He went to NYU where he learned to operate a camera with the street sense of Shirley Clarke and handle actors like John Cassavetes. Much of *Mean Streets* was shot in California but that didn't matter: the language and obsessions oozing from Robert De Niro and Harvey Keitel were pure native stock. Marty waited years to get *Mean Streets* off his chest, and in it, it seemed, was a moviemaker to grow up with.

Later some said Marty deserted his muse when he went to Arizona to make *Alice Doesn't Live Here Anymore.* But you have to get out of the neighborhood sometime. The film was a commercial success and Marty became "bankable," which is what Hollywood calls sure things.

It was heartening to hear that Marty would shoot *Taxi Driver* on the old turf. But he didn't return with the same adolescent flash. The gutter opera had turned to careful raunch; the manic camera that spoke of "becoming" was gone too, replaced by artful composition. De Niro and Keitel weren't even Italian anymore. The cinema punk had gone stylish. Certainly many of the obsessions remained—the fearful and looming portrayal of

From *Village Voice*, 5 April 1976. Reprinted by permission.

blacks, the clumsy violence, the ritualistic males—but if the neighborhood in *Mean Streets* had Scorsese by the balls, in *Taxi Driver* he was exorcising old demons.

We asked Marty about the past and present and what you can't shake no matter what.—M.J.

"How did things go at the opening?"
"Fine. Very good, in fact. Hollywood Boulevard theatre seems to be doing very good, I mean, really excellent."

"What about the reviews?"
"Reviews? Reviews is very, um—they're very respectful, but they're not.... They don't understand the ending and they don't know if this kind of violence is really, you know.... Actually, they're wondering why we didn't explain what this character's about. They're trying to find reasons why he did everything. And they get very upset at the ending because that may mean something else. See, everybody wants the picture to end like *Hamlet,* everybody's like dead all over the place, you know, and he looks up and points a finger at his temple and shoots himself three times, you know. That's where everybody thinks it should end, because then it's just like a ... you know. I don't think a Western is bad—I like Westerns—somebody gets killed and everybody goes home. Everybody forgets about the picture."

"Well, maybe you could tell why Taxi Driver *ended that way."*
"Well ... [Laughter] the whole thing has to do with, you know, the whole process that the character goes through to the point at which he wants to sacrifice himself.... And it's going to be a blood sacrifice, right? Then you might as well do it right, and you might as well show every detail. I mean, I'm talking about the character. Travis goes through every detail, and the only thing is that he blows it, because he doesn't get killed."

"Is that why he puts his finger to his head, he's upset that he didn't get killed?"
"Yes. It's also kind of mocking, mocking himself.... It's the final irony. And then the camera going back over things is really kind of, like a reexamination of the elements of the sacrifice."

"So, it's a ritual?..."
"A ritualistic, religious experience. Like the Mass. Christ came down and said you don't have to kill any more lambs, right?"

"Did He?"
"Yeah. He said, I'm gonna go up on the cross and it's going to be a human sacrifice and I'm going to be—I'm the son of God and uh, [laughter]....
Do you understand my point? The idea of Christ coming to fulfill...not to, not to destroy, but to fulfill, you know, the prophecy and the idea was, you know, no more ritualistic blood sacrifice of lambs."

"You mean, Travis thought if he did that killing, New York City would be clean?"
"Yeah."

"Is that idea coming from inside Travis, or from you?..."
"That's part of my thing, and it's part of Paul's thing [Paul Schrader, the screenwriter]. Uh, you know, Paul had a religious background, a depressed background, the whole thing. He was in the Special Forces, in the marines. You only get that by watching the kind of knife Travis is using at the end. It's called a K-bar. Only Special Forces use it. Uh, the way he, uh, the way he, uh exercises it, uh...The haircut, that's very important at the end— because the Special Forces, before they went out on patrol in North Vietnam, they would shave their hair like that."

"Are we meant to see Travis as a kind of average person, a well-adjusted guy?"
"No. By the time you see him, he's ready for a breakdown. Travis is right on the edge, you know. Right from the first frame, he's on the edge and we just wait the hour and 51 minutes for him to go over. But...I think that he has right on the surface a lot of the emotions, a lot of the problems, that most everybody has in them. I have them, Paul has 'em."

"Do you generally approve of your characters?"
"Absolutely."

"What about their attitude toward black people?"
"Well, Bobby De Niro in *Taxi Driver* is a racist character."

"What about the point of view of the movie, though? I mean, whenever we look at a black person, we see somebody who's majestically evil looking."
" . . . Looking into his eyes. Remember that shot when he, says fucking Mau Mau land and suddenly Bobby looks over, sees this guy? . . . The guy was such a sweet guy. He was an extra. A very sweet guy. He was sitting there all night for that one shot. The shot was in slow motion, though. That's why he looks evil." (Snicker)

"What about the black woman in Mean Streets*?"*
"Absolutely. Yes. He says she's beautiful, she's beautiful, but she's black. You gotta realize where these guys are coming from."

"Do you worry about the fact that people are going to think that that's the way you look at things or is that the way you look at things?"
"We were brought up that way. You don't lose certain things. You get to deal with certain things, right? I mean, how do, how do you say 'Oh, I mean, in the Italian-American neighborhood I never heard the word, "Nigger."' [Laughter] Never. You know, how do you say that? I mean, that's not true. It just isn't true. I mean, if you're gonna put something up there about yourself you might as well try to do it as honestly as possible."

"When you were growing up I mean, did you buy those values?"
"Buy what values?"

"Let's say, values toward black people and toward violence? I'm curious about how you related to all that stuff as a child."
"You relate to it in many different ways. I mean, in one way I was involved with it, but I was also involved with the Church at the time, you know?"

"Did they counteract each other?"
"Yes, Sure. Sure, but at the same time, at the same time, you know, you're in the streets and you're watching the stuff and, um, you get involved with it. You get involved with codes of behavior, you know, and how do you act, how should you act in a situation like this? You know, can you make yourself a special person because you're not, you know, uh, the

toughest guy on the block? You know, how do you do that? Because there are ways, you know, you can survive, you know, and you know, 'respect' is a key phrase."

"One thing I always wanted to ask you—what's a mook? You never find out in Mean Streets *what a mook is."*
"Well, no, it's not, you don't have to know what he's saying, that's the point. I found out in a discussion—some guy told me it's a, it means, it's a slang for big mouth, like shooting off at the mouth, like very often, they call a guy a dun, remember at the end of *Mean Streets* he pointed a gun at Michael, he says . . . DD—Disappointed Dunsky. . . ."

"What's that?"
"D-Dunsky is a word for dun. Dun is like a Don. Like Don Corleone."

"So in other words, a guy who's a disappointed Mafia leader?"
"Yeah, disappointed—a dun can mean a man of respect, you know, an honorable man."

"How similar was your childhood to what went on in Mean Streets? *Did you live through things like that?"*
"You live through them . . . above some of them; you see some of them and some you can't talk about, you know what I mean?"

"How angry do you feel about things?"
"If I didn't feel angry, I wouldn't have to make *Taxi Driver*."

"Do you feel angry the way that De Niro felt angry in that film?"
"Oh, yeah."

"The movie's like a nightmare to me."
"Yes, it's a nightmare. Yes."

"I know Hitchcock works straight from his dreams. Do you ever do that?"
"Oh, sure, I had scenes in *Mean Streets* that are dreams which I actually shot. You see the way it opens now, he jumps out of bed? Well, there was a dream before that. Took a shot of him lying on the ground—with a flame

going out of his heart, some sort of flame in his chest, like it was supposed to be an X ray of him dying—you could see his soul burning up."

"Are there details in Taxi Driver *that come out of your dreams?"*
"All the slow motion. People in slow motion on the street. A lot of Bobby's close-ups are slow motion. I wanted to extend the moment. You go inside his head, really, and also, it's accentuating his acting, his looks."

"Did you ever have nightmares like that?"
"No, but that's—very often when I get angry, that's the way I feel."

"How would you—can you—talk about that anger?"
"Uh, gee, I should be paying you $45 a session. . . ." [Laughter]

"Do you see a shrink?"
"Oh, yeah, for the past few years. . . . You talk about anger, like jealousy, for example, you put this woman as a goal, and then Travis puts all these self-destruct mechanisms, uh, in his actions with the girl, so that he knows that he can't get her. Takes her to a porno movie, deep down knowing that he's going to fuck up, you know . . . the conscious mind it's fine, but the subconscious is saying you better screw up again and you don't deserve her, understand?"

"Yes."
"Well, uh, there's a self-destruct mechanism that he puts in the relation-ship, see? So, uh. . . . So, we talk about the anger and the jealousy and we come up with the whole thing he does in front of the mirror, which is really the key to the picture, you know. . . ."

"Is that scripted, or did? . . ."
"No, that wasn't scripted. We said, Bobby, let's do something like that. Talk to yourself in the mirror. And when I shot the rehearsals, I kept saying keep repeating it. Repeat it. Because I couldn't hear him. And it sounded great to me. I wanted to make sure we had it on sound. And the repetition was what I liked. That's what we used. The repetition of, 'Are you talking to me? Are you talking to me?' That's what I liked a great deal. But there's

a lot of, um, you were asking the thing about the sessions, you know, like you think you put all that up on the screen. You think that you're gonna, in a way — exorcise those feelings. Then, after the picture's over, you watch it on screen and maybe besides the usual postpartum blues you have after a movie, there's a period you go through when you realize, my God, you know, it isn't enough to just put it on the screen. You've still got to work at changing the feelings, you know, the feelings of anger and the feelings of — whatever."

"How do you manage to feel close to your feelings and emotions when you're making a movie? It's such a complicated process?"
"You laugh a lot. Especially with actors that I like, you know. I have fun with them and, uh, you get the violence though, and the violence is so, uh, inch by inch, A-B-C. There's no fun in that. It's a pain in the neck, so in between jobs, you know, you wait two hours, because makeup has to be done."

"You say the violence in your films is ritualistic, but the way you shoot it is realistic."
"Right, the violence has got to be plain, straight, and fast, and awkward, awkward and stupid looking, just the way it would happen in real life. It's got to be just as if the Daily News photographer went there and shot the whole thing. It's gotta be just like a tabloid."

"It's not much fun to shoot those violent scenes?"
"Oh, it's really not that much fun, no. No. Then you have to plug your ears because the gunshots are so loud. Everybody's getting headaches. Murray Marston had to come in every morning and get his hand cut off [snickers].... And uh, meanwhile, mind you, I'd taken Bobby out to dinner twice — through the blood and the Mohawk haircut. And nobody, nobody paid any attention. This was like 99th and Broadway in one of those Cuban-Chinese restaurants, you know. I looked like a regular, one of the Saturday night crowd."

"How do you feel about New York now that you don't live here anymore?"
"Well, I'm here most of the time really, I mean this is . . . L.A.'s one big office. It's got palm trees, and you look out the window, 'cause I'm look-

ing out the window now and it's got trees outside. That's about it. It's an office."

"Are you going to make more movies in the streets of New York?"
"We are gonna come back to do *New York, New York.* But only some of it. I would like to make this film look like a film that was made in the '40s. You know, shoot in studios and have some fun with that."

"It's a musical."
"Yeah."

"Does anyone get killed in it?"
"No. No."

"I'm trying to figure out what a musical by Martin Scorsese could possibly be like."
"First of all, it's not a musical, it's a film, which has music in it, that comes from an actual source, in other words, big bands, everybody gets up and sings — sing! — right? — music!"

"Set in, like, 1940."
"Opens on V-J Day. A guy comes out of the war, and loves jazz. And he plays a sax, and he plays sax rather violently, too — so he's got a strange way of playing music. He hears some new music being played in Harlem, it's the beginning of Charlie Parker, and all that sort of thing, he gets fascinated by it, and he tries to incorporate it, with the Big Band Sound. It's really a story about him and a girl who sings in the band, and they're very young, they get married, on impulse. Both characters are on the edges of emotion all the time — like, he'll get up and play a solo, an unannounced solo — and throw off the rest of the band . . . that kind of guy."

"In other words, it's a little like Taxi Driver, *it's still the same character propping himself up."*
"Yeah, yeah, but he's *talented,* and the thing is that the talent, her talent and his talent, get in the way of the relationship and they have to split."

"Did you always want to be a Hollywood director? . . . when you went to all those movies, is that what you wanted to do?"
"I didn't know what a director was, I just wanted—I guess—to make the movies. I don't mean—not the details, but I always came back thinking how I would have done the film."

"When I see Taxi Driver, *I notice a couple of heavy allusions. I mean, when Travis drops the Alka-Seltzer in the glass, is that like, a take from Godard?"*
"It's exactly that. The script just says he pours the Alka-Seltzer in and, Jesus, think about what it refers to—the shot of the coffee cup in *Two or Three Things I Know About Her, she* was all the way into the black coffee, and the coffee looked just like a galaxy, and they're talking about the state of the universe."

"Well I guess Travis is a lot like the character in Diary of a Country Priest.*"*
"Yeah, that's my favorite of the Bresson pictures."

"In fact, when Travis pours that peach brandy on bread, and he starts talking about how his stomach can't. . . ."
" 'Cause he, that's again a self-destructive thing. Don't forget that what the priest is doing in *Diary of a Country Priest.* He had *cancer,* that's what he had the guy drinking this rotgut wine for, you know, he's making sure he dies. "But I mean—you should just understand—the way I like to work, is I'm prompted by a lot of things, other books, things that happened to me in personal life, or that I do in life, some people will get it, some won't, that's fine."

"Like what in Mean Streets*?"*
"Uh, *Mean Streets* is a very, very. . . it's really, obviously, personal, you know, because it deals with semi, semiautobiographical, such as we were talking about before, saying that you really experienced those things, well if you didn't really experience them, experience them spiritually or you hear about them, or you live through certain things like them, over a period of years, you know, if you compress them, you lie, you know, that's what you do."

"Why does the murderer in Mean Streets *let his hair down at the last minute?"*

"Several reasons. First one is—a ritual, he puts his hand over the glass, you know, 'cause what I had, I had—also, a physical problem, and I had to work it in the script."

"What physical problem?"

"Physical problem was that, the kid who did the scene was in another picture and he couldn't cut his hair. Now, I knew that we had to write that in the script, and figure out a way that would work in terms of the whole picture—so that it should be done so that it's almost like a ritual."

"It never occurred to you that there would be any sexual ambiguity in it? I mean, the guy lets his hair down in the men's room."

"Oh sure. Because nobody will know exactly what's going to happen. Everybody... something sexual's gonna happen, and... bam!"

"Why do people always bleed from the neck in your movies?"

"... For anybody it's ... I think it's—you really, to me, you really want to know?"

"Sure...."

"To me, I like the idea of spurting blood, it reminds... it's like a... God, it's... it's really like a purification, you know, the fountains of blood... but it's realistic, all realistic. That's my own head, you know... the guy puts the blood... I said, give me a little more... he says, 'there's gonna be a lot,' I said, that's gonna be okay [Laughs]. And... that's it, no explanation for it, nobody asks any questions. I like the idea of getting shot... I can't, I can't respond to that, I mean just why he gets shot in the neck, but... it's a personal thing, but like... it's based on something I have... whatever."

"Okay, I'll accept that."

"Oh boy."

"You want us not to print that stuff about your neck?"

"About the neck? No, you can run it. What about it? I do what I feel, not what comes out of my head, it's like a fountain, washing, the fountain, like in the Van Morrison song, you know. 'Wash Me,' you know, the whole idea of standing in the waterfall?"

"Do you actually feel cleansed after you've made a film?"
"For a while—I'm discovering now that a lot of other feelings just don't go away. I'm very disappointed. [Laughs] You know, it's the whole feeling that I used to have with the Church, you know, not being worthy, not being worthy enough to be a priest, not being worthy enough to do this, because you're not good enough, you know what I mean?"

"You wanted to be a priest, when you were a kid?"
"Yeah."

"Did you feel that there was some reason why you didn't do it besides the fact that you decided you didn't want to do it?"
"Uh, well...I couldn't...I realized I couldn't fit in the institution, let me put it that way, I couldn't fit in the institution of the Church...I was...I was considered, you know, I was thrown out."

"Did you do something special that got you thrown out, or...."
"Oh, well, I had great, great grades, and then I, uh, caused havoc. Caused great havoc, and you know, I just would bring in all kinds of things and cause all kinds of trouble in the classroom, and...I cut up a lot, too, I did a lot of cutting up you know, in a sense...class clown, I guess, that's the thing, and I was thrown out."

"Do you still feel ambivalent about not being a priest?"
"No, no, I think I can't fit in that. The institution, I mean, I can't fit in that."

"How are you fitting into the institutions in Hollywood?"
"Not very well. No director ever does in this situation. I mean, this is not the old Hollywood, this is a different kind of Hollywood."

"Do you feel like you missed out on the romance?"
"It's still pretty romantic."

"Do directors hang out together? Do you know Spielberg?"
"Sure."

"How would you have directed Jaws?*"*
"I would never do a picture about water."

"What if it was a movie about mussels?"
"Depends on how they're cooked."

Taxi Dancer: Martin Scorsese Interviewed

JONATHAN KAPLAN / 1977

THIS INTERVIEW TOOK PLACE May 25, 1977 during a break at Goldwyn Studios, where Martin Scorsese has been dubbing his new film, *New York, New York.*

MARTIN SCORSESE: Hello, I've had two hours sleep. I'm exhausted.

JONATHAN KAPLAN: *Well, here were are. How do you feel about the picture?*

MS: This picture, *New York, New York*? I got pretty much what I wanted on the screen. More so actually. I got things as the picture developed that I didn't expect. Once I got the lean of it, in other words, where it was going to, it became more a dramatic story, and I took more of the music out. This wasn't even in the editing, I'm talking about the shooting.

JK: *What initially attracted you to the picture?*

MS: I liked the whole idea of the premise—a love story set in the big band era in the Forties. For whatever reasons, I liked the idea. It was just one of those things. I planned to do it before *Taxi Driver,* but because of commitments, whatever, I had to do *Taxi* first. In fact, I started work on *New York, New York* before *Taxi.* When we got back to *New York, New York,* it became a little bigger than we thought because of this concept I had of doing the picture in the old style, which is, you know, sound stages and back lots.

From *Film Comment,* July/August 1977. Reprinted by permission.

A movie called *New York, New York* shot entirely in Los Angeles. Made in Hollywood, U.S.A., which reflects back to the old films I used to see as a kid, which reflected a part of New York—I was really living in New York, but that was a fantasy of New York up on the screen. So in the picture, I tried to fuse whatever was a fantasy—the movies that I grew up with as a kid—with the reality that I experience myself.

J K : *Can you describe your working method on this picture?*
M S :   The working method was kind of strange because Earl Mac Rauch worked on the script for a long time, but Earl, he is a very interesting writer. He is more of a novelist. Whenever we would ask for a change of two or three pages, he would bring twelve pages in and they were terrific. A whole new direction, whole new character things. He is a good writer and what happened was it became unmanageable in terms of making a shooting script. So eventually, at a certain point, my wife, Julia Cameron, started working with him and then about a month before the picture started shooting, Mac felt that he had given as much as he could to it. He couldn't go any further. He worked on it for two years. So then, Bobby De Niro and I had some ideas about some improvisations, and I had known Liza Minnelli for about a year and a half and we could feel comfortable in terms of the improv, but you just can't do a whole picture on improvisations. We needed the structure. So Mardik Martin of *Mean Streets* came in. Mardik structured it with Julia. He wrote some scenes, some key dialogue.

J K : *And this went on during the whole picture?*
M S :   Yeah, fourteen weeks became twenty-two weeks. Mainly because of the fact that it was a musical. Irwin Winkler and Bob Chartoff and I had never done a musical before so we underscheduled the picture mistakenly.

J K : *You mean in terms of the production numbers?*
M S :   Actually, the big musical number "Happy Endings" was perfectly scheduled. It was shot in ten days. Of course, eventually, it was cut out of the picture.

J K : *Not entirely . . .*
M S :   Well, there are two shots left—the staircase and the popcorn. It works much better. But the entire "Happy Endings" number, along with all

the other scenes we liked, are in the television version, which is three to three-and-one-half hours. Tom Rolf just cut it. So what happened was that when we started making the picture, I did this all-out work on the production number. I made it as good as I could because I didn't know what the script was eventually going to turn out like. Even though I had a feeling at that point that it was going to be more personal than I had thought, and I was going to base it on myself, our relationships, our marriages. Sure enough, in the picture, the character (Jimmy Doyle/Robert De Niro), his wife (Francine Evans/Liza Minnelli) was pregnant, my wife was pregnant, Bobby's wife was pregnant, it was crazy time.

J K : *Art imitates life imitates art—*
M S : Imitates life. It was just madness. It went on and on like that. It was fun, it was crazy, it was upsetting, it was terrific; what eventually happened though, the improvisation procedure cost some time. We couldn't have done without Mardik supplying the structure, and Julia helping out. Also Irwin, too, helping out a great deal. Of course, without Mac's script—I mean, he worked two years on it—we wouldn't have had anything.

J K : *What does Mac think of the film?*
M S : I don't know. I don't think he has seen it.

J K : *I don't know of another film that has been so widely screened during the editing process. How did you deal with all that feedback? I mean constantly being inundated with differing opinions, etc.*
M S : Well, at a certain point, you have to leave it. I left it for about three weeks. I left in a way that was not leaving it. I mean nobody knew I left it. They sensed I wasn't around as much. "What's Scorsese doing? What's he playing the fuck around? What is this? Isn't he serious about the picture?" I mean when they got to that point, I just said, "Leave me alone for a goddamn three days. Let me goddamn think about the goddamn movie. Everybody's given ideas, ideas, ideas, I appreciate it all, but at this point, it's total clutter. I can't see the picture and I don't know what the hell anybody is talking about anymore."

J K : *The first cut was what? Four and a half hours?*
M S : Four and twenty-nine. And it worked.

J K : *It worked great.*

M S : But it wouldn't be for the theatrical audience. Once we started cutting it down and finally got it down to two hours, forty-five, that was when we were in the ballpark area. I reshot the key things, a couple of things at the end, because up until that point, I had been so close to the subject matter, the characters, that I couldn't see how they should end as characters.

J K : *It's a very organic process.*

M S : Yes, exactly. Really, in a way, I didn't shoot an ending, and we knew it. So we just waited. It was really that kind of a picture.

J K : *You rely so much on improvisation. What would you do if you found yourself confronted with an actor who couldn't improvise?*

M S : A lot of it has to do with casting. There are certain people who are just immovable. You try to stay away from them, but sometimes, you get stuck. The majority of actors, I find, give them the script and say "This is the dialogue" or "I'll write the dialogue for you in a minute," which automatically gives them a feeling of great insecurity and/or a feeling of great looseness and they can be relaxed to a certain extent. And you say "Here's the idea, and here are the sections—you go from here to here to here. Maybe you could think of how you want to say it. Why don't you say it in your own way." And so you're stumbling around and you find new things and you write them down.

J K : *So you have an improvisation and now you set it.*

M S : Yes, you finally set it. You do it four or five times, but you finally set it.

J K : *You do it four or five times in rehearsing, or on film?*

M S : You do it in rehearsing. But what happened eventually in *New York, New York,* the rehearsing caught up with us. So you are standing around the set rehearsing. That is where a lot of the time went to a certain extent.

J K : *Can you talk about a scene, a moment, a piece of business, anything, that was not scripted at any point that is in the final theatrical cut?*

M S : The breaking of the glass, when Jimmy knocks on the door.

J K : *In the proposal scene, at the justice of the peace?*
M S : Yeah, I got that idea at the end of the day. We had been rehearsing the shot all day. I kept thinking when he would knock on the glass that he would put his hand through it by accident. I said to myself "Gee, this is terrible. Bobby's going to cut his hand. We have to be careful. I'll tell him not to knock the glass so hard." And then I thought, what if he actually *does* put his hand through it? So I asked about the window. I asked the A.D. and other people. They said "Oh, that will take time. You know, the windows, it's a big deal." Within fifteen minutes, we had two of them (breakaway windows), and then, of course, when we had the two, we got five more. And it went on like that, and we did it, and it worked. That kind of thing works. It was 5:30 in the afternoon, and we were trying, but we hadn't even taken a shot. So by the next day, we developed the point in the scene where he literally gets on his knees and tells Francine that he doesn't want her to be with anybody else. That element was added, see, totally unscripted. That's what we were looking for. The scene in the script at that point was a farce scene. We said we needed something else.

J K : *Something real.*
M S : Yeah. Something where maybe this is the area where we can "lock-in," "lock-in" meaning that we could get a certain kind of honesty between the characters. And we asked, "Will it work with the humor and everything?" and I said "Yeah, I think it will," and then Bobby came up with the idea of putting his head under the car. But then he said he thought it was too much. But I said "Let's shoot it anyway." You know, that's how it went, like that.

J K : *In general, if you had the time, you shot more than one alternative for a given scene?*
M S : Yes, I really covered myself, and that came in handy, you know.

J K : *What are some of the problems of doing a musical?*
M S : The playback system.

J K : *Staying in synch?*
M S : The singing and dancing, staying in synch. And the way I shoot the music—every eight bars or four bars or twelve bars, there is a new shot.

J K : *This is all choreographed beforehand?*
M S : Drawn pictures, everything. I mean other people shoot it differently.

J K : *All in one master?*
M S : Yeah.

J K : *What else?*
M S : Well, Bobby learned to play the saxophone in synch. And it had to be in synch. The shot may have been beautiful, but the technical advisor would say "I'm sorry, the fingering was way out there" and we would have to shoot it again.

J K : *The fight in the car, how long did it take to shoot?*
M S : Two days. One day for the masters, and then we had to stop.

J K : *Because they were both so bruised?*
M S : Yeah. Everyone was tired. The next day we did some close-ups and *that* is when we all went to the hospital, really. Liza almost broke her arm, Bobby hurt his knuckles, I hurt my knuckles. Of course, I wasn't in the car, it was from something else, I don't remember. But we all got x-rayed.

J K : *And what was scripted in that, was there scripted dialog?*
M S : Yes, there was scripted dialog. Some of the dialog is in there. But the emotional thing became mainly improvisation. At one point I was with Bobby and I said "You know what, I think she should hit you here." He said "Yeah, yeah, that's good." The next day when the three of us got together, Bobby had an idea for rearranging the scene. I said no, I didn't want to rearrange the scene, but we knew something heavy was going to happen. But Bobby said "Look at it this way" and I said 'Yeah yeah, it might work," and I remember thinking to myself I shouldn't say this, and I started laughing to myself. Liza said "What?" and I said, "But then, if we are going to do it that way, *he* should hit *her* at this point, towards the end, you know, six months, seven months pregnant, it doesn't matter." And that's the way it happened. It happens in the first takes, and if you want, you tone it down, that's all, or you bring it up.

J K : *Let's talk about sets for a minute. Particularly the trees set at the Meadows Club. Did you anticipate the kind of reaction where people are going to say "What is it supposed to be? Real? Fake? What's going on?"*
M S : Yeah, I knew that was going to happen. We showed the film to a bunch of students and one of them said "Did you intend for that set to look realistic or the way it looks?" I said "Yeah, yeah, well, the whole film is on sets, do you realize that?" They all said no.

J K : *Of course some sets look very—*
M S : Real. I know. But if you look closely, they are all stylized. Boris Leven did that—the production designer.

J K : *What was the most common reaction you got from all the rough cut screenings that you had? Was there one scene, one character, plot point, something that people—*
M S : Liked?

J K : *Or didn't like.*
M S : The biggest thing was the "Happy Endings" production number. But a lot of people felt it overbalanced the picture. I mean it was eleven minutes long, and eventually I realized it *did* overbalance the picture, and I had to cut it, and I did, and it was very painful. We made a short of it and it's also in the television version. But it does overbalance the film, because at the end, people felt in the montages in the end, Bobby's character was weakened.

J K : *But the production number was in a way a stylized microcosm of the whole picture.*
M S : Of course, I know. But they don't want to see it. Believe me. We like it. We are just crazy film buffs. It was a direct homage thing, a loving thing to the Fifties, early Fifties production numbers, Forties, whatever, but they don't want to watch it. Even *if* they like it, you could sit in the back of the screening room and see them moving around—restless. They want to know what is going to happen to the characters. And you know what happened, actually, was that the characters became stronger than the music.

J K : *So what are you up to now? What's next?*

M S : I've got two more films that will be done by the end of this year: *The All American Boy* about a friend of mine, Steve Prince, and *The Last Waltz*, you know, with The Band. Now, I'm going to do a play with Liza—almost like an extension of *New York, New York*. The same Francine Evans character. Only after she has made it, and now she has to find a new image. A where-do-I-go-from-here sort of thing, at age thirty-one, I've had it. That kind of character.

J K : *This might be sort of a strange question, but how are you going to put yourself in it? I mean is there a character that you can hang yourself on?*

M S : Herself.

J K : *Her?*

M S : Yeah, herself. The character. She's a workaholic. Complete crazy, crazy person who ruins everybody who comes near, marries her, disaster. Right? Another person, disaster. Always with the wrong person, and gets crazy and finally winds up alone. And likes it. (*Laughter*) I don't know if I like it, but I wind up alone when the time comes. But that way I am undertaking a fantasy. This is going to be my first fantasy film—

J K : *Play.*

M S : (*Laughter*) Play, play, whatever.

Martin Scorsese's Elegy for a Big-Time Band

TERRY CURTIS FOX/1978

MARTY SCORSESE IS LAID BACK. Literally. It is 5 o'clock of a
Sunday afternoon and Marty is leaning all the way back into a Hotel Pierre
couch. The television is soundlessly beaming *Lonely Are the Brave* into the
suite's living room, while one of the various sound-producing machines
that travel when and where Scorsese does is playing Italian popular
music—preparation, perhaps, for Mama Scorsese's birthday celebration
later that night. As the rest of the city is coming out of lazy Sunday, Marty
is having his wake-up cup of coffee. "I hope the caffeine works," he says.

One expects everything of Marty Scorsese: He is that peculiarly American
phenomenon, the mass-cult figure. Scorsese occupies a unique niche in the
Hollywood hierarchy: He is revered by both the industry and the critics, as
an extremely personal, highly idiosyncratic director who is still somehow
in touch with the street. Scorsese is always mentioned as part of the New
Hollywood litany, but he is also, almost inexplicably, apart: Despite a filmography that jumps over genres and styles with deliberate eclecticism, his
movies always read autobiography. If *New York, New York* failed dismally at
the American box office, it is not because the picture overwhelmed Scorsese: It is because a particularly abrasive part of Scorsese overwhelmed the
movie. Musical fans simply could not go in and have a good time.

What one didn't expect is *The Last Waltz. The Last Waltz* is a rock-concert
film, a cinematographic record of the Band's final stand at San Francisco's
Winterland in the fall of 1976. Before it only hacks were supposed to do

From *Village Voice*, 29 May 1978.

rock-concert films. The last time Marty touched the stuff was back in his NYU days, when he edited first *Woodstock* and then *Medicine Ball Caravan*. He may talk about how important these two projects were for his artistic development, but the line on opening day was that *The Last Waltz* just wasn't the sort of thing a Great American Director should do. It's not Important enough. It could only have been done as a lark.

"I shot the whole thing incognito," Marty says. "I was supposed to be resting, taking time off between shooting and editing *New York.* It was all very secret. Irwin Winkler [*New York, New York*'s producer] didn't know I'd done it until it was over, and then, when he found out, he was furious. But all during the concert, it was like a rumor—he's here shooting, he isn't here shooting. I'd shot 22 weeks on *New York, New York,* prepared this film in three weeks, shot one day, and then I sat down. I just sat, for four hours, downstairs at the Miyako Hotel. I couldn't get up. It was perfect.

"We went in thinking, we'll document the Band's last concert and maybe we'll get something, maybe we won't. Then when the footage came back and we looked at it on the KEM, I just said, 'Wow. This is fantastic. We've got a movie.' "

Things do not always work out as planned. Between Thanksgiving of 1976, when the Band played at Winterland, and the release of *The Last Waltz* this April, just about nothing Scorsese planned on did. *New York, New York* failed in the States. (Recent indications are that the film is doing quite well abroad, and will probably recoup its investment.) *The Act,* Liza Minelli's stage vehicle that Marty attempted to direct as a sequel to his dark, ferocious musical, floundered on the road, and Scorsese was replaced by an uncredited (but highly publicized) Gower Champion. Worst of all, his marriage to writer Julia Cameron broke up shortly after the birth of their daughter.

"The movie was therapy," Marty says. "It was the only thing that held me together."

The Last Waltz was not just work; it was a special kind of anchor. Scorsese's love affair with rock and roll, his commitment to music as a form, is at least as deep and abiding as his love and commitment to film. He has always *used* music in his films, knowing just what the kid would listen to in *Alice Doesn't Live Here Anymore,* manipulating the track of *Taxi Driver* with disc-jockey ease. The cultural conflict in *Mean Streets* is most directly expressed as a war between two styles of music, Italian and rock. Indeed, until Jay Cocks read him the Raymond Chandler quote from which he drew the final title, *Mean Streets* was called *Season of the Witch*.

"The music was just always there," Marty says, and when he says it, he means just about all the music there is. His travelling tape collection includes *Don Giovanni*, his radio is tuned to rock and roll.

The Last Waltz was conceived as "an opera." Scorsese borrowed the set of *La Traviata* from the San Francisco Opera, and he and head cinematographer, Michael Chapman, sat down with a set of lyrics to each of the songs, scripting line by line color changes intended to emphasize the content of each musical moment. If Scorsese's fiction films have musical structure, then *The Last Waltz*, with its meticulous script and preplanned camera angles, was constructed in the same manner as his narratives.

Unlike most rock-concert pictures, *The Last Waltz* is an extremely formal film. Coming off *New York, New York*, Marty shot the movie with the same dark, totally interior look. This is a movie in which daylight is never seen, in which the world is totally artificial, limited to stages and studios. Scorsese managed to put crab dollies on the Winterland stage in places that would not obscure the audience's view. With Bill Graham's permission, he dug through Winterland's floor to anchor a tower that could hold Vilmos Zsigmund's position at the back of the hall, providing wide-angle long shots Scorsese was afraid he would otherwise not be able to get. Each of the cameramen on stage had specific instructions, including tracking directions, although little more than six inches of tracking space were available. Only David Myers, who can be seen periodically floating around the stage, had hand-held mobility. Scorsese gave Myers a single, simple instruction: Nothing Myers shot could *look* hand-held.

As important as the highly polished shooting style was the decision, made early on, to refrain from cutting back to the concert audience. Indeed, the audience is almost absent—we hear them applauding, and every once in a very long while one of Zsigmond's long shots includes silhouettes of the front rows. This is no *Woodstock*: The point of *The Last Waltz* is the music, not the listeners.

"I had the feeling," Marty says, "that the movie audience could become more involved with the concert if we concentrated on the stage. Besides, after *Woodstock*, who *wants* to see the audience anymore?"

The result is a movie that is about music and musicians, about living the life of rock and roll. In addition to the concert footage, Marty interspersed three studio-shot numbers, which gave him a chance to practice his pyrotechnics, as well as his own interviews with members of the Band, which give the film its rough balance. Although he never met any of the Band before agreeing to shoot the concert, he and Robbie Robertson almost immediately became close friends. Robertson actually moved into Scorsese's Los Angeles house.

Scorsese denies that his friendship with Robertson greatly influenced the film, but *The Last Waltz* does make clear that Robbie Robertson was the leader of the Band. For one thing, he's an articulate musician. For another, he has a ton of stage presence, which translates perfectly onto the screen. And, of course, he does play lead guitar. "Levon Helm looks great," Marty says, "but he's trapped behind those drums."

True. But it is also true that Marty, who may be right when he calls himself "the world's worst interviewer," functions best as a documentarian when dealing with subjects he knows intimately.

It is not just that Scorsese knew where his cameras could go but he was not embarrassed to let unkind moments intrude upon the general celebration. (Compare, for example, the treatment of Ronnie Hawkins in *Last Waltz* with his treatment in *Renaldo and Clara*: In Scorsese's film, Hawkins is clearly a man far out of his depth when trying to front the Band he formed. There is no question, watching him, that he doesn't belong in this company. In Dylan's disaster, Hawkins is taken at false face value. At the same time, while this is ostensibly a film about the Band, Scorsese's editing makes no bones about how much a Dylan event it becomes the moment the singer walks on stage. Everything else disappears behind his presence, and Scorsese, despite his friendships and commitments, does nothing to hide or minimalize this effect. It is not merely the best rock-concert movie ever made; it is as intensely personal as anything Scorsese has done.

Late in the film's editing, at editor Jan Roblee's suggestion, Scorsese placed the footage of the Band's last song—Holland-Dozier-Holland's "Don't Do It"—at the beginning of the film. The concert thus becomes a flashback, while the interviews and studio shots are a meditation on the half-life of collective efforts and the weariness 16 years of road life can bring. Marty says the entire movie is about "Stage Fright," but a more appropriate metaphor is suggested when the Band, obviously stoned, attempts "Give Me That Old Time Religion." The improvised version is at once completely a Band song in its modalities, harmonics, and instrumental breaks, and a lethargic failure, falling apart before anyone can finish. "It's not like it used to be," someone says, and that seems to be the point of the film. Having become the Band, the members are, at the point of breaking apart, undefined by their success. They are no longer able to produce the work that sustained them.

"I'm slowing down," Marty says. "I mean, I have *projects,* but none of them are ready yet. They'll have to wait until I am ready or else they won't get done. I want to get away from big budgets. I don't know what I'm going to do next. But I can't keep up the kind of thing I've been doing the past two years. I mean, I've even read in *The Village Voice* how I left New York. I never left. I've just been out there working, and then on the road with *The Act,* and then editing this one. I've got to find a place here, now. I mean, I can't keep living in hotels..."

Marty Scorsese is no longer laid back. He is standing up now and serious. "I really have to think very carefully about what to do next. Because I'm convinced I have very little time left—physically. I just believe it. And I've got to do what's important—whether it's a rock-concert film...or a 16mm documentary...or nothing."

He turns and looks at the television.

"In L.A., when we were editing, we watched too much daytime television. We'd get up so late, so wiped-out, that's all we could do. I'm not going to watch daytime television in New York.

"I don't know what there is to write about me anymore. Just where I am, now, I guess. It's like the Band—just because the Band broke up doesn't mean the music's over. It's just a hiatus, a stopping, before something different, more complex, the next step."

Martin Scorsese looks out the window. He is waiting for the night.

Raging Bull

MICHAEL HENRY/1981

QUESTION: *Robert De Niro brought you Jake La Motta's autobiography when you were preparing* Taxi Driver. *What attracted you to this character? Did your vision of him evolve in the years preceding the shooting?*

ANSWER: I remember having read the book in California when I was finishing *Alice Doesn't Live Here Anymore*. I also remember long conversations with Bobby during the night in my office at Warner Brothers. Honestly, it wasn't like a bolt of lightning. No matter what anyone claimed later, I didn't even notice Jake's opening sentence: "When my memories come back to me, I have the feeling that I'm watching an old film in black-and-white." My reasons for shooting in black-and-white, as you know, have nothing to do with this quotation. When we were screening Bobby's training sequences, which had been shot in 8mm, I was struck by a remark made by Michael Powell: "But his gloves are red!" Yes, Michael Powell, the man who made *The Red Shoes*! Nowadays, boxers use gloves and pants that are colored, whereas our memories of boxing from the 40s are in black-and-white, like the newsreels and photographs of that time. Powell was right. You also know how much I worry about the instability and the changes in color film stock. The final reason was that several films on boxing were in preparation: *The Champ, Rocky II, The Main Event, Matilda*. I wanted *Raging Bull* to be very different visually and to evoke, if a reference is necessary,

---

This interview took place in Paris during the night of February 11–12, 1981. A translation of "Nuit blanche et chambre noire" from *Positif*, April 1981. Translated by Peter Brunette. Reprinted by permission.

the admirable photography of James Wong Howe in *The Sweet Smell of Success*.

Q : Raging Bull *is, along with* Mean Streets, *the film with the longest gestation period of all your films.*
A : I had worked on *Mean Streets* for so long, it was so close to me, that I knew almost word for word what the characters had to say, the way they had to dress or to move. *Mean Streets* was a fragment of myself. *Alice* was an experiment — and a lot of work. *Taxi Driver* was once again a film that was very close to me, one I had to make at any cost. We were completely confused during that period, and didn't know whether to start with *Taxi Driver* or *New York, New York,* which seemed less risky. I think that I had already begun the preproduction of *New York* in 1974, when I went to see Bobby in Parma, on the set of *1900,* to make sure that he still wanted the role of Jimmy Doyle. It's then, during that very uncertain period, that we spoke seriously, one on one, about *Raging Bull,* about the book, about our favorite scenes. We thought of it as a small-budget film, we even thought we could write it ourselves. The one sure thing was that it wouldn't be a film about boxing! We didn't know a thing about it and it didn't interest us at all!

Q : *The book is edited like a Warner Brothers film from the 30s. It has a dramatic structure that's very studied, in fact too studied to seem like an autobiography.*
A : Jake is constantly analyzing himself in the book. He very pedantically explains why he did this or that. But I didn't think that Jake was really able to analyze himself like that. Or maybe he didn't give us all the reasons. And how could he? All that stuff went back so long before. We felt that the book had been put into shape by Peter Savage, an amazing character. He appears in *Taxi Driver* and in *New York, New York,* and he made two films with Jake. He put a dramatic structure on Jake's chaotic existence. It wasn't so much Jake speaking about himself as Pete explaining Jake to Jake!

Q : *The book privileges the relation between the two men. Certain events weren't witnessed by Jake and so it's Pete's point of view that takes over at that point. You joined Pete, the friend, and Joey, the brother, who is in the background in the autobiography, into one character.*

A :   Yes, because I just couldn't buy this idea of undying friendship that jus-
tifies and links all the episodes. The book's psychology is close to that of
the 50s. This is not a reproach—I love tons of movies from that period!—
but for me there were too many overlapping points of view. Even though
Pete has since begun practicing hypnosis, he wasn't inside Jake's skin. How
could he know what was happening inside Jake's body, his impotence, his
fears? I no longer knew who Jake was. The champion who was surrounded
with respect or a hothead who was always getting in trouble? Joey and Pete
gave up boxing, but Jake was still the champ! How could I separate the true
from the false? It's said that Joey did a lot of dirty work for his brother, and
Pete said he did even more than was in the book. Who knows? It doesn't
really matter, it's not really them any more on the screen. I'm the younger
brother! I have a brother who's 7 years older, and I know this situation well.
We're not speaking any longer of real individuals. That's why we combined Joey and Pete. There was a lot that they had trouble admitting. Take
their break-up: they didn't speak for seven years. Why? We tried to explain
it—it's the longest sequence in the film—but in fact we still don't know
why. Only God knows what happened between two brothers. The only
certain fact is the 7 year silence. When I said to them: "There must have
been something, right?" They laughingly replied "Oh it wasn't as serious
as all that!" Seven years of silence, not as serious as all that? Everybody
always gives false reasons. What did Renoir say in *Rules of the Game*?

Q :   *"Everyone has his reasons." In* Raging Bull, *Jake doesn't have a past, or at
least you invoke it only in a refracted way. You skipped his training years. Why?
Where they too close to* Mean Streets?
A :   No, that wasn't it. I love the scene of the fight with the poker players,
where Jake and Pete are like idiots at the door because they won't let them
in. It was also in the first version of the script. Mardik Martin had kept the
attack on the bookmaker—and I knew exactly how to film it. We also hoped
to bring in the character of the priest, who I was to play. Our favorite scene
is the one in which Jake jumps on Pete's girlfriend after she's just read the
letter Pete has sent her from prison: it's a great scene, not because it's the
rape of a young virgin, but because it demonstrates the extraordinarily complex relationship between the two friends. Pete, you know, got a bullet in
the arm while protecting Jake: it's an episode that we really wanted to keep,
but which we finally took out. That one was authentic, but the others?

Q: *What was Mardik Martin's contribution before you asked for Paul Schrader's help?*

A: Mardik did two and a half years of research and interviews. He took off in all directions, and he even spent a year writing a play about Jake. The more eyewitness accounts he got, the more things got mixed up: there were about 25,000 shades of gray. No well-defined black and white: just gray! It was maddening. And on my side, I was struggling to finish *New York, New York* within the limited budget and taking into account the structural deficiencies of the script. When I was celebrating my 35th birthday at Sam Fuller's house, I got it into my head that I could integrate, in *Raging Bull,* a followup to *Italianamerican,* where I was going to talk about the death of my grandparents, and the third part of the triptych begun with *Who's That Knocking at My Door?* and *Mean Streets*! This shows you what a state of panic I was in! I was working simultaneously on *New York, New York, The Last Waltz, American Boy,* and *The Act.* My second marriage was falling apart. Domenica had just been born and I already knew that she wouldn't be living with me. I told Mardik that I had to get myself together and that we had to find a way to get my grandparents into this film about boxing. In fact, I couldn't concentrate any more, I was lost. Bobby, who had just come back from *The Last Tycoon,* was overwhelmed too.

Q: *Is this when you met Norman Mailer?*

A: He encouraged me a lot. The script was way too long. Everything was there, Jake's childhood, his father, the prison, and even his testimony before the Kefauver Commission in New York—but I didn't want to hear about any boxing matches! "He's a fantastic guy," Mailer told me. "I never used any real people in my novels except Jake. He's been very underestimated, both as a man and as a boxer. You have to make this film." He was alluding to *The American Dream,* of course. Do you know that when Mailer met Jake in a bar, and told him "I could have been a boxer," Jake, staring at his beer, coldly replied, "No, you're not disturbed enough."

Q: *That's when Paul Schrader came on the scene. What did he bring?*

A: At this stage, we were lost. We had to find a new structure. Schrader had worked on it for six weeks, to help us out. "Jake has to masturbate in his cell," he told me at dinner. I found the idea interesting. In the novel, there was a complete obsession with the female sex. It was a new approach to the subject, basing it on sexuality. I said okay. Schrader had the idea of opening with the speech on the stage and linking that with Jake's first defeat, in Cleveland. An unjust and inexplicable defeat. Anyway, it didn't matter: the essential thing was for the audience to sympathize with Jake right away. So Schrader cut the whole first part of the novel. But Peter and Joey were still distinct, the session before the Senate committee was still there, and we also saw Jake's gambling house at Kingston, Long Island. Paul, who's fascinated by gambling, wanted a very spectacular decor. I was happy with the Copacabana and the Debonair Social Club, one of those masculine sanctuaries where men can be alone and do their business quietly together. Something like Scala in Hollywood, where people in the business go to negotiate contracts. The ritual isn't very different, you know.

Q : *Was it you or Schrader who lessened the domestic violence portrayed in the book?*
A : It was me. Schrader had kept the scene in which Jake knocks out his first wife during a party and, thinking that she's dead, imagines different ways to get rid of the body. They weren't even 20 years old at that point, and they were living like animals. There was also the scene where his wife climbs up on the fender of his car to keep him from starting it. This violence came too early. I was happy with just the table overturned and a couple of swear words. For Jake and Pete's scene in the parking lot, Paul had them fighting. Jake wanted his brother to punish him, and let himself be humiliated, screaming "I was on the mat!" I finally chose to keep it much simpler.

Q : *With Schrader gone, there was only you. You were the only one left to harness yourself to the task?*
A : Well, that was our original dream, don't forget. When he left, Schrader told me, "You pulled *Mean Streets* from your guts. Do the same thing now, but this time just use two or three characters. With four, you won't make it." After that I went through a serious crisis. I didn't want to do the film any longer, I didn't want to do it at all. Physically, I was also in terrible shape. I spent four days in the hospital hovering between life and death. I was lucky, I survived, the crisis passed. My suicide period was over. Bobby came to see me. We spoke very openly. To want to kill yourself over work, to dream of a tragic death—there's a moment where you have to stop let-

ting go, even if it's stronger than you. We were talking about ourselves, but I suddenly understood the character. When Bobby asked me pointblank: "Do you want us to make this film?" I answered yes. It was obvious. What I had just gone through, Jake had known before me. We each lived it our own way. The Catholic background, the guilt feelings, the hope for redemption. Maybe it's a little pretentious to talk about redemption. More than anything, it's about learning to accept yourself. That's what I understood the instant that I answered yes, without really knowing what I was saying. When I got out of the hospital, we left for San Martin, an island in the Caribbean where there are no films and no television. We were on the same wavelength, and now we were talking the same language. In ten days, we wrote a hundred-page script. On the last page, I added a quotation from the Gospel of St. John, the exchange between Nicodemus and Christ. Jesus told the High Priest that it was necessary to be reborn of the spirit before one could enter the Kingdom of God. I wasn't planning to use it in this form, but I wanted to warn everyone who would read the script just what it meant to me.

Q: *In removing La Motta's youth, you also took away certain "extenuating circumstances" from your character. He became more opaque, just like his feeling of being guilty, his certainty that God was punishing him for the bad that he had done, especially for the unpunished murder of the bookmaker, all of which became more diffuse.*

A: I was right, no? That guilt, please understand this, doesn't come from a specific act, but is part and parcel of the character. If you had inherited this guilt from birth, what chance would you have had to escape? If in the deepest part of yourself, you're convinced that you're not worthy—as I have been, and as I might be again some time—what can you do? You're condemned, no?

Q: *The film caused some very gut-level reactions: why devote a film to such a disgusting human being? However, what the hatred for Jake translates into is the fear of knowing that you too are a sinner and that you are waiting to be struck by lightning at any moment.*

A: Ah, fear! What torture! You know his tactic in the ring. He could take more than anybody because he had an abnormally hard skull. Punch and get punched until the adversary got tired out. *Raging Bull* is the story of a man who is facing a wall. Of course, there is, in superimposition on the screen, the reminder of matches and dates, there are historically correct episodes, especially the one in Miami, but it's really about what happens inside of him. The Kefauver Commission? Why did he spit it out? Why wasn't he killed? That wasn't our problem, it was the problem of the Family. Here's a man who is methodically destroying himself, who is pulling others down with him, who falls into the deepest hole—and who pulls himself up again. Pulls him up again toward what? It doesn't matter. To live with a strip-teaser? Yeah, so what? Are you better than a strip-teaser?

Q: *Isn't that one of the meanings of the parable of the Pharisees? Who are you to cast the first stone? Who are you to condemn her? It's up to the spectator to decide, in his soul and conscience, like at the end of* Taxi Driver *or* American Boy: *is this man a criminal or a brother?*

A: Yes, and that can go a long ways. You can't act like Jake, of course, but isn't there something rotten in everything that surrounds us? Well. . . . If I said yes to Bobby, it's because I unconsciously found myself in Jake. I felt that this character was the bringer of hope. It was for this hope that I made the film. Jake, I think, understood that. He admitted that it was him—and that it wasn't him—up there on the screen.

Q: *The criminal and the saint—these are the two contradictory postulations that you like to bring together in one individual. During our last meeting, in Rome, you said that the most primitive consciousness is closer to the Spirit than any other.*

A: Yes, it's closer to God. Jake is an animal—and isn't.

Q: *He lives like an animal, but he is capable of conceiving something else. When he's at his lowest point, in the cell in Miami, he has this great outcry: "I'm not that guy, I'm not me!"*

A: "I'm not that guy!"—that's the key. And I shouted the same thing to Bobby. It's strange, but no one has ever talked to me about this before. But everything I wanted to say is there. Will French Catholics understand me? For Italian-Americans it's different: they're born that way, convinced that they don't deserve what has happened to them.

Q : *And especially not success! In sports as in show business, there are those who construct a career and those who follow a vocation. Jake is one of the latter, and you are too. The metaphor was already clear in* New York, New York.

A : I think I know what you mean. You're putting into words what we feel in a pretty confused way. In the ring, Jake does what he has to do, that's all. He can't behave otherwise. He couldn't do anything else. You should see them when they're together, Jake, Pete, Joey. "Who's the champion here? Who's the champion?" asks Jake, and he repeats it, very softly, like a litany. "Vocation"—yes, in this sense, like a priest.

Q : *You intervene in person in the final sequence, when Jake is getting ready to go on stage. You remind him of the demands of show business.*

A : This ending was in the script right from the beginning. And you know why? In one of the sequences cut by accident in *New York, New York,* the one in the Up Club, Lenny Gaines said to Bobby: "Relax. Take a twenty minute break. Have fun." He was speaking about life in general, of course. Here Jake asks me "How much time do I still have?" And I answer "You've got five minutes." Bobby and I felt this profoundly, especially me, since I'm incapable of relaxing, I'm always tense. I completely immerse myself in a film. On the set of *Raging Bull,* I was so much taken by the character that I often forgot my marks. The man with his face to the wall in the cell is me.

Q : *All of us are in that prison with our face to the wall, no?*

A : Yes, sure. I'm there in any case. What is it that confers a sort of grace on him at that moment? That's the mystery. Something happened to him, and it happened to me too, and that's why I'm here now. Something that allowed him to say "I'm not that guy." We were thinking—but it was really only a joke—of having a white light break into the cell or of tracing the shape of the cross with beams of light.

Q : *A redemption maybe, but also, above all, a vital start, a reconquering of the self.*

A : It was a catharsis. How do you accept who you are? If you don't accept yourself, you self-destruct. Do you remember, in *America America,* when the Turk Abdul says to Stavros: "Go ahead, take the knife, it'll go quicker. Finish it now." I know what Kazan means. Suicide is the simplest. With people who were strangers to me, who knew nothing about the film, I never spoke of redemption, I used the word "resolution."

Q : *In the book, the character of the priest is central. One imagines him being played by Spencer Tracy or Pat O'Brien. In the film, though, he's only a silhouette.*
A : We could have remade *Boys Town*. We played with that idea for a while, before deciding that it wasn't really important to show Jake's beginnings. He's there and he does what he has to do, and that's it. You have to accept him the way he is. You don't believe it? Too bad! Thanks for coming. I'm not mad at you. You'd be better off leaving and going to see *Moonraker*. Thanks and goodbye. I heard so much nonsense, if you only knew! Father Joseph? Oh, yeah. I only kept him for Webster Hall. That's where my parents used to go dancing. It became the Ritz, one of the temples of New York disco. And then you see him again in the home movies. The whole parish knew him, they all went to him for confession. Like the priest in a small Sicilian village. Webster Hall is pure nostalgia. There was dancing and fighting between rival clans. In the film, the fight at the entrance is between the Italian-Americans and the more recent Italian immigrants, the "greaseballs," as the bouncer says. That's the only time the colors were right on the set! The costumes, the lighting, everything was perfect. And as in *Knocking* and *Mean Streets,* I think I really captured the strangeness of that way of life.

Q : *The iconography of* Mean Streets *keeps popping up: the home movies, the holy pictures and the statue of St. Francis of Assisi in the father's apartment, the relation between Joey and Jake, which is the same relation as the one between Charlie and Johnny Boy.*
A : Absolutely, and I was very aware of that, even if I didn't want to remake *Mean Streets*. The cross in the apartment is my mother's. It was in *Knocking,* and the statue, too, I think. Jake shot them in 16mm. 16mm in the forties! He must have been rich. In *Mean Streets,* I only had 8mm, the format that less rich families had to use. We reshot Jake's little bits of film with an Eclair. We had some problems with this because the original negatives were very dark and were often only three or four feet long! The Technicolor expert did great work, desaturating the colors, even putting color on the perforations, like in the scene of the wedding on the terrace

in the Bronx. I considered for a moment using the still photos, as I did for the fights, then I remembered my parent's wedding in 1933. It was so hot they had to hold the reception on the roof. The funniest thing is that the day of the shooting I was sick and I let my father play director, and you can imagine the chaos! One of my favorite moments is there, when the camera reframes, on the right, on an extra who's sitting apart, on the edge of the roof. That's how I see myself, with this feeling of being a stranger, of being completely lost.

Q : *Jake's environment doesn't really explain his character. There's something irreducible, which escapes analysis, that interests you, right?*
A : Now we're getting to the heart of things! That's what I realized at San Martin—before the death of Haig Manoogian, who I want to tell you about later. Why not narrate the lives of these people in big blocks, clearly distinct from each other? You'd find them at different stages. Like that conversation that started in a little Latin Quarter hotel in 1974 that we renew from year to year in different places. We have to proceed like that, I told Bobby, because there's no way to explain everything that happens in between. There aren't any words to speak about it. No words to say what happens in the cell. Not even religious words. He just stops destroying himself, that's all.

Q : *The first "flashback" seems to be set off by Jake practicing "That's entertainment," his entry onto the stage. The link is striking.*
A : We found it by accident one night at the editing table, when I was in despair about being able to connect Jake's bloated face of the 60s with his young face of the 40s. Two tracks accidentally overlapped and bang! The sound connected the two eras. There's another moment, even stranger, when Vickie moves her lips but no sound comes out of her mouth. After Jake has beaten them up, her and Joey, he finds her packing her suitcase. That came at the end of the shooting. After everything that had happened, any dialogue seemed meaningless. We tried everything, but no response worked. She's there, she's waiting with her whole body that he's touching and, if you notice, her lips are moving but you don't hear anything, because there's nothing left to hear at this stage. There are no words for such a situation.

Q : *Several different times you isolate different parts of Vickie's body, with very tight shots, especially at the swimming pool. Then, at Webster Hall, you have this blonde Irish woman sit at a table where there are only brunettes, no doubt Italian. Under this fetishistic look, Vickie seems only a mental image.*

A : And how! She doesn't exist for herself. Look at those snakes that keep surrounding and entwining her! These "semi-toughs," who aren't as bad as all that, after all, much less than in the book, because, after all, I love all those people! Even Salvy, the fake judge. But not more than Michael in *Mean Streets,* who doesn't manage to become a real tough guy, the kind that you don't get too near to, but whom you respect and offer allegiance in embracing him. To come back to Vickie, if Jake takes her under the paternal roof, it's because he knows that she doesn't deserve it. Like J.R. in *Knocking* when he makes love with Zina Bethune on his mother's bed. Where else to go? We don't have an apartment, we don't have any money. . . . It's a very authentic moment and I love it that at the end of the sequence they are framed only from the back. I had the feeling that if the audience identified with them at that instant, they would identify with them all the way to the end.

Q : *The television set that doesn't work is a great metaphor for Jake's frustrations. It seems to echo the one with the golf ball which comes before they make love.*

A : Each time that you see Jake and Vickie in an intimate moment, their relationship is coming apart a little more. The first time is the only satisfying one. It's also the most chaste. The next time, before the third match with Sugar Ray Robinson, it's only about sex and frustration. Later, when they're in bed, he asks her "Who do you think of when we make love?" After, it gets worse and worse. We had the television set in there from the beginning, it was in Mardik's script. At that time, the sets were always breaking down. I chose *Of Mice and Men* because it was on that Sunday— I checked it. And also because there are similarities between the two films. I love Aaron Copland's score; I used the last third of it, the length of which corresponded exactly with our sequence. In the early 60s, at NYU, I acted in *Of Mice and Men* with Gregory Rozakis, who played the young guy with TB in *America America*. A little later, *Variety* announced, God know why, that I was getting ready to shoot a student film with Rozakis and . . . Jake La Motta! That was a sign of fate, no?

Q : *It also seems like there's a very carefully worked out evolution in the mise-en-scene of the fight scenes. The first one, in Cleveland in 1941, uses reaction shots, and even some long shots from the top of the stands, as in certain contemporary films of the match. It makes you think of Capra and of* Meet John Doe *during the riot scene. There is also the light from the flashbulbs which recalls the realistic photos of the 40's. After that, the framing and the lighting become more and more unreal. The last fight with Robinson, for example, is choreographed in a completely abstract space, like the numbers of* The Last Waltz *that you shot in the MGM studios.*

A : Capra? No, I wasn't thinking of him, I don't remember *Meet John Doe* very well, but you're right, there's a escalation, a progression in the horror, and thus an increasing stylization. The first match is the only one in which we used the reactions of the audience. The last meeting with Robinson is completely abstract. There are wide angle and foggy shots because at this stage no one is worrying about the punches which landed so well. The ring is twice as big as it was in reality. It's not a matter of literally translating what Jake sees and hears, but to present what the match means for him, all the while respecting, as much as possible, historical truth. To do it in such a way that you are more and more implicated in what is going on in this miserable ring. It's not only a question of point of view: it's not enough, I'm sure you realize, to shoot subjective shots or in slow motion.

Before shooting, I went to two boxing matches, five-round matches between unknown boxers. The first evening, even though I was far away from the ring, I saw the sponge red with blood, and the film started to take form. The next time, I was much closer, and I saw the blood dripping from the ropes. I said to myself that this sure didn't have anything to do with any sport! From what point of view should it be filmed? I hesitated for a long time. Believe me, it's not simple. It's like math or chess. In the old days, the newsreel guys didn't worry about it: they filmed the entire match from the same angle, outside the ropes, of course. That was shown during the intermission, between the two films on the main program, and I still remember how impatient and angry we were that we had to suffer through 15 rounds at a stretch.

It wasn't simple! It wasn't as simple as having Bobby gain 50 pounds. With the exception of the match against Dauthille, where we were outside the ropes, I was in the ring the whole time with the camera, just as attentive to the physical reality of the punches and the panting as I was to the psychological dimension of the encounter. When Jake let himself get massacred by Robinson, the television commentator yelled "Nobody can take such punishment!" He was right and that was why I gave such a stylized vision of this punishment—abstract, if you wish, but not unreal for all that. I had to use a lot of blood because we were shooting in black-and-white, but that's just secondary. The real violence is inside. I know from my own experience that a broken nose doesn't bleed that much. This vision became a mental projection.

Q: *Between the highly emotional scenes, in and out of the ring, you allow your-self some breaks, like the discussions between Jake and Joey, that are filmed in a very simple manner. Suddenly, you look at these crazy people with a certain serenity, a certain distance.*

A: After Paul Schrader gave us the overall structure, Bobby and I kept condensing and simplifying. The masturbation scene, for example. Bobby talked me out of it: "What? I'm going to masturbate right after they've beaten me up?" It's enough for him to bang his head against the wall, it's the same thing. We shot tons of inserts that were meant for the montage sequences, before the meeting with Cerdan (in which you can see Audie Murphy, who had just finished *Bad Boy*) or for the last fight with Robinson—where Vickie's face was, for example, supposed to substitute for Sugar Ray's. I didn't keep any of that. I also cut the press conference, which you can see an extract of in the trailer. In Miami, during the breakup, we had planned a long speech in which Vickie explains herself, but it wasn't necessary.

After filming the fights, not without difficulty—and I've only mentioned a couple of the problems—I asked myself: does all of this have any meaning? Is there a good reason for printing all this film? Why move the camera? Is it really necessary? If I could, I would be happy to shoot it all in one take three hours long. I made this film for myself, no? Films are the most important thing in my life. OK, that's understood. You still have to find reasons to manipulate this tool which has been given to us. Yes, the scene between Joey and Jake in the kitchen is very simple. Just like the one with the television set. I wanted to take a break to try to understand what was happening in their heads, the absurdity of that implacable logic.

A filmmaker friend whom I respect a lot once told me in Rome: "It's not your best film." Inwardly, I wanted to reply: "Do we always have to make our best film each time or are we building an oeuvre that will last?" He continued: "It's not violent enough. You fell in love with your actors, you didn't restrain them enough, they imposed their own rhythm at the expense of the deeper meaning." I started asking myself some questions: In looking for simplicity, had I become lazy? Was I too easy? Not explicit enough? During the shooting, I had asked myself these questions, but in the opposite way: Isn't it too obvious? Too explanatory? In reality, I just did what I thought was right. Some people think that something important happens in the prison in Miami, other people don't. What can I do about it?

Q : *The progression of Jake La Motta toward self-consciousness, toward a certain powerful decision, even if it's schizophrenic, doesn't it reflect your own attitude toward the project and more generally toward cinema itself?*
A : I don't know. The film really doesn't help me to see these things more clearly, nor does it help me to understand others or myself. What really interests me is hope. In the pit of his dungeon, Jake doesn't have anything, he's lost it all. Vickie, his brother, his house, his children, his championship belt. Before, we saw him undergo a terrible punishment from Dauthuille. He let himself be massacred, then, in the last seconds, he had a surge of pride and demolished his opponent. In other words, he's never really gotten what he deserves. He hasn't paid. After which, he meets Robinson. What does he see there? He sees his blood squeezed out of the sponge, his body that they're preparing for the sacrifice. For him, it's a religious ritual and he uses Robinson to punish himself. As I told you, everything happens in his head. He thinks he's at the end of his martyrdom, but there again his pride carries him away. When they stop the fight in the thirteenth round, he yells "I didn't hit the floor! I didn't hit the floor!" He rebels one more time. Then the posing for the photographers at the swimming pool in Miami, and you see everything that he has to lose. Vickie, the kids, the Cadillac, the nightclub. He loses all that immediately and now, in his cell, all that's left is himself. He's facing the wall, facing himself, and he screams: "I'm not that guy!" He has fallen so low that he can only come up to be reborn. When we find him in the strip-tease joint, he has changed. A customer treats him like a clown and he answers, without any aggression, "That's why I'm here." He has found a kind of peace with himself. He's no longer the same man. Of course, it's not ideal, but he could

have fallen even lower. His job isn't degrading, he has stopped destroying himself like so many of his friends. He has survived.

Q : *How did the idea of quoting from* On the Waterfront *come to you? Is it an indirect comment on Jake?*

A : Jake often quoted it on the stage. Mardik's script included a soliloquy from Shakespeare. Michael Powell talked me out of it; he found the character original enough that he didn't need any quotations. Against his advice, I decided on Kazan. At this point, I wasn't listening to anyone, I was acting like a kamikaze. Just like when I was making *Mean Streets,* I was convinced that this would be my last film, the end of my career. So I had a good time. I saw *On the Waterfront* when I was 12 years old and never forgot it. It's so beautiful, that monologue of Brando's, so funny and so sad: "Let's be honest, I'm just a bum . . ." And, even more, it was the story of two brothers, like *Raging Bull.* But I didn't want people to take the monologue as a comment on the relation between Jake and Joey: Jake isn't accusing his brother, because without him he would have lived in the same way. Bobby and I explored all kinds of different ways of saying the lines. We did at least twenty takes. The most interesting one, the one we used, is also the simplest, the least expressive. A small, thin voice, that's all. Bobby would have liked us to use three different takes in a row, but the most monotonous one was the best. I thought of the end of *Taxi Driver:* on the screen, the reading of a letter moves me even more because the face and the voice betray no emotion. The coat-stand in the dressing room is an homage to Ermanno Olmi, a reference to the death of the hero in *Il posto* that stunned me.

Q : *As the film continues, what words are incapable of saying becomes clearer, retrospectively, in the light of the parable of the blind man and the Pharisees that you put at the end.*

A : I didn't want to quote the dialogue between Nicodemus and Jesus because it could have been confusing. In re-reading the new English Bible, I fell upon a passage from Saint John, "The healing of the man born blind." The Pharisees interrogate the parents twice about the miracle. The parents are afraid because the whole thing is political. Then the Pharisees called the child: "He who approached you is surrounded by prostitutes, pimps, tax collectors. Do you understand that this man is a sinner and that you must not go near him?" And the child responds: "All I know is that once I was blind and now I see." Jake La Motta, at least as he appears in the film, is someone who allowed me to see more clearly. Like Haig Manoogian, to whom the film is dedicated.

When I took his first course, in the 60's, he transmitted the spark to me, he gave me the energy to become a filmmaker. His house became a second home for me, I was always there. I saw him again last May, when I was on the campus of NYU, when I was finishing the first cut of *Raging Bull*. The simplicity of the black-and-white was also a return to NYU. We laughed about *American Boy,* which I had come to talk to the students about, and suddenly he said to me, with great seriousness: "Do you still see a lot of films today? I really don't feel the need any more. Now it's all science fiction. Today, films don't have any resolution, that's the problem." What did he mean? I wasn't sure, but three weeks later he was dead—and the very same day Steven Prince, the protagonist of *American Boy,* lost his father. Both were buried on the same day. So *Raging Bull* is dedicated "with love and resolution" to the one who gave me inspiration, to the one who gave me, at the same time as a camera, the eyes to see.

Scorsese's Past Colors His New Film

MICHIKO KAKUTANI/1983

WHEN MARTIN SCORSESE FIRST read the script for *The King of Comedy* in 1974, he dismissed it as a one-gag film. The story of an ambitious young comic who kidnaps a famous talk-show host in order to get himself on television didn't interest him at all. Years passed, and Mr. Scorsese directed, with much acclaim, such movies as *Alice Doesn't Live Here Anymore, Taxi Driver, New York, New York* and *Raging Bull*.

When he read the script of *King of Comedy* again in 1979, he says he finally understood what it was all about. Indeed the film — which opens this Friday at the Coronet — had taken on an intensely personal resonance for him. It would provide him with a means not only for making important stylistic experiments, but also for taking stock of his own career — for reassessing his early ambition and the consequences of his more recent success.

In *The King of Comedy* Robert De Niro plays a novice comedian named Rupert Pupkin, who will do anything, *anything,* to get Jerry Langford, a television personality played by Jerry Lewis, to invite him to perform on his show. Pupkin wheedles, he whines, he makes a complete pest of himself, and when that doesn't work, he resorts to kidnapping and ransom. His ambition is blind and crazy, says Mr. Scorsese, and it is based on his own youthful will to succeed at any price.

From *New York Times,* 13 February 1983. © 1983 by The New York Times Co. Reprinted by permission.

"I can identify with Pupkin," he says now. "It's the same way I made my first pictures with no money and with the constant rejection — going back and going back and going back until finally, somehow, you get a lucky break. Actually luck doesn't have that much to do with it; it's just this constant battering away at this monolith. Pupkin goes about it the wrong way, but he does have drive. I remember I'd go anyplace, do anything. I'd try to get into screenings, get into any kind of social situation to try to talk up projects. It's important who you meet — after all, if you meet 40 or 50 people, the one person who will produce your first film might just be there."

It took almost a decade of struggling — after receiving a master's degree from New York University's film department in 1968, he edited documentaries and made commercials — but Mr. Scorsese's hustling paid off. Made in 27 days for $650,000, his third feature, *Mean Streets,* earned critical acclaim at the 1973 New York Film Festival and helped establish him as one of the country's outstanding directors — a reputation he would enhance with each successive film.

In retrospect, however, he says that that success incurred heavy personal costs — three marriages fell apart, and his friendships, too, suffered from the pressures of his work. Intense, driven and passionate in his love of film, Mr. Scorsese, at 40, speaks in rapid staccato sentences — sentences that pile up on each other as though he cannot talk fast enough to express all his thoughts. Though his conversation often erupts into bursts of good-natured humor, he also possesses the nervous introspection of someone who has always been a loner.

"I wanted to look at what it's like to want something so badly you'd kill for it," he says of *King of Comedy.* "By kill I don't mean kill physically, but you can kill the spirit, you can kill relationships, you can kill everything else around you in your life. It *does* affect personal relationships, and the final line for me *at the time* was that if I had to make a choice between work and a relationship, the personal relationship would go by the wayside. I don't have regrets — whatever's happened over the years, I think happened for the better, but maybe the reason I made this picture is because I hope I wouldn't think the same way now."

If Rupert Pupkin represents the unaccommodated ambition Mr. Scorsese possessed as a young man, the Jerry Langford character serves as a kind of metaphor for the success the director — and his star, Robert De Niro — have since achieved. Like Langford, he worries about the demands of others who want to latch onto the coattails of his good fortune, and like Langford, he has experienced the isolating consequences of fame.

"It does cut off your social behavior," he says, "In the period of the last three or four years, I've cut off a lot of the people around me—usually they need something, they want something and they think you can give it to them, but you can't. You have to be very, very careful. And while it's nice to be the center of attention, the danger is it may alter your perceptions. The most important thing for a director is his sense of the relationships between people. This social behavior I find fascinating, and very often, if you walk into a room and *you're* the center of attention, it's harder to pick up on these things. So what you have to do is go to things that are more deeply rooted—things that haven't altered, things that have obsessed you for years, things that you really know."

One of the things that Mr. Scorsese has captured best in his films is a sense of American life—not so much life lived in the mainstream, but life lived on the margins, where the promises of the Dream seem both alluring and elusive. Charlie, the young would-be hood in *Mean Streets* works for his gangster uncle and aspires to rise in the world of crime. Alice, liberated from the past by her husband's death, sets off for Monterey, hoping to make a new life as a singer. And Jake LaMotta in *Raging Bull* and the Jimmy Doyle and Francine Evans in *New York, New York* also harbor dreams of success.

Through these characters and a kind of documentary approach, Mr. Scorsese has created perfectly observed worlds: in *Mean Streets,* a portrait of life on the Lower East Side, as it is played out in the local pool halls and bars; in *Alice,* a portrait of blue-collar life amid the motels and diners of the Southwest; and in *Taxi Driver,* a portrait of night-life in New York. The last movie in particular purveys a dark vision indeed; it portrays the city as a place where alienation erupts into violence and despair. But while his movies often seem to be making certain social observations—*King of Comedy,* for instance, may be viewed as a kind of comment on America's obsession with celebrity—Mr. Scorsese says that those aspects do not really interest him. *Taxi Driver,* he explains, "is much more Dostoyevskian than political."

More than any of his contemporaries, in fact, Mr. Scorsese has been concerned with using film as a means of exploring his own behavior and preoccupations. The random violence in his movies, the sense that anything can happen, stems from the aimless street action the director witnessed as a child growing up in Manhattan; and the fact that all his heroes, Pupkin and Langford included, are outsiders, afflicted with guilt and hungry for recognition or human contact, also has autobiographical roots.

The son of a clothes presser, the director grew up in Little Italy, where asthma and a frail physique prevented him from taking part in the macho, street-smart life around him. He spent most of his free time going to the movies, and those movies made him want, more than anything, "to be part of that incredible world of the creation of films." "Films are like having a person around," he says. "And to have films be so much a part of your life that you can't live without them is kind of nice, and I thought that's what I wanted to achieve for other people."

In *Mean Streets,* Mr. Scorsese created a dark, vital portrait of street life on the Lower East Side—the very life he once felt so excluded from. Although the picture chronicled the attempts of young men trying to make it as small-time gangsters, it was more concerned, at heart, with exploring the hero's struggles to reconcile the moral dictates of his conscience with the brutal code of life around him. It raised the question, says Mr. Scorsese, of "how does one practice Christian ethics and morals when you're in a world of that sort—and can you be a hoodlum and also be a saint."

The religious themes, of course, grew out of Mr. Scorsese's own Roman Catholic upbringing and his adolescent determination to become a priest. Although he later dropped out of the seminary and has since become an agnostic—"I lost my faith in the man-made aspects of the religion"—he says he still harbors a "fascination, not necessarily with the Church, but with the teachings and trying to understand what the teachings are about." Indeed his films are all animated by this spiritual vision; they are inquiries of sorts into how to live and find an honest, noninstitutional faith.

In Mr. Scorsese's first feature *Who's That Knocking at My Door?,* a young man attempted to reconcile sexual desire with his Catholic sense of guilt. In *Taxi Driver,* the demented hero's ascetism and isolation turned him into a kind of saint-run-amok, his determination to purge New York of its pimps and prostitutes, possessed all the fervor and intensity of the Old Testament God. And in *Raging Bull,* the story of the boxer Jake LaMotta's rise and fall took on mythic qualities of suffering and redemption.

Not surprisingly, *Raging Bull* also reflected certain spiritual struggles Mr. Scorsese was experiencing at the time. It was 1978, and the director had just finished making *New York, New York*—a picture, he says now, that marked the end of his love affair with film. Employing painted backdrops and big musical numbers, the movie had been intended as a kind of homage to the Hollywood films of the 40's that Mr. Scorsese loved so much, but in shooting the picture, he found that it was "nightmarish" to try to recreate what no longer existed: the "factory" provided by the old studio system was gone, and the visual style of the old movies proved difficult to merge with his own.

To make matters worse, Mr. Scorsese was also feeling overextended: while finishing *New York, New York,* he was also involved with making *The Last Waltz,* a documentary called *American Boy* and staging Liza Minnelli's Broadway show *The Act.* He was traveling too much and spending too much money, and he had begun to question all his values. "Your values are upside down when the fun begins to take over, and you don't even know where you are," he says. "I think L.A. became too much during that period, too much of a movie star town, and I realized I didn't belong."

And so, before beginning *Raging Bull,* Mr. Scorsese took a 10-day vacation and did a lot of thinking. He thought about how messy his life had become and he thought about how the success he had wanted so much had turned out to be so hollow. Somehow, in the midst of this, he says he had a kind of revelation about how to make *Raging Bull.* In *New York, New York,* he had already touched upon the consequences of success—the marriage between the Liza Minnelli and Robert De Niro characters falters when her career takes off and his does not—and he realized that a similar parable was provided by the story of how Jake LaMotta won a boxing championship at the expense of his family and self-esteem.

The movie not only transformed Mr. Scorsese's personal dilemmas into a critically acclaimed work of art, but it also represented a kind of stylistic breakthrough. In the past, his films had possessed a nervous, eclectic style. They were filled with references to previous films—the Wizard of Oz homage in *Alice,* the *Star is Born* allusions in *New York, New York*—and his hectic, expressionistic camera work often jarred with his tendency to work with actors in a naturalistic, almost documentary, fashion. Largely in reaction to the high stylization of *New York, New York,* he had tried to simplify his technique in *Raging Bull*—the movie was even shot in gritty black and white—and in doing so had managed to integrate all these disparate elements into "a complete cohesive style." In *King of Comedy,* the director's camera is even more static; it represents, he explains, an effort to simplify things further.

In a sense, Mr. Scorsese has tried to do the same thing with his life. At the end of 1979, he left Los Angeles and moved back to New York, and now lives quietly in Lower Manhattan. The apartment has the same empty, almost antiseptic look of Jerry Langford's apartment in *The King of Comedy*, and it is filled with the sort of provisional furniture—metal bookcases and cheap metal and rattan chairs—someone acquires in the wake of a divorce. The television set is frequently left on without the sound—to give the illusion that someone else is home—and Mr. Scorsese says the first thing he does every morning is check the TV listings to see what movies are on.

Although he has remained in touch with such friends as Brian De Palma, Steven Spielberg and George Lucas, he sees far less of them than he did during the late 60's and early 70's, when they were all starting out together. Most of his time, in fact, is spent working. At the moment, he is making plans to shoot his next picture based on Nikos Kazantzakis's *The Last Temptation of Christ*.

"It's calmed down a lot," he says. "It may be kind of boring and lonely at times, but it's better for the work and it's better for you as a person. At 40, you do start to think about things differently. I must say, I can understand why people eventually stop making pictures—because to make films in such an impassioned way, you really have to believe in it, you've really got to want to tell that story, and after a while, you may find out that life itself is more important than the filmmaking process. Maybe part of the answer for what the hell we're doing here has to be in the process of living itself, rather than in the work." He pauses, and then laughs. "Of course," he adds, "you're talking to a person who's leaving this Sunday to look for new locations for the next picture."

Chalk Talk

PETER   BISKIND   AND

SUSAN   LINFIELD/1986

MARTIN SCORSESE'S NEW FILM, *The Color of Money*, picks up the story of Fast Eddie Felson, the pool shark played by Paul Newman who we last saw twenty-five years ago in Robert Rossen's *The Hustler*. Scripted by novelist Richard Price (author of *The Wanderers, Bloodbrothers,* and *The Breaks*), the film stars Newman as an older and perhaps wiser Eddie, and Tom Cruise as the young player who becomes his protégé and eventual rival. *American Film* spoke with Scorsese and Price in New York about the making of *Money.*

QUESTION: *How come Marty Scorsese is making a sequel?*
MARTIN SCORSESE: It's not a sequel. Let me give the rundown. I was in London for about a week in September of 1984, after the shooting of *After Hours.* Paul Newman called me while I was there and asked if I'd be interested in this project. When I first spoke to Newman on the phone, he said, "Eddie Felson." I said, "I love that character." He said, "Eddie Felson reminds me of the characters that you've dealt with in your pictures. And I thought more ought to be heard from him." I asked, "Who's involved?" He said, "Just you and me." I said, "OK, what have you got?" He said, "I've got a script." So he sent it to me and the next day I read it. I had a lot of reservations about it. I felt that it was a literal sequel: There were even a few minutes of film inserted in it from the first picture. It had its own merits,

From *American Film,* November 1986. Reprinted by permission.

but it certainly wasn't the kind of thing I wanted to do. And so I made an appointment to see Newman when I got to New York.

Now, I know that he's not afraid to play people who are not necessarily "nice." Many characters in my pictures are also what we would call unsympathetic. So, I like the guy and he likes me and we respect each other's work—maybe we can find a common ground. And this character of Eddie Felson is the only common ground that we have. And, of course, Fast Eddie lives and thrives in my favorite places, which are bars and pool rooms. But I have to ask myself: Can I, from my generation of filmmakers, work with somebody from his generation? I've admired and appreciated the guy since I was twelve years old and in a movie theater. But can this happen?

At about the same time, I found out that there had been a book called *The Color of Money* by Walter Tevis, who wrote *The Hustler.* I read the book, but I didn't really think it had anything in it in terms of a film, either. So I thought: Let's drop the book, just keep the title. I asked Richard if he would get involved in it. It was totally starting from scratch.

RICHARD PRICE: To write the script, I spent a lot of time traveling with pool hustlers. If I'm doing a movie about pool hustlers, and if pool hustlers are sitting in the audience opening night, I don't want anybody getting up in disgust. I don't want anybody saying, "This is bullshit." I want people to say, "This is true." As true as drama and fiction can be true.

The nature of pool is such that on one night, if there's a $7,500 pot, sixty of the one hundred top pool hustlers in the nation will be under this tin roof. You can go and say, "Hey, I'm doing a movie," and they're all your friends, they all want to show you the inside, because they're all dreamers in a way. They all knew *The Color of Money,* the book, and they all knew the movie *The Hustler* because that was a romanticized version of their lives. You can be like one of those guys in a red vest playing in the lobby of the Roosevelt Hotel and writing little pamphlets on trick shots, too, but you know, pool is really just hustlers. It's kids in Members Only clothing with those sort of long, outdated hairdos and those marshmallow shoes.

Q: *What's the thrust of the script?*
MS: I felt that Eddie Felson was a very strong guy. I thought if something that bad happened to him in the first film, he would get stronger. He says, "You want to see bad, I'll show you bad." In twenty-five years he's become a sharpie and a hustler of a different type. He doesn't play pool anymore;

he doesn't have the guts to do that. But he sees young talent, takes it, and makes money with it. He takes this young kid under his wing and corrupts him. And then somewhere along the road, in the education process, he reeducates *himself* and decides to play again. It's about a man who changes his mind at the age of fifty-two.

The first time I met Paul Newman, I asked him why this guy would start playing pool again at fifty-two. I asked Paul, "Why do you race if you don't win every time?" There is really no answer. We looked at each other for a while and I said, "That's the picture."

Q : *There's no ethnic material in this script. But both of you have frequently dealt with Italians and Jews.*
R P : This is more urban stuff than ethnic stuff. But I feel like everybody's a Jew in the world.
M S : I feel everybody's Italian.
R P : But all Italians are Jews.

Q : *How did the three of you work together?*
M S : In writing sessions, it was the three of us constantly reworking, constantly coming up with and batting ideas back and forth. Eventually, the writing sessions took on the aspect of rehearsals. So by the time we did the picture, I'd already had two weeks of rehearsal—it was the most preplanned film I had ever made. This was also the way that I've worked with Bob De Niro. We'd get something we'd be interested in—maybe he'd be interested first, or I'd be—and we'd get together and see if both of us could find ourselves in it. And then we'd get a writer. It always comes down to whether I can see myself in the film, if I can express myself in it through the mouthpiece—in this case, through the persona of the Paul Newman character. And could Paul express himself in it.
R P : I know this: If these guys had left me alone to write what I wanted (because I'm a novelist and all that), it would not have been as good a screenplay by any stretch of the imagination. I'll be the first to admit that. It would have been different, and it would have had its merits, but in terms of the requirements of the film, it would never have been as good.
M S : Remarkable meetings.
R P : Four o'clock. "Why does this guy have to play pool, anyhow?" Paul says, "Guys, I don't know, I have to go race, so I'll see you in about a million years." He'd come back with a big steel bowl of popcorn.

M S : I gained seven pounds.

R P : That's because you put butter on it.

I learned a lot about writing dialogue from working with Marty and Paul. I've always taken pride in writing these great lines, but it was literary dialogue, an urban literary dialogue. An Elmore Leonard line or a George Higgins line looks great on the page, but when somebody is saying it, you feel like you have to stand up and say, "Author! Author! Perfect ear!" It sounds like a David Mamet thing. You just look at each other and go, "Wow, that is really true dialogue." And everybody is at the mercy of the dialogue because the dialogue is so, like, perfect.

So, they sort of decalibrated my dialogue. I didn't go for the razor every three lines. It's like, instead of acres of diamonds, let's just make it a tomato box of diamonds.

M S : How about one diamond? I'd say, "It sounds like it's written." Very blunt. Paul would say, "It sounds like a bon mot."

R P : A what?

M S : It means it's written. Sounds like a play.

R P : *Now* my problem, frankly, is going back to a book. Because I had to unlearn a whole lot of novelistic stuff to do a screenplay. I've got to go back to baseball from softball, which I'm playing now. For example, I don't know how to write a sentence more than five words long.

M S : Working with me — any word longer than two syllables is no good!

R P : It's not just from you, but it's the momentum, the pace. I feel like I'm Leroy Neiman and there's a camera over me and I'm doing a quick sketch of horses neck and neck. I can't go into depths of character, because everything has to play out one-dimensionally on the screen. There's no internals. You can't stop and sniff the roses; you're playing beat the clock. My pacing is all off. My thought processes are jacked up too high. I've got to go back to a slow pace and think: Now, what do I really want to say?

The other phrase of Newman's that was great was when I would have an idea, but it was sort of unformed and obscure and it existed exclusively in my mind. Newman would say, "I don't understand, what's going on here?" And I'd explain and he'd say, "Well, let's call that our delicious little secret."

M S : The audience will never know!

R P : But the killer was, I'd go into meetings and my hands are shaking, and Newman's looking at the script, and I think it's like the Koran, it's so perfect. And he goes, "Guys," going dot dot dot — and I was looking at Marty and Marty's looking at me, and he's like my mother saying, "Didn't I say you're gonna get a beating?" — and then the rest of Newman's dreaded sentence would come: "I think we're missing an opportunity here."

M S :   When a guy says something like, "I think we're missing an opportunity here," our reaction is: Let's hear what he has to say. What opportunity? We think we hit on them. But what do you think we missed — because if you think we missed, for example, the opportunity that the character could be in a Nazi uniform or blackface or something, then we are talking totally wrong. But usually he was right.

R P :   I remember the moment in Connecticut when I realized that the picture was going to really get done. Newman turned to Marty and said, "Are you good at holding actors' hands?" And he said, "Oh, yeah, excellent, excellent." Newman goes, "Let's do it." I'm thinking: Shit, man, we've been doing this for six months; what do you mean, "Let's do it"? Oh, you mean we were just *playing* at doing it?

M S :   How many times do I have to tell you that? I had just come off *The Last Temptation of Christ,* man [a project of Scorsese's that fell through at the last minute]. That's why I kept telling you over the phone, "Don't tell people. Don't say anything."

R P :   Is it still too soon?

M S :   It hasn't been released yet! It still has to be released! He's walking around saying, "We're making the picture." I'd say, "Shut up, you jerk, we're not making anything." First Fox decided not to do it. It's not the kind of picture Fox does. Then began the long problem of going from Fox to Columbia. Even with Tom Cruise involved as the kid, it was still difficult to get a "go" on the picture.

Q :   *I thought Paul Newman was one of those automatic "yeses."*

M S :   I don't know. I think in a case like this, given the kind of film that it is, even with Newman and Cruise — it's not what the studios need. We are now talking about censorship in America, which is worse than the blacklist, and the kind of difficulties certain unique sensibilities have. We now have to do it with a lot of style, and very cheap, in order to get projects done. There's no guarantee of anything in this business any more unless it's a big epic — invading cannibals.

R P :   *I Eat Cannibals Who Massacre Zombies.*

M S :   Then Columbia decided not to do it. And Katzenberg and Eisner at Disney grabbed it.

Q : *Did Disney bother you?*

R P : They were great. I'd do a pornographic movie with them. *Bambi Does Dallas*.

M S : Portions of Paul Newman's and my salary had to be put up as insurance against going over budget.

Q : *It's incredible that people like you and Newman had to put up part of your salaries.*

M S : I don't know. The kind of picture I make is sort of in the margin at this point.

R P : What's the median age of the moviegoer now?

M S : Two. They're kids.

R P : Two of them added up *together* make two. Who goes to the movies? Didn't they say that ninety percent of the audience would not have seen *The Hustler?*

M S : It is a crime what's happening in the American industry. If the situation is not totally bleak, it's news to me. I just lock into certain projects. Hopefully, I can still get *The Last Temptation of Christ* made someday, but it won't be in this country, and it won't be financed by this country. At all. Forget it. That film has nothing to do with the American industry. I mean, I love Spielberg pictures. You have those wonderful little kids. But I don't think everyone should have to make them.

R P : It's true. Now you've got all of these prepubescents. It's not even the Brat Pack. It's the Wet Pack.

M S : I did a half-hour TV show with Spielberg called "Mirror, Mirror" — although the network neglected to tell anyone it was on. But I can't imagine directing one of those special effects . . . talk to the blue screen!

R P : Since *Color of Money,* I've turned down fifty projects. Basically, it feels like people sit down and say, "All right, what's the trend now? What's hot? We have to get somebody to capitalize on this trend." There's not even anything like generic caper movies any more. It's all tailored to, well, there's a kid with two heads, and we'll use this girl who's got no arms at all, and it's wacky and her father's having a sex change, and it's really wild.

Q : *Richard, did you do the scripts for the movies of* Bloodbrothers *and* The Wanderers?

RP: No, I wouldn't go near them because I didn't want anybody telling me what to do on my own book, which is the nature of the game. The best thing is just to take the check; let them make a bad movie rather than no movie.

But I've always loved movies. And I always knew that because two of my books were made into movies, I could write scripts if I wanted to. And I knew I wanted to eventually.

MS: That's why I worry about you, Richard. You've got this whole thing about writing scripts. Here you are, you're a novelist, you actually have this gift—you can sit down with a blank piece of paper and somehow the words come out and you have total control over it. And you want to be a screenwriter!

RP: Well, my last book was a very tough project—it was like giving birth to a cow—and I'd just had it for a while, and I wanted to have fun.

MS: I can't believe you said that.

RP: I got tired of the loneliness. I wanted some group interaction. When you get out to Hollywood, everybody starts stroking you because you're a novelist and they're kind of in awe of people who can really write. You get hooked on the contact, the phone calls, the plane tickets, the meetings. It beats work.

Then there is the fact that you make about one-tenth the money when you're writing novels. Once you're making screenwriter money, it's very hard to voluntarily cut your income by ninety percent. That's a bitch for anybody. Your life changes. I bought a loft in SoHo, my wife is pregnant. (I got fertile.) But Marty says to me, "Hold on to writing novels."

MS: Yeah. You gotta prepare yourself for cutting the life-style. You have to get used to the moments when you don't have the money. The only thing you have to rely on is yourself and your own talent. Don't get sucked into all that nonsense. Don't get used to the planes and the meetings and everything else. People are told they'll have four campers with three telephones in each. But that's not necessarily what's important in making a movie. It's not important to make it bigger and with more money. It's important to remain true inside yourself and keep your own thinking straight. That's going to show up on film.

...And Blood

RICHARD CORLISS/1988

TWO GUYS, TOUGH GUYS, sit in the waiting room of
Martin Scorsese's Manhattan offices. Are they auditioning for
Scorsese's forthcoming Mafia movie? Are they a pair of Willem
Dafoe's roustabout apostles? No. They are not even waiting to see
the director of *The Last Temptation of Christ*. They are waiting to see
anyone who wants to see Scorsese. Lew Wasserman may have been
depicted as a Christ killer, but his company only distributes the
movie. Scorsese made it. And have people made threats? In a generous, full-disclosure interview of more than two hours, this is the
one question he is reluctant to answer. "Well, let's say there are a
lot of people around. Privacy is gone, and everyone is very careful."

Very careful, and very open. Those attitudes marked both
Scorsese's ballsy adaptation of the Nikos Kazantzakis novel and
his conversation with me, a week after *The Last Temptation's*
opening. ABC News' Person of the Week was happy to discuss the
film with someone who had logged as much time with the
priests and nuns as he had. And to explain how personal and
universal—how, even, paramount—was his quest to make this
picture.—R.C.

RICHARD CORLISS: *Was your family religious?*
MARTIN SCORSESE: My parents grew up Americans, Italian-Americans. Their idea was survival; my father went to work when he was nine

From *Film Comment,* September/October 1988. Reprinted by permission.

years old; there was hardly room to sleep; you had to fight, you literally had to fight with your brothers and sisters for food and attention; if you got into trouble, you had to know enough to stay on the streets for two nights. It was survival. And I don't think the church figured into their life that much. Italian-Italian Catholics, like my assistant Rafael Donato, who says, "We're really pagans. Pagans in the good sense. We enjoy life, we put the church in a certain perspective." My parents were able to do that. When the church wanted to delve into personal lives, how many children they should have, my parents shied away from that. They figured that wasn't any of the priest's business. *I* was the one who took the church seriously.

My grandmother was the one who had the portrait of the Sacred Heart. Also the niche with the statue of the Virgin Mary grinding the snake under her foot. Also the beautiful, gigantic crucifix over the bed, with Jesus in brass and the palms from Palm Sunday draped over the crossbar. And remember when you'd go into church and you'd see Jesus on the cross? And he's bleeding from the wound on his side? And there's this angel below him with a cup? And the blood is dripping into the cup? The most precious blood! A great title for a film: *Most Precious Blood.*

R C :   *The scene where Jesus returns from his first temptations in the desert to open his robes and pull out his heart is right from that iconography.*
M S :   Actually, that scene, which was not in the Kazantzakis book, was written by Paul Schrader, a Dutch Calvinist, and it was kind of nudged to me as Catholic. He also wanted to show that the supernatural and the natural exist on the same plane. But we were doing that all along. He wanted to show the angel at the end turning into a gargoyle, and slithering off a table. I leveled that all out. I wanted it to be like when I was growing up, and my grandparents and parents and aunts would tell me stories — ghost stories — that took place right in our apartment. The supernatural and the natural on the same plane. Only here you're dealing with the messiah. So if a snake goes by, the snake is going to talk. In voice over. Don't even try to do Francis the Talking Mule. Or Leo the Talking Lion. Forget it! It's Harvey Keitel's voice, or mine, saying, "Do you recognize me? I'm your heart."

So when we got to do the Sacred Heart scene, here's what I thought was more important. You have these guys bickering all the time, just like in the gospels. It's all there: "I'm the one, I'm the one, I'm gonna sit next to him when the Kingdom of Heaven comes. I'll be at his right hand." "No, *I'm*

gonna be at his right hand!" Hysterical stuff! So they're all bickering, and
Judas is being a pain, as usual. And then Jesus shows up, and it's party soli-
darity. It's the Democratic convention, everybody getting together. Unity.
And his presence is shining so strong at that moment that they have to be
unified behind him. Then again, you could say that the apostles are seeing
him just back from the desert, with the light from the campfire, and the
music around, and the glow behind his head, just a little touch of De
Mille. It *could* be mass hallucination, mass hypnosis. We don't know. It's a
symbol to bring them all together—especially Judas, who kisses his feet
and says, "Adonai!" All of a sudden Jesus is God? Wait a second! Yes—
Judas needs this. So do the others, to be convinced that this is the man.

R C : *Is this Jesus God, or a man who thinks he's God?*
M S : He's God. He's not deluded. I think Kazantzakis thought that, I think
the movie says that, and I know I believe that. The beauty of Kazantzakis'
concept is that Jesus has to put up with everything we go through, all the
doubts and fears and anger. He made me *feel* like he's sinning—but he's
not sinning, he's just human. As well as divine. And he has to deal with all
this double, triple guilt on the cross. That's the way I directed it, and that's
what I wanted, because my own religious feelings are the same. I do a lot
of thinking about it, a lot of questioning, a lot of doubting, and then some
good feeling. A lot of good feeling. And then a lot more questioning, thinking, doubting!

R C : *This Jesus is also a mortifier of the flesh, like the medieval flagellants and
mystics.*
M S : I think mortification of the flesh is important. I don't mean that you
have to go around whipping yourself, but disciplining is important. This
kind of movie, on a $6 million budget, *that's* a discipline. When you're in
Morocco, and the sun's going down, and the generator's breaking, and the
actor's wig is coming off, and you know you don't have $26 million and the
10,000 extras like Bertolucci—that's discipline. You design it another kind
of way. Except that, as [cinematographer] Michael Ballhaus would tell me
whenever I got depressed, "That's the way this picture has to be made."
    You know, the Roman soldiers who surround the temple, at the end?
Just five. Same five guys. They were also the guys who were rioting when
Jesus starts throwing things. And they were the Levites who come down

the stairs, and also the guys who go up the stairs *against* the Levites! Five guys from Italy. We had twelve uniforms, but we couldn't afford the other seven stunt men. So it's a strong punishment.

R C :   *And the "fantasy" or "hallucination" that Jesus has at the end of the film, it's really a diabolical temptation?*
M S :   Exactly. You know, the one sexual thing the priest told Catholic boys they could not be held responsible for was nocturnal emission. It was like an involuntary fantasy. And with Jesus it's the same thing. How can you hold him responsible for this fantasy? Of course, Catholic boys were taught that, if you entertained fantasy for a while, it became an occasion of sin. That's another good title for a movie: *Occasion of Sin!*

R C :   *Your apostles, they don't speak like the holy figures we've heard in other biblical epics. They speak like characters from a Martin Scorsese picture.*
M S :   Schrader said this to me: "Unless you have them speaking in ancient Aramaic with subtitles, whoever stands behind the camera is going to be doing his 'wrong' idea of the dialogue of the time. You'll do your wrong idea. I'd do my wrong idea. Twenty years ago George Stevens did his wrong idea." And he's right. But I did want to break away from the sound of the old biblical epics, to make the dialogue plainer, more contemporary. That's mainly what Jay Cocks and I did the last six drafts of the script. We rewrote 80 percent of the dialogue, arguing over every word. Jesus says to Judas, "You have the harder job." "Job?" Is that the right word, the simplest, the most effective? Make it more immediate, so people have a sense of who these guys were, not out of a book or a painting, but as if they lived and spoke right now.

The accents do that too. The apostles, most of them, were tough guys who worked with their hands. Peter, the fisherman, was like a rough guy from the docks; he had a Brooklyn accent. Vic Argo, who played Peter, would walk around the set with a cigar in his mouth all the time. And when it was time to shoot, he'd say to me, "I have to lose the cigar, right?"

R C :   *And the bad guys, Satan and the Romans, they have British accents.*
M S :   Anyone from the outside is going to sound different. And anyone in authority should have a British accent. It sounds authoritative to American ears. Just as any British actor is supposed to be better than any American

Robert De Niro and Harvey Keitel, *Mean Streets*, 1973

Dianne Ladd, Valerie Curtain, Vic Tayback, and Ellen Burstyn, *Alice Doesn't Live Here Anymore*, 1974

Robert De Niro, *Taxi Driver*, 1976

Martin Scorsese directing Robert De Niro, *Taxi Driver*, 1976

Robert De Niro, Liza Minnelli, and William Tole, *New York, New York*, 1977

Liza Minnelli, *New York, New York*, 1977

Rick Danko, Levon Helm, and Robbie Robertson, *The Last Waltz*, 1978

Robert De Niro, Martin Denkin, and Kevin Mahon, *Raging Bull*, 1980

Willem Dafoe, *The Last Temptation of Christ*, 1988

Robert De Niro and Ray Liotta, *GoodFellas*, 1990

Robert De Niro and Nick Nolte, *Cape Fear*, 1991

Daniel Day-Lewis, Winona Ryder, and Miriam Margolyes, *The Age of Innocence*, 1993

actor. Don't they tend to win the Oscars, just for sounding British? I love British actors, and I love American actors, but there's a reverse-snobbism thing there. Also, the British empire was a lot like the Roman empire. They occupied America, and a lot of other places, just like the Romans occupied Judaea.

R C : *When people in theaters hear these accents, do they giggle at the wrong time?*

M S : Some critics called the movie unintentionally funny, but Jay and I don't think so. Sometimes what's said is serious, sometimes it's ironic, and sometimes it's meant to be funny. One of the elements we kept from the book is that Lazarus never quite heals properly. I mean, the guy's been dead for three days. Forget it, he's a little dull! That's why Harry Dean Stanton [Saul] says, "How're ya feelin'?" It's all done with a sense of humor. And if you see it with an audience, they're going with it. They're laughing hysterically at the cast-the-first-stone scene with Zebbedee, where Jesus says, "Take this rock—mine's bigger." An audience picks up on it. They pick up on it as a story. As a movie.

Jay Cocks went to the first public showing at the Ziegfeld in New York, and there were two black ladies behind him saying, "Hallelujah!" and "That's the way He said it!" And when the last temptation comes on, they say, "Oh my God, no! No!" And when he gets back on the cross: "It was a dream! It was a dream!" Which is exactly the way it should be.

R C : *The film has certainly made a lot of people think, for the first time in a long time, about Jesus and his message of love. You didn't mean to be, primarily, a bringer of the Word.*

M S : No, but I've always taken that word—the idea of love—very seriously. It may not be a stylish thing these days to say you're a believer, especially to say it so often in the papers, as I've been saying it. But I really think Jesus had the right idea. I don't know how you do it. I guess it has to start with you, and then your children, your wife, your parents, friends, business associates—you start branching out a little bit, it starts to spread, until you create a kind of conglomerate of love. But it's hard. That's why Judas' line in the movie gets a great laugh: "The other day you said, 'A man slaps you, turn the other cheek.' I don't like that!" Who does!? We agree with you, Judas. How do you do it?

R C : *Barbara Hershey, who plays Magdalene, gave you a copy of* The Last Temptation of Christ *in 1972. Did you read it then and know immediately you wanted to make a movie of it?*

M S :   No! It took me six years to finish it! I'd pick it up, put it down, reread it, be enveloped by the beautiful language of it, then realize I couldn't shoot the language. I read most of it after *Taxi Driver* [in 1976] and then finished it while I was visiting the Taviani Brothers on the set of *The Meadow* in October 1978. And that's when I realized that this was for me. I'd often thought about doing a documentary on the Gospels—but Pasolini did that.

Paul wrote two drafts of the script, and Paramount backed us. Boris Leven, the production designer, made a trip to Morocco and Israel, scouting locations, working out a look for the film—all those arches!—and making beautiful sketches. It was great, because he was one of the first people who made me conscious of design in films when I was a kid. My family didn't go to the theater, so I'd never seen theater design. Then I saw *The Silver Chalice* in 1954, and it was the first time I'd seen a movie presentation of theatrical design, something that wasn't supposed to be quite real. I'd seen movies with dream sequences, but nothing like this, where the whole film was done in an obvious style. And here we were 30 years later making another biblical epic. It's such a shame Boris died before *Last Temptation* got made, but a lot of what he did survives in the film.

By now it's 1983. And the budget is starting to climb from $12 million to 13 to 16, and the shooting schedule is getting longer, and we're going to shoot in Israel, where we're a day-and-a-half's flight from Hollywood if anything goes wrong, and they're not exactly crazy about the casting— Aidan Quinn they could accept as Jesus, but some of the others made them nervous. And then the religious protests started, and a theater chain said it wouldn't show the movie. Well, if you have a picture that's pretty expensive by now, and you're not sure it's going to be profitable, and you can't show it in a lot of theaters, and you're getting flak from organized groups. . . .

So they dropped it. Then Jack Lang, the French Minister of Culture, tried to help finance it with government money. And there was a big storm over that, over there. Meanwhile, my agent, Harry Ufland, kept shopping it around to other studios. He kept the idea alive, he kept my *hope* alive, for three years. That's why he's listed on the credits as executive producer. He was great. But he was involved with other projects. Then I got Mike Ovitz in January of 1987, and within three months we had a deal at Universal.

R C : *Kind of ironic, since Universal has this rep as the black suits and black hearts of the movie business.*

M S : I never thought I could make a movie like this for a place like Universal. They represented a certain kind of filmmaking. But from the moment I met Tom Pollock and Sid Sheinberg, I felt a new attitude, a new openness. I've never felt such support from any studio. They never said change one thing. They made suggestions; everybody made suggestions. And they knew it was a hard sell. But from the very first screening of the three-hour cut, they were moved, they were teary-eyed, they just loved it. I just hope they get through everything. But the toughness you used to hear about Universal against filmmakers, that's how tough they're being in defense of this movie. The more they get slapped, the more they hit back.

R C : *Maybe they fought harder because of the charge that the film would fan the flames of anti-semitism.*

M S : Of all the things that come out: anti-semitic! I was totally shocked by this turn. I couldn't believe it. I mean, if they have problems with a businessman trying to make money, then he's a "businessman"! He's not "Jewish." It's disgusting. Obviously it just shows them for what they are. And even Rev. Hymers later apologized for his tactics.

But the whole point of the movie is that nobody is to blame, not even the Romans. It's all part of the plan. Otherwise, it's insane. I mean, the Jewish people give us God, and we persecute them for 2000 years for it!

R C : *At least the controversy helped bring your film to a wider audience.*

M S : I do hope the controversy doesn't keep this movie from being shown on cable. When even Bravo, the very best cable channel, buckles under to 30 or 40 protest letters and withdraws Godard's *Hail Mary* from its schedule, you have to be concerned about the life of your movie. You have to be concerned about a lot of things when that happens.

R C : *Between 1983, when Paramount passed on the project, and '87, when Universal said go, you made two other films that might be called commissioned projects.*

MS: After *The Last Temptation* was cancelled in '83, I had to get myself back in shape. Work out. And this was working out. First *After Hours,* on a small scale. The idea was that I should be able, if *Last Temptation* ever came along again, to make it like *After Hours,* because that's all the money I'm gonna get for it.

Then the question was: Are you going to survive as a Hollywood filmmaker? Because even though I live in New York, I'm a "Hollywood director." Then again, even when I try to make a Hollywood film, there's something in me that says, "Go the other way." With *The Color of Money,* working with two big stars, we tried to make a Hollywood movie. Or rather, I tried to make one of my pictures, but with a Hollywood star: Paul Newman. That was mainly making a film about an American icon. That's what I zeroed in on. I'm mean, Paul's face! You know, I'm always trying to get the camera to move fast enough into an actor's face—a combination of zoom and fast track—without killing him! Well, in *The Color of Money* there's the first time Paul sees Tom Cruise and says, "That kid's got a dynamite break," and turns around and the camera comes flying into his face. Anyway, that night, we looked at the rushes and saw four takes of this and said, "That man's gonna go places! He's got a face!"

But it was always Work in Progress, to try to get to make *Last Temptation.* And now that *Last Temptation* is finally done, I'll be doing another movie about the difficulty of defining love. It's one of three *New York Stories*; Francis Coppola and Woody Allen are doing the other two. Richard Price has written the script for me, based on something I've been thinking about for maybe 15 years. It tells the end of an affair between a famous painter, about 50, and his young assistant, whom he uses as a subject for his work. It's based on the diaries of Anna Polina, one of Dostoyevsky's students. It begins at the end of the affair and goes to the *very* end of the affair. The dialogue is very snappy, because Richard has that touch, but basically it's about a guy's relationship to his work and the people around him. Is he able to love? Is he a loving person? Is this his idea of love? And if so, is it valid?

And then I'll do a gangster picture, *Wise Guy.* I'll be going back to my roots—it's a real assault on these two guys living it up. And I'll be working on style again. The breaking up of style, the breaking up of structure—of that traditional structure of movies. I like to look at that kind of movie; I don't like to do them. I get bored.

R C : *In a way, it must be hard not to get bored, now that you've achieved this film that has obsessed you for so long.*

M S : I'd like to take a year off from my more personal projects and do a Hollywood genre film, with a good script, some wonderful actors. You learn craft. Every time you go on the set, even though you plan everything before, you realize how little you know. Or maybe I've just forgotten! The guys on the set ask, "What do we do now? Should we pan him over?" "I don't know, I'll probably lose it in the cutting anyway." So what I'm doing now is thinking fast—I've always talked fast, but now I'm thinking fast. Always editing in my head: compression, compression, compression. Of course, I've just made a movie that's two hours and 40 minutes!

I get stuck in between the European films of the Forties, Fifties, and early Sixties and the American films. And I don't know. I don't know if I belong anywhere. I just try what appeals to me. And to get the money from America—which is very hard to do and stay within the system. I'm so glad *Last Temptation* was financed in Hollywood, that it's an American movie, that an American studio was willing to take the flak. And I would like to do a movie with widescreen and a couple thousand extras, if I could keep my interest going. My everyday interest. Because I don't enjoy shooting movies. There's too many people around, too many things to go wrong, too many personalities, and you have to be very... rational. I don't like being rational. I don't like being held back.

R C : *Answer a few points of contention, if you will. Some people, seeing the early scene in Mary Magdalene's brothel, think that Jesus is watching Magdalene perform in a sex show.*

M S : Jesus and the other men are not voyeurs. They're waiting, they're not really watching. Some of them are playing games; two black guys are talking; Jesus is waiting. Magdala was a major crossroads for caravans, merchants would meet there. And when you were in Magdala, the thing do to was to go see Mary. But the point of the scene was to show the proximity of sexuality to Jesus, the occasion of sin. Jesus must have seen a naked woman—must have. So why couldn't we show that? And I wanted to show the barbarism of the time, the degradation to Mary. It's better that the door is open. Better there is no door. The scene isn't done for titillation; it's to show the pain on her face, the compassion Jesus has for her as he fights his sexual desire for her. He's always wanted her.

RC: *At the last supper, Jesus says, "Take this and drink this, because this is my blood." And when the cup is passed to Peter, he tastes blood.*
MS: That's the miracle of transubstantiation. And in a movie you have to see it. Blood is very important in the church. Blood is the life force, the essence, the sacrifice. And in a movie you have to see it. In practically every culture, human sacrifice is very important, very widespread. When I was in Jerusalem, Teddy Kollek, the mayor, showed me the Valley of Gehenna, where the Phillistines sacrificed their children.

RC: *The last temptation is one of a long, normal, and still basically sinless life. Except that Jesus commits adultery with Mary's sister Martha.*
MS: I don't know that it's adultery. It might have been polygamy. There is some evidence of a Hebrew law at the time regarding polygamy for the sake of propagation of the race. But remember again, this is the Devil doing fancy footwork. "You can have whatever you want. And look, I'm *sorry* about what happened to Mary Magdalene. Really sorry, won't happen again. In fact, this time, take two! You need more than one—take two!"

RC: *In the Gospels, does Jesus know from the beginning that he's God?*
MS: Maybe, maybe not. There are hints both ways. In Matthew, the first time you see Jesus, he's being baptised by John; and God's voice comes out and says, "This is my beloved son in whom I am well pleased." But I think that was more to emphasize Jesus over John the Baptist. Because John was the one getting all the attention. I mean, this man had a presentation! He knew how to draw the crowds. But except in Luke's gospel, where the twelve-year-old Jesus is presented to the elders, the question of when Jesus knew he was divine is cloaked in mystery. So we're not saying this is the truth, we're just saying it's fascinating, it's so dramatic, to have the guy make a choice. As if he *could* make a choice—I mean, if he's two natures in one, he *has* no choice. But the beauty is that it gives the *impression* of choice. And eventually he has to say, "Take me back, Father." It's wonderful.

RC: *The final words of the movie—Jesus' final words—have baffled transla-tors for centuries. How did you decide which words to use?*
MS: Very hard to translate and get the power and the meaning. "It is fin-ished." "It is completed." "It's over." Can't use that—too Roy Orbison. What was the translation we were taught in Catholic school? "It is con-

summated." The Kazantzakis book used "It is accomplished." Because Jesus had accomplished a task, accomplished a goal. I shot three different versions. What I wanted was a sense of Jesus at the end of the temptation begging his Father, "Please, if it isn't too late, if the train hasn't left, please, can I get back on, I wanna get on!" And now he's made it back on the cross and he's sort of jumping up and down saying, "We did it! We did it! I thought for one second I wasn't gonna make it—but Ididit Ididit Ididit!"

RC: *So how do you feel after a decade of trying to get this temptation on film?*
MS: I thought for one second I wasn't gonna make it. But Ididit Ididit Ididit!

Scorsese: A Bicoastal Story

AMY TAUBIN/1988

"FORMAL STORYTELLING WITH A camera is very difficult for
me. I'm constantly learning it from the beginning. I guess you never stop
thinking about whether you really can tell a story with a camera. I'm nervous every morning before I start."

Indeed, Martin Scorsese is the most overtly anxious director I've ever
encountered. Apparently, it doesn't interfere with his productivity. But it
just seems unfair that the maker of some dozen feature films that range
from extremely interesting to extraordinary—and, along with Kubrick, the
only post-1960 major American auteur—should be so painfully afflicted.

I am sitting on a staircase in what was once Duke Ellington's townhouse
on Riverside Drive at 106th Street, where Scorsese is shooting his segment
of *New York Stories*, a three-part omnibus film. (The other sections are by
Francis Coppola and Woody Allen.) Scrunched down on the step below is
cinematographer Nestor Almendros, and next to him, seated in, yes, a
director's chair, is Scorsese, with producer Robert Greenhut, publicist Marion Billings, and script supervisor Martha Pinson clustered protectively
around him. The atmosphere is solicitous, slightly suggestive of a hospital
waiting room, the small talk and bits of advice or reassurance staving off
some never-to-be-spoken terminal terror. In this scenario, Scorsese functions as an amalgam of doctor, patient, and next-of-kin. During rehearsals
and takes, he is impressively concentrated, quick-witted, and authoritative.
In between, he turns convulsively self-conscious, humming the opening of

From *Village Voice*, 25 October 1988. Reprinted by permission.

the "Tannhauser" overture, tracing fragments of camera moves with his hand, and alternating overeager repartee—his delivery's as forced as Rupert Pupkin's, but fortunately lacks that character's maniacal aggression—with cheery bursts of encouragement ("Good thinking, Joe, let's keep up our incentive.")

Here, I must invoke the Heisenberg Uncertainty Principle. Most of the production team have worked with "Marty" for years. I am a stranger, the first journalist, so I'm told, allowed on a Scorsese set since Siskel visited *New York, New York*. Would the director's demeanor been different had I not been there? I don't know, but I took his behavior as a form of graciousness. Five minutes won me totally to his side.

The project, which, says Scorsese, "came about through Woody Allen," placed no constraints on the directors except that the stories take place in New York City, and the productions abide by budget and schedule. ("Movies would be great without a schedule," jokes the director. "You could sit around all day and think about the shot.") Scorsese took the opportunity to realize a 15-year-old dream about a 50-year-old artist and his relationship with a woman in her early 20s who's been both his assistant and lover, but now wants her own career and emotional independence. "It begins at the end and goes right to the very end," he says (a typical Scorsese one-liner).

"The difficulties in the relationship seem to feed the work—the moment she says she's leaving, he starts to paint really well. Even in the student/teacher relationship, there are creative jealousies and a constant testing of each other. I always find it interesting when a pupil has to move on," Scorsese explains, and then adds, "I like both of them. I can't help it." (The ex-couple is played by Nick Nolte and Rosanna Arquette.)

Scorsese originally conceived the central character as a writer, but Richard Price, who did the script, suggested making him a painter. "Until about two weeks before we started shooting," explains production designer Kristi Zea (she did *Married to the Mob*), "Marty thought we shouldn't see his paintings." When he changed his mind, Zea selected large landscapes by Chuck Connelly as appropriate for Nolte's character.

This morning's scene is a black-tie art party (Japanese waiters in red eye makeup) held in the home of a major collector—art, courtesy of Holly Solomon Gallery. A gray-bearded Nolte (looking a lot like Don Judd) is holding court. His dialogue starts with a joke about an early commission from "army intelligence" and ends with a zingy reference to Vietnam. The first shot, a 360-degree dolly, involves a complex coordination of moves by the camera, Nolte, and some two dozen extras.

The actors, camera, camera operator, assistant director, grips, and other assorted crew are crowded into one small room—so small that the director and the cinematographer are exiled to the outer hallway. Scorsese shouts his "And ACTION!" through a walkie-talkie and, with Almendros, watches the shot on the video tape monitor. (He won't use the video for serious acting scenes; he needs to watch the actors in the flesh.) The AD functions as a go-between, giving the cues and conveying Scorsese's comments to the crew.

Scorsese has preplanned all the shots. He shows me the tiny squiggles on his script. "I used to make bigger drawings," he says. After countless rehearsals, he suddenly realizes that the camera move should start slightly later. Six actual takes go by before he likes one well enough to print. "One problem [in the shot] is okay; two, I can't handle it." By the 12th take, not only is the move more elegant, but the bit of story it tells has come into focus. "Close to perfection," comments Almendros. Answers Scorsese, "Yeah, I like it to be a little off."

During the changeover, I get 15 minutes to ask questions. We start easy—what about the relationship of the emblematic New York filmmaker to Hollywood?

"In order to make movies, you need to go to Hollywood. I made *Boxcar Bertha* for Corman. *Mean Streets* was shot in Hollywood with Corman producer Paul Rapp. He taught me how to make a movie in 21 days. It's been difficult to make personal movies within the system. Movies are too expensive. It's hard to keep exploring. I use myself as a measuring rod, try to stay as honest as I can."

Scorsese is reluctant to talk about *Last Temptation*. Clearly the reception has been wrenching. "The movie was locked by early July, before we showed it to the fundamentalists. But I wish," he plaintively adds, "it had had the opening we planned for it."

I tell him about my response to the film—that I kept thinking about how the Christ imagery must have been at the root of his involvement with visual representation, and that I was moved by his need to make something that would become part of the history of that representation.

"I really enjoyed making those little images. The Bleeding Heart. Digging in those wounds." Although he claims never to rescreen his films once they're finished, he has been looking at *Last Temptation.* "I like to hear the stories told over and over again."

The next project is *Wise Guy,* adapted from the Nick Pileggi novel. Scorsese and Pileggi are writing the script. "It'll be different from the traditional gangster picture. But I'd like to do some genre movies — maybe another musical. I could get more money if I made genre. We only had a little crane on *Last Temptation.* I'd enjoy using a really big crane."

You've Got to Love Something Enough to Kill It: The Art of Non-Compromise

CHRIS HODENFIELD/1989

MARTIN SCORSESE IS READY to make another gangster movie. He has these memories from his days growing up in New York City's Little Italy: mental snapshots of mobsters in sleek, stylish suits, passing out favors. This would be the '50s and '60s: graceful days before the drug trade busted up the old traditions. He just has an urge to record the gone regime of stylish killers.

This project—based on Nick Pileggi's book, *Wise Guy,* which has nothing to do with the TV show—sounds like a real crowd-pleaser, the kind of solid commercial fare you need after you get crucified for making *The Last Temptation of Christ.* Then he starts telling you about it—this short, intense guy with the thick, beetling eyebrows—and he starts talking faster and faster in feverish bursts, and his eyes go from woefully sad to explosively happy in a heartbeat, and he makes it sound like a hell of a story, lots of action, very funny. Then he sits back and cackles and adds the one caveat that makes the tale sound truly Scorsese: "I hope it will infuriate the audience."

Provocations come easily to Scorsese. And who knows what will happen? Movies have a way of changing on him. In 1977, he talked delightedly of his next feature, *Raging Bull,* which he promised would be a madcap lark, and bunches of fun. Then dreadful things happened in his life. Divorce, scandal, write-ups in the newspapers, late-night misery. He got various friends working on the *Raging Bull* screenplay, and they added their own

From *American Film,* March 1989. Reprinted by permission.

highly personal tumults. ("If it's not personal," Scorsese says, "I can't be there in the morning.") *Raging Bull* worked at being close to the truth of a boxer's life. It became the story, starkly enough of a man who hits people for a living. All of the anguish and despair in the boxer's life, and Scorsese's life, were there to see. If you were infuriated by the sight of it, tough luck.

There are filmmakers who give you nice moments of truth on their way to selling you a big lie. Then there are the storytellers who fib, vamp and deceive their way to eventually coming up with a larger truth. And finally, there are those who don't care what they heave onto the screen, as long as they get paid.

Scorsese may not always know what the truth is, but at least he's in search of it. In today's market, that takes courage. Even his mere entertainments—*Alice Doesn't Live Here Anymore, The Last Waltz, After Hours, The Color of Money*—have an edge of risk and uncertainty. The pictures of his renown—*Mean Streets, Taxi Driver, The Last Temptation of Christ*—are riddled with the energy of obsession.

Scorsese's movies have rewarded him with the reputation of a gritty guy from New York's teeming streets. But he's really a man of high-boulevard style. He's exchanged the downtown loft scene for a town house in Manhattan's Upper East Side. He likes to be able to walk from his home to his office in the Brill Building, charging over to midtown with his white poodle.

When we found him recently, Scorsese was just finishing up his segment of *New York Stories,* a three-part compilation film he was making with Woody Allen and Francis Coppola. For such a ball of electricity, he appeared to be almost in a state of contentment. His uniform seems not to have changed in years: a fine tailored shirt, beautiful leather shoes and incongruous blue-denim pants. The clothes symbolize the inner man. In short, conflict. And conflict, as Laurence Olivier once observed, is the essence of drama. This man is all drama. Sometimes he appears to be frail, asthmatic, coughing like Camille and preparing to die; usually, though, he's ready to give enormous attention to just about anything. Scorsese is an educated, cultured man of considerable sensitivity and idealism, but he will jab you off-balance by confessing to a violent, self-destructive past. He instantly sweeps you up with his jovial, irascible energy, and everything in the world suddenly seems like great theater.

These days, Scorsese's been reading books and "reassessing" things. With the current feature not yet out, he's still suffering the bruises and notoriety of *The Last Temptation of Christ.* The story itself—Jesus wrestling with his divine and human natures—offended certain conservative Christians. But just as many cineasts were offended and unnerved by the cinematic elements, Scorsese's combination of his two grandest loves: old-fashioned, Bible-epic pictorial sweep along with early '60s, French New Wave anarchism.

The visual surface of the movie screen is his central devotion. He compulsively thinks up all manner of stylistic flourishes to liven up a scene, and, in this, he is in league with visual kingpins like Alfred Hitchcock. Reeling camera moves are as essential to his truth as the blood sacrifices are to his plots. It's as if he wants to create an intensity on screen that matches what he perceives/suffers in real life.

I recall seeing him in early 1976, talking to a group of film students. It was just after the release of *Taxi Driver,* and he was asked what it was like dealing with film studios. Now, although *Taxi Driver* went on to gather fine profits and weird infamy, it was only intended by Columbia Pictures to be a fast cheapie. Scorsese bared his soul with a story.

It seems that on the 10th day, rain forced a stop in the shooting. They were filming inside a coffee shop, a simple scene of Cybill Shepherd and Robert De Niro just talking. "I placed them by a window," he explained, "so you could see all of Columbus Circle, the cars, the whole city, everything. New York City is *the* character in the movie. A bus goes by the window; there's thousands of people. By one o'clock in the afternoon, a big thunderstorm breaks. And it doesn't let up. What are you going to do?"

He sent everybody home for the day. The alarmed studio bosses said, well, maybe he just ought to film the actors against a white wall. Scorsese replied that he would shoot anything he could, but he would not shoot that scene against a white wall.

"That night, I went through a lot of crises," he told the students, "and made a lot of phone calls. I said to a friend, 'That's it. If they don't like the way I'm gonna make the picture, then I won't make the picture.'"

The next morning, after quiet declarations were made, Scorsese was told that everything was taken care of. He could proceed.

"That's when you realize that you really have to love something enough to kill it," he declared.

The composition was worth dying for. Like a good Catholic schoolboy, Scorsese instinctively understands the power of imagery. During his sickly youth, he often passed the days drawing elaborate comic-book storyboards for the movies in his head. (Today, the opening credit on his movies is "A Martin Scorsese *Picture*.") The flow of his imagery is easier to understand if you visit him in high-energy New York City, where, just walking down the street, you see a swirling parade of elliptical shapes, passing faces, shadowy characters in doorways. It helped me understand very suddenly how, at their best, Scorsese's movies are a torrent of images and that he is really just a mad painter.

"If I could just get them on film fast enough!" he agrees, laughing. "If I could make the camera move faster, I would. We tried to, Michael Ballhaus [cameraman on *Last Temptation*] and I, but it was dangerous; the camera would just go flying off the track. Go right into the actor!

"Really! That's the way I see it, walking to work! And I walk very quickly, because that's the way I grew up. I grew up downtown on the Lower East Side. Around the corner was the Bowery, and it was pretty scary. All the derelicts, and some of them were violent. There was no such thing as 'the colorful bums.' I felt sorry for them, but the idea was to survive walking down the street going to school.

"It's living with fear, but I don't think it's necessarily that. They say my films are about paranoia, but, to me, it's just pure survival."

Being consumed by the image has nothing to do with a director's search for truth, of course. Plenty of high-powered hambones out there possess nothing *but* a gaudy visual style. Like his *New York Stories* cohort, Allen, Scorsese doesn't mind putting his personal life up there on the screen, too. Before film school, Scorsese studied to be a priest. His first feature, an enhanced student project called *Who's That Knocking at My Door?* (1968), was about an intensely religious guy and his struggle with a more worldly girlfriend. *Mean Streets* and *Taxi Driver* both involved what he called "false saints." All of this had autobiographical meat. And for years he wanted to make a movie about Mother Cabrini. Even *The Last Temptation of Christ* was, he says, a little embarrassing in what it revealed about his profound religious beliefs. "I'm always thinking about it," he admits. "I believe it!"

New York, New York (1977) was supposed to be about two married musicians who have trouble mixing love and careers. But, with Scorsese heading into a divorce, and his wife, Julia Cameron, rewriting Earl MacRauch's and Mardik Martin's script, it came to be about the *impossibility* of mixing marriage and career. It should not be an impossible mix, but it was to him at that turbulent time of his life.

An unwieldy combination of splashy musical numbers and doomed romance, *New York, New York* may not be a likeable stop in the Scorsese filmography, but it marks an important stage in his life. His three previous movies having proved very successful, Scorsese suddenly found himself a star. He was not up to the task, and, as he commenced the Band documentary, *The Last Waltz,* he jumped on a Mr. Toad's wild ride of rock 'n' roll whoop-de-doo that took a couple of years to wind down.

(A later marriage to the young actress Isabella Rossellini dissolved, and now he is happily married to Barbara [De Fina], who produced *Last Temptation* and *The Color of Money.* It has often transpired in his life that friends and wives become collaborators.)

Scorsese was just getting back on his feet when John Hinckley claimed that the bloody climax of *Taxi Driver* inspired him to shoot Ronald Reagan. Scorsese responded with another movie about a demented loner who "claims" a famous person for his own, *The King of Comedy.*

His best films, he says, are the ones he made for himself. "I didn't think *Mean Streets* could be released. That's not phony humility. *Taxi Driver* was a low-budget film, and I loved Schrader's script so much it was as if I had dreamed it. De Niro felt the same way. We were like the Three Musketeers together. When it became a hit, it was a surprise to me, believe me. And *Raging Bull,* I figured, was the end of my career. It was like a punch in the face. It was a violent movie that would shake them and make them feel something.

"I had decided that *Raging Bull* would be pretty much the end of my working in America. Luckily enough, we got the money to make it because De Niro was a star. I thought it was a swan song for Hollywood. By the time it was released in '80, I thought it was the end; that I was going to be living in New York and Rome, and I was going to make documentaries and educational films on the saints. I was going to make films for television, that sort of thing."

Scorsese says this in all sad-eyed sincerity. It is true, though, that in 1983 Paramount killed his treasured *Last Temptation* project, and he didn't know if he would ever make it. He remembers having lunch that year with director Brian De Palma, who was depressed about the brutal reviews of *Scarface.* "We were sitting there at Hugo's thinking, 'What can we do?' And Brian said maybe we should do some teaching. And we looked at each other. The salaries in teaching..." his voice trails at the ignominy. "And what would you do in teaching?

"There doesn't seem to be anything else I can do," Scorsese offers plaintively. "I can't write novels. I could write scripts, but I'd only want to direct them."

It should have been amusing to hear one of America's premier directors take himself so seriously, but, of course, that seriousness is what makes him what he is. What was crazier was to hear him judge his career as being so precarious, as if he were just another steelworker.

"You've got to be realistic," he presses on. "There's no such thing as a guarantee of anything in life. Anything. To make the movies I made in Hollywood, it's like a gift. And sometimes," he said, brightening, "they even pay me for it!

"The trick in taking a lot of chances is if you can do it for a price. The days of *Raging Bull*—when we went overbudget shooting 10 weeks of fight scenes that comprised nine minutes of time in the completed film—those days are gone. Unless you have an absolute guaranteed box-office star name. Then . . . maybe."

Hence, he brought in the striking-looking *Last Temptation* for a paltry $6.7 million. He was helped considerably by his actors, who worked for deferments and peanuts.

Actors usually love the very attentive Scorsese. He himself has taken small, seething roles in *Taxi Driver* and Bertrand Tavernier's *Round Midnight*. Ellen Burstyn, Robert De Niro and Paul Newman have all won best acting Oscars under his tutelage. And it's no wonder that Marlon Brando has tried to enlist him as a director, first in 1974, after he saw *Mean Streets,* and again two years ago, when he invited Scorsese and De Niro down to his island in Tahiti.

"He says, 'Come down for five days,' and we ended up staying three-and-a-half weeks," Scorsese recalls. "It's the only time in my life when I ever forgot what time it was or what day it was. It was remarkable. I was very sad to leave. The ideas he was telling me were wonderful."

The event is doubly intriguing, because Brando and De Niro could almost be considered actor-brothers. Each has perfected an artist-of-the-streets style; each has inspired a slew of questionable imitators.

"It was as if they'd known each other for years," Scorsese marvels. "They had kind of an affinity for each other. Everybody was extremely relaxed, one of the best times I ever had in my life. They were more outdoors people than I was, of course. Boats would fall on my head. I was the comic relief, I guess. I didn't know what the hell was going on.

"I was never involved with any acting schools or acting techniques. I always say to actors, the hardest thing you can do in a movie is sit down and talk to somebody. Yelling and ranting and raving, sometimes that's very easy to do. The real communication between two people, the subtlety... I think Brando and De Niro broke through there. They made realism a virtue, I think. Brando created that style, and De Niro moves ahead with it. They have emotional depth—they're not just walking through a scene having their faces photographed.

"The best collaborations I had in my life were with De Niro. A lot of people don't understand when I say please leave the set. 'What's this? Genius at work?' No, it's distracting. Some of the stuff I used to do with Bob was so personal and, for the actor, so painful that the only way he could do it was with me, and nobody else, watching. He could make some mistakes. And very often those mistakes wouldn't be mistakes at all. It's the searching process. Intimacy and trust is the thing."

What does De Niro want out of a role?

"The truth of the situation. How would a person really react, I think. He may tell you something else. I can only tell you that when we work, we use that phrase, 'It's not right. Something's not right.' If I see honesty in front of that lens, I'm satisfied behind the f---king camera—I tell you that."

Scorsese got another chance to explore the truth of the situation in his chapter of *New York Stories* (the three segments are unrelated except for the locale). Called *Life Lessons,* starring Nick Nolte and Rosanna Arquette, and written by novelist Richard Price, it is yet another story ripped right from the headlines across Scorsese's soul.

"In the late '60s, I wanted to make a film out of Dostoyevski's *The Gambler.* Paul Schrader tried in the early '70s, but it didn't work out. And then around '72 or '73, Jay Cocks gave me a Christmas present of a new translation of *The Gambler,* along with *Diaries of Paulina,* who was Dostoyevski's mistress, and a short story that she wrote about her relationship with him. All in the same book. He was like 50 or so, and she was one of his students, around 23.

"After the affair had gone down, he exorcised Paulina out of his system by putting her as the main female character in *The Gambler.* And, as you know, he had to write the book in four weeks to pay off debts. At the end of four weeks, he married his secretary, and that's when he finally got Paulina out of his system.

"There are scenes in *The Gambler* that are quite extraordinary about the relationship, the humiliation and love and battles between the two. So, over the years, I was trying to work out something with that. I found that elements of their relationship found their way into my movies. In *Raging Bull*. A little bit in *Taxi*, which was Schrader's thing. And in *New York, New York*, a lot of it! The difficulty in being with each other, the difficulty of loving."

He strokes his Mephistophelian beard and searches the air in front of him. "How should I put it? The amount of pain in a relationship, and how the pain works for and against the people. How they *need* the pain. How long can you go with that pain in a relationship, from one relationship to the next, to the next? Just building up pain. Not only in yourself, but giving it to the other person, without everybody just caving in. Or committing suicide. There are many forms of suicide; you can die spiritually and live another 50 years and be a piece of wood.

"That's what fascinated me most, the passion of a relationship. It doesn't always have to be so destructive. I found all these ideas in the books and in Paulina's diaries. And her story is great, because you read *The Gambler* first, and you get his interpretation of it. Then you read the diaries, and you see a reality. 'He came to the door, it's Fyodor again, he's crying. I hate when he does that.'" He laughs uproariously at the thought. "She must have been beautiful.

"Instead of a writer, we made the man a famous painter in Soho who's extremely rich but still lives in the lofts, wears a $16,000 watch but has it covered in paint. The guy has constant relationships with these women, these assistants, and obviously these relationships are dead from the beginning. Because at a certain age—53, 54—and you're famous, doing a lot of stuff, and you keep getting involved with girls who are 23—they're kids, they're like daughters. You've got to let them go out, to let them grow. They'll hurt you. And you'll hurt them, too. They'll gain a lot, hopefully, in what he calls life lessons. 'You'll get life lessons from me,' he says. And they're emotionally murderous. They're like beatings.

"I think he comes to resolve that he is going to go on with this series of relationships, deal with the pain and the humiliation and the passion of it, and resolve that he will be alone with his work. He's not the person they should be with." Again, a painful laugh. "Who knows if he should be with anybody?"

Scorsese draws himself up and wonders. "How much does the pain fuel the work? At the beginning of the picture, he's got a show opening in a few weeks, and he can't paint. The minute she tells him she's not in love with him, he starts to paint.

"But I must emphasize," he cautions, "it's light comedy."

Comedy would seem to be a natural terrain for Scorsese; his normal speech shoots off like a rapid-fire Borscht Belt comedian's string of firecrackers. Whether or not he ever makes a true comedy, he at least feels a profound need to make a commercial picture and pay back Universal Pictures for backing him up on *Last Temptation*. Scorsese's problem is that while he grapples with the truth in a movie, he usually clashes with the audience's expectations. The filmmaker doesn't often serve up drama's most attractive device: wish fulfillment.

It is significant to him, for instance, that his dark, schizo *New York, New York* opened a mere three weeks before *Star Wars*, which, he says, "brought about a whole new period of filmmaking."

But an even more important movie opened the year before, in 1976. And that was *Rocky*. Its triumphant ending seemed to galvanize the Hollywood bosses. At a stroke, much of the brave, adventurous moviemaking of the previous decade was suddenly brought to a halt.

"Gone," Scorsese agrees. "Wiped out. Oddly enough, I like the ending of *Rocky*, myself. I don't like the picture that much, but I like the ending. I felt good. A lot of the pictures I love and adore through history are pictures that make me feel good.

"But to make a picture like that," he says, shaking his head, "I could never do it. Not that I make pictures to make people feel bad. Go see *Last Temptation*! He transcends; he goes into heaven. What more could you want from life than salvation? For all of us! You'll feel great!

"But this is what scares me. You have films with happy endings, which show the triumph of the human spirit, in films like *Rocky*. And then you have pictures that are a little more realistic and deal with certain emotions and psychological character studies, and they don't necessarily have that uplifting effect. In the '50s through the '70s, they seemed to exist together. Now, it seems that some films don't even have a right to exist.

"With the advent of *Rocky* and *Star Wars* and the Spielberg pictures, on the best side they're morally uplifting; you leave the theater the way you did at the end of *Casablanca*. And on the worst side, they're sentimental. Lies. That's the problem. And where I fit in there, I don't know.

"We've got some pet projects we want to make here in the future, but in between I want to make some good commercial pictures. *The Color of Money* was a good commercial exercise for me. I learned a great deal about structure and style. Learned what may not have worked.

"It's very hard for me to do the uplifting, transcendental sentimentalism of most films, because it's just not true." He draws himself up with a mocking self-righteousness. "And it's not because I'm this great prophet of truth—it's just like embarrassing to do it on the set. How would you stage the scene? What do you tell the actors, you know?

"There's no doubt we've got the problem that movies are considered mainly to be escapism. You want to have fun. I even shirked, let's say, from seeing every Bergman picture after a while. It was like doing homework.

"I prefer the escapism of fantasy, rather than the escapism of incredible sentimentality. What I'm afraid of is pandering to tastes that are superficial. There's no depth anymore. What appears to be depth is often a facile character study."

His face empties. "But they're making a product, and a product's gotta sell. And what sells is fantasy and sentimentality. You've gotta make money. And you make money [by] giving the audience what the hell they want!"

Combating this, however, is his readiness to infuriate, to go against audience expectations. A guy who wants to show the human side of Christ and the spiritual side of gangsters has to be ready for anything.

His dilemma may be that he is, through and through, a very emotional man. Whatever emotion he deals with, he will be hot on the subject. Around him, however, has grown up a generation that is cool, informed and wised-up to everything under the sun. And perhaps there are people—even among those in charge—who would rather not deal with the heavy, human, emotional soup in any way but a cool, detached way.

Scorsese hears the theory and nods matter-of-factly. "Because they don't want to be sucked in and taken advantage of," he says, with no great feeling. He looks down at his hands. They are rather large and striking hands for so small a man. "I don't blame them." Then his eyes come up, emphatic, definite and level. "But you've got to deal with the emotions some time or another."

Martin Scorsese's Cinema of Obsessions

AMY TAUBIN/1990

MARTIN SCORSESE IS A small, fragile man in a pressed, custom-tailored suit and immaculately polished soft Italian shoes. Now that he's shaved off his beard, his eyebrows seem even more imposing. They're the first thing you notice about his face, before you catch the flight-or-fight expression in his eyes.

At 48, Scorsese is an anomaly among contemporary film directors. For 20 years, he has managed to make utterly personal, deeply autobiographical movies that are bankrolled by the film industry. He's both an art-film director—the American equivalent of a Buñuel or Truffaut—and a "player" in Hollywood. Because his films deal with urban culture in knowing detail, and because their vocabulary is based in Hollywood, their effect on American audiences is something no "foreign" film can achieve. Scorsese does not make *homages* to American cinema. Rather, he shapes its syntax to his own experience.

His latest film, *GoodFellas,* is also his largest, budgeted at about $25 million. Whether or not it's a commercial success, there's a sense within the industry that Scorsese has been elevated to the ranks of the untouchables. The failure of any single film would no longer prevent him from getting others off the ground. Scorsese doesn't agree. He's as anxious as ever. "I just keep hoping," he says with a nervously flashed smile, "I get to make the pictures I want to make."

From *Village Voice,* 18 September 1990. Reprinted by permission.

In his tiny apartment with a wide-screen view of Central Park, Scorsese keeps an Eames chair right up against the floor-to-ceiling windows. This is one of the places where he takes phone calls and watches old movies: 900 feet above the street. Scorsese is a man who knows the edge. His elegant image is self-conscious, if not self-mocking (which is not to say he doesn't get a kick out of it). He's incapable of hiding the extreme shyness that might motivate his will to power. In a dark (most likely Armani) suit and nattily, knotted silk tie, he looks like a proud child actor playing the part of a Sicilian grandee.

As seemingly dissimilar as Scorsese is from Henry Hill, the protagonist of *GoodFellas,* the director points to one parallel between them. "Henry says that as far back as he can remember he wanted to be a gangster. From the moment I enrolled in NYU film school, I knew I wanted to be a director. Within a year I was planning my first feature." There is another similarity; like Henry, who first appears in the film as a child, Scorsese has always been intensely aware of the privilege and violence of "wiseguys." At a press conference for the film, the director is asked how he can look at these mobsters with such a nonjudgmental eye. "It's what I thought about these people when I was eight," Scorsese replies. But unlike Henry, he was too sickly as a child to be one of them.

In Little Italy, where he spent much of his childhood, Scorsese led a sheltered life. Asthmatic from the age of three (he carries an atomizer and uses it frequently), he was barred from the obvious routes to becoming a somebody on Elizabeth Street, exempted from the male rites fetishized in his films. "On my block, people took games seriously," Scorsese recently recalled. "They had bets going on them. If a kid dropped the ball, they could get very mad. I wasn't good at sports; they became anathema to me." He spent a lot of time in church and going to the movies with his father. "Having asthma, I was often taken to movies because they didn't know what else to do with me."

One of the movies Scorsese remembers "being hypnotized by" as a boy was Michael Powell's *The Red Shoes.* He says he was drawn to the hysteria and elegance of the picture as well as its characters: to the impresario, with his "cruelty, beauty, and self-hatred"; to the choreographer "who spoke his lines the way he danced"; and to the ballerina (Moira Shearer) who, like Christ in Scorsese's *Last Temptation of Christ,* is torn between her special calling and her desire for a sexual and familial life. At the climax of *The Red Shoes,* the ballerina, desperately attempting a reunion with her lover, hurls herself down a flight of stairs above the Cote d'Azur railroad station, loses her balance on the parapet, and falls to her death on the tracks below. Imbedded in Scorsese's memory bank—along with Jennifer Jones's bleeding hands at the end of *Duel in the Sun*—is the close-up of Shearer's broken feet, white tights stained as red as her shoes. For what it's worth: The director who does business from a chair placed at a dizzying height is phobic about flying.

Ambivalence is central to his style. Scorsese's Italian-American trilogy— *Mean Streets, Raging Bull,* and now *GoodFellas*—mixes anthropology with psychodrama, revulsion with empathy, from the perspective of an insider who was also an outsider. *Mean Streets* is the most overtly autobiographical film. ("It was about my friends and myself and about trying to break away.") *Raging Bull* is the story of a man who gains fame and fortune by brutalizing others legally. *GoodFellas* is about the guys who take the other route, becoming gangsters so they won't have to stand in line to buy bread. At once a depiction and a critique of upward mobility, the films have elevated their director's status, even on the street. Nicholas Pileggi, who co-wrote the script for *GoodFellas,* based on his bestseller, *Wise Guy,* says that *Mean Streets* is the favorite film of the gangsters he interviewed.

On Sullivan Street, where I do my laundry, the guys in the candy store watch *The Godfather* on videotape, on a daily basis. *Mean Streets* isn't part of their repertoire. When I mention Sullivan Street to Scorsese, he snorts: "That's compromised. It's the Village! People reciting poetry in coffee shops." Further east, where he grew up, (and where he says "the last bastion is Mulberry Street"), the guys who live like Scorsese characters might fixate on seeing their daily rituals set to golden oldies and depicted in such florid detail. They might disavow the mocking critique of male violence, the comedy of male excess and female domesticity. Outside the subculture, it's possible to miss both the unsparing accuracy and the anguish, to see these films as urban exotica—a celebration of blood and pasta. In any event, what makes Scorsese attractive to the industry, besides the undeniable skill and economy of his filmmaking, is that the critique doesn't obliterate the blood. "Violence is a form of expression," he says curtly. "It's how people live."

As Scorsese tells it, Warner Bros. liked *GoodFellas* so much that they considered giving it a mass release. "Deep down, I knew it wasn't that kind of picture," he says. But Warner decided to test their hunch at a sneak preview in plush Sherman Oaks. "People got so angry that they stormed out of the theater. They thought it was an outrage that I had made these people so attractive." Indeed, what attracted him to Pileggi's book was its matter-of-fact, even affectionate attitude toward outrageous behavior. He enjoys the wiseguys for their energy and single-mindedness, however murderous, while debunking their mystique. "I liked the everyday banality of it. Daily life in the Mafia on the lower echelons as opposed to the bosses of crime families. The real worker bees. Coming from an area where that was part of the life-style, I also found it very funny. They are human beings, human beings have a sense of humor, and the humor is more extreme among people living an extreme life." (Or, as Freud put it: criminals and humorists "compel our interest by the narcissistic consistency with which they manage to keep away from the ego anything that would diminish it.")

What blew them away in Sherman Oaks was not just the sight of Joe Pesci hacking away at a half-dead, flayed open body; it was Tony Bennett on the soundtrack, launching into "Rags to Riches" as the last blow is struck. *GoodFellas* mixes comedy and melodrama into a rock 'n' roll Grand Guignol, further complicating its point of view. "I never intended to make a straight genre film," Scorsese says. "My films never go from A to B to C." Rather than fitting emotions into a conventional dramatic structure, Scorsese allows emotional change to shape the picture. *GoodFellas* has an astonishingly peculiar shape. It starts with an hour-long roller coaster ride that winds up exactly where it began. Then there's a relentless downhill slide climaxing with frantic depiction of a coke-soaked day in which everything Henry has to keep track of—stirring the sauce, delivering the guns, cutting the coke, avoiding the helicopter—has equally absurd value. Finally there's a grim denouement of betrayal and revenge: the music fades but the killing continues. As the film relinquishes its breathless pace, the viewer begins to feel the nausea and disgust that sheer kinetic involvement had masked.

Scorsese's ebullient editing—that sense of being on a roll, of a process taking you over, so that you keep being surprised by what you're seeing— is one with the experience of his characters. "I wanted *GoodFellas* to move as fast as a trailer or the opening of *Jules and Jim* and to go on like that for two hours." Speed dominates other aspects of his filmmaking as well. "On film," he says, "it looks better if the actors do it twice as fast."

But the power of Scorsese's films is not merely kinetic; it's visceral. His earliest memories of movies are seeped in blood and he remains fascinated by images of what violence does to the body. In *GoodFellas*, the most brutal murders are shown not once, but twice, so that we see the act not only within the flow of the narrative but as a fetishistic spectacle that stops the narrative cold. It isn't a laughing matter the second time around. In the end, violence is the means by which he shows us that the body bleeds—to death. And male identity cuts two ways: It's not only the capacity to inflict pain, but also to withstand suffering. "I enjoyed making those little images of the bleeding heart," he once said about *The Last Temptation*. "I enjoyed probing the wounds."

His anxieties notwithstanding, Scorsese clearly relishes being in business with the studios. Another layer is imposed on the kid and the artist—the serious but streetwise businessman. It's a persona he's still trying on. "I want to be a player," Scorsese says. "To be a player in Hollywood, you have to take a lot of bruising."

An enthusiast with an immense store of knowledge, talking film with dazzling fluency, he can't help but impress the dealmakers. Although he has never produced a megahit, Scorsese has, during the past five years, cut deals with most of the major studios. "What they all want, of course, is another *Taxi Driver*." His subsequent films were hardly that. Even a critical success like *Raging Bull* was not a big money-maker, while *New York, New York,* and *The King of Comedy* were regarded as "difficult." Given the uneven progress of his career in the early '80s, it's remarkable how secure Scorsese's position now appears. It's not all mystique: the box-office success of *The Color of Money* (his least personal film) probably made *GoodFellas* possible.

There's no doubt, however, that his fortunes improved after he became a client of Michael Ovitz, the agent frequently labeled the most powerful man in Hollywood. Scorsese had been trying unsuccessfully for 10 years to make *The Last Temptation of Christ*; within three months of signing with Ovitz in 1987, he was in production.

Although most of Scorsese's films have been studio-financed, they don't go through the usual in-house process of development and packaging. How exactly does an auteur from Little Italy convince a bunch of corporate executives whose primary responsibility is to their shareholders to hand over $25 million for a film about gangsters that hardly conforms to the rules of the genre?

"You don't lie to them," he says directly. "They've got to respect your work so they know you're not just coming in there to make fools of them or take their money. And they've also got to like the script, although they never fully understand what it is until they see it. So they give attention to other things like the casting—they had several suggestions which fortunately didn't pan out because I knew from the beginning that I wanted Ray Liotta to play Henry Hill. Mike Ovitz was helpful in protecting the work and working it out so that the studio and I each got what we wanted. We're not talking about a blockbuster. We're talking about something which, if handled properly, can make some money."

Scorsese hadn't thought there was a part for Robert De Niro in *GoodFellas*. "In the pictures where Bob and I work together, he's in almost every scene." But when he was having difficulty casting the icy hijacker/killer Jimmy Conway, De Niro suggested himself for the part. Neither man will discuss their working relationship. When Scorsese directs DeNiro, absolutely no outsiders are allowed on the set. "When I work with actors like Bob," he says, "we improvise. We work it out in advance, rewrite the scene, and then we shoot it." Occasionally, the improvisation continues, even while the camera rolls. (When Scorsese played his famous cameo in *Taxi Driver*—"Do you know what a 44-magnum can do to a woman's pussy?"—the tables were turned and De Niro directed him. "If it wasn't for Bob, I don't know that I could have done it.") In any event, De Niro's presence in *GoodFellas* encouraged the studio to cough up a few million more dollars.

Scorsese has a gift for getting all kinds of people on his side. It's not merely that he's funny, smart, and surprisingly open. He's at once the surgeon and the patient, a man with awesome skill and authority who evokes in others the desire to protect. His jackhammer speech and gestures erupt out of agonizing self-consciousness. His relief when his passionate grasp of an idea or process overcomes anxiety is palpable. Scorsese's crew of regulars— writers, producers, assistants, technicians, and even actors, some of whom have worked with him since his first film—are constantly worrying about Marty. Is he tired? Is he depressed? Is he doing too much? Not that these aren't reasonable fears. (Scorsese's work load at any given moment would tax a person 20 years younger who hadn't been asthmatic all his life.) But the director's fragility is also functional: it makes it hard for those around him to separate their involvement in the work from their concern about his well-being.

The artist who wants to be a player has one film in pre-production, a remake of the 1962 thriller *Cape Fear,* with De Niro in the Robert Mitchum sadistic-killer role. Scorsese hopes to follow up with an adaptation of Edith Wharton's *The Age of Innocence*. He's also planning a film set in 4th century Byzantium and several other projects with Pileggi. He doesn't intend the Italian-American films to stop at a trilogy. "No doubt I'll always be interested in underworld stories. But no cutesy films about mama's pasta and people getting married. I can't stand that. It's completely fake."

His enhanced status has opened up other options, like executive producing. *The Grifters,* adapted from the Jim Thompson novel and directed by Stephen Frears, will be released this fall. He's also involved in a script by Richard Price to be directed by John McNaughton of *Henry... Serial Killer* fame. "I can't do the day-by-day production stuff. I don't know anything about money. And now that I've found out it's not going to be that artistically satisfying, I have to be careful how much time I apportion to it."

There's another perk that comes with success as an auteur: Scorsese has become a crusader for film preservation, lobbying the studios, and running a foundation out of his office that locates original materials to be archived. Like the goodfellas who become gangsters so they don't have to stand in line to buy bread, Scorsese can get his hands on any film he has a passion for. He watches movies constantly, though he finds it impossible to look at his own (except for *Last Temptation*). "That's what I do," he says. "Sit here, watch movies and talk on the phone. That's it."

He still gives vent to his anxieties about every project. About *Cape Fear.* He shudders to think where he's going to be in November. He'll need a pith helmet with netting because mosquitos love him. And he doesn't know how to make a straight genre picture. He's never done it. "There are certain rules—how you move the camera." And he wants to have it both ways—to make an A-to-B-to-C film, but a bit twisted, like his other pictures. "At the end of *Cape Fear,* there's a scene with a boat breaking up. It's just like a real movie," he says with mock incredulity. "Like the movies we watch up here. I don't make real movies like that."

The notable objects in Scorsese's midtown office are a bookcase filled with reference sources essential to a film archivist, and a large desk covered with papers. The walls are cluttered with movie stills, photos, framed strips of 35mm, and posters: *East of Eden, The Life and Death of Colonel Blimp.* . . . Ask him about one or another of his mementos and it's more than likely he'll reply with only slightly studied casualness that it's a gift from this or that studio production head. Tribute to the Sicilian grandee.

Directly behind his desk is a print reproduction of a Titian altar piece — Jesus on the cross. If Scorsese is in his chair and you are seated directly opposite him, his head appears superimposed on the crucifixion. It's probably an accident, but the irony of the composition is worthy of his films. Like the man said: players have to take a lot of bruising.

Martin Scorsese Interviewed

GAVIN SMITH/1990

GAVIN SMITH: *What was it that drew you to the* GoodFellas *material?*
MARTIN SCORSESE: I read a review of the book; basically it said, "This
is really the way it must be." So I got the book in galleys and started really
enjoying it because of the free-flowing style, the way Henry Hill spoke,
and the wonderful arrogance of it. And I said, oh, it would make a fascinating film if you just make it what it is—literally as close to the truth as
a fiction film, a dramatization, could get. No sense to try to whitewash,
[to elicit] great sympathy for the characters in a phony way. If you happen
to feel something for the character Pesci plays, after all he does in the film,
and if you feel something for him when he's eliminated, then that's interesting to me. That's basically it. There was no sense making this film [any
other way].

GS: *You say dramatization and fiction. What kind of a film do you see this as
being?*
MS: I was hoping it was a documentary. [*Laughs*]. Really, no kidding. Like
a *staged* documentary, *the spirit* of a documentary. As if you had a 16mm
camera with these guys for 20, 25 years; what you'd pick up. I can't say it's
"like" any other film, but in my mind it [has] the freedom of a documentary, where you can mention 25 people's names at one point and 23 of them
the audience will not have heard of before and won't hear of again, but it
doesn't matter. It's the familiarity of the way people speak. Even at the end

From *Film Comment,* September/October 1990. Reprinted by permission.

when Ray Liotta says over the freezeframe on his face, "Jimmy never asked me to go and whack somebody before. But now he's asking me to go down and do a hit with Anthony in Florida." Who's Anthony?

It's a mosaic, a tapestry, where faces keep coming in and out. Johnny Dio, played by Frank Pellegrino, you only see in the Fifties, and then in the Sixties you don't see him, but he shows up in the jail sequence. He may have done something else for five or six years and come back. It's the way they live.

G S : *How have your feelings about this world changed since* Mean Streets?
M S : Well, *Mean Streets* is much closer to home in terms of a real story, somewhat fictionalized, about events that occurred to me and some of my old friends. [*GoodFellas*] has really nothing to do with people I knew then. It doesn't take place in Manhattan, it's only in the boroughs, so it's a very different world—although it's all interrelated. But the *spirit* of it, again, the *attitudes*. The morality—you know, there's none, there's none. Completely amoral. It's just wonderful.

If you're a young person, 8 or 9, and these people treat you a certain way because you're living around them, and then as you get to be a teenager and you get a little older, you begin to realize what they did and what they still do—you still have those first feelings for them as people, you know. So, it kind of raises a moral question and a kind of moral friction in me. That was what I wanted to get on the screen.

G S : *How did you feel about* Married to the Mob, *which satirized the Mafia lifestyle?*
M S : I like Jonathan Demme's movies. In fact, I have the same production designer, Kristi Zea. But, well, it's a satire—it's just too many plastic seatcovers. And yet, if you go to my mother's apartment, you'll see not only the plastic seatcovers on the couch but on the coffee table as well. So where's the line of the truth? I don't know.

In the spirit of Demme's work I enjoyed it. But as far as an Italian-American thing, it's really like a cartoon. When he starts with "Mambo Italiano," Rosemary Clooney, I'm already cringing because I'm Italian-American, and certain songs we'd like to forget! So I told Jonathan he had some nerve using that, I said only Italians could use "Mambo Italiano" and get away with it. There might be some knocks at his door [*Laughs*].

G S : *Do* GoodFellas *and* Mean Streets *serve as an antidote to* The God-father's *mythic version of the Mafia?*

M S : Yes, yeah, absolutely. *Mean Streets,* of course, was something I was just burning to do for a number of years. [By the time I did it,] *The Godfather* had already come out. But I said, it doesn't matter, because this one is really, to use the word loosely, anthropology — that idea of how people live, what they ate, how they dressed. *Mean Streets* has that quality — a quote "real" unquote side of it.

GoodFellas more so. Especially in terms of attitude. Don't give a damn about anything, especially when they're having a good time and making a lot of money. They don't care about their wives, their kids, anything.

G S : The Godfather *is such an overpowering film that it shapes everybody's perception of the Mafia — including people in the Mafia.*

M S : Oh, sure. I prefer *Godfather II* to *Godfather I.* I've always said it's like epic poetry, like *Morte d'Arthur.* My stuff is like some guy on the street-corner talking.

G S : *In* GoodFellas *we see a great deal of behavior, but you withhold psychological insight.*

M S : Basically I was interested in what they *do.* And, you know, they don't think about it a lot. They don't sit around and ponder about [*laughs*] "Gee, what are we doing here?" The answer is to eat a lot and make a lot of money and do the least amount of work as possible for it. I was trying to make it as practical and primitive as possible. Just straight ahead. Want. Take. Simple. I'm more concerned with showing a lifestyle and using Henry Hill [Ray Liotta] as basically a guide through it.

G S : *You said you see this as a tragic story.*

M S : I do, but you have a lot of the guys, like [real-life U.S. attorney] Ed McDonald in the film or Ed Hayes [a real defense attorney], who plays one of the defense attorneys, they'll say, "These guys are animals and that's life," and maybe not care about them. Henry took Paulie [Paul Sorvino] as sort of a second father; he just idolized these guys and wanted to be a part of it. And that's what makes the turnaround at the end so interesting and so tragic, for me.

G S : *In* Scorsese on Scorsese *[published by Faber and Faber] you said that, growing up, you felt being a rat was the worst thing you could be. How do you feel about Henry and what he did?*

M S : That's a hard one. Maybe on one level, the tragedy is in the shots of Henry on the stand: "Will you point him out to me, please?" And you see him look kind of sheepish, and he points to Bob De Niro playing Jimmy Conway. And the camera moves in on Conway. Maybe that's the tragedy—what he had to do to survive, to enable his family to survive.

G S : *This is "Henry Hill" as opposed to Henry Hill—purely an imaginative version of this guy?*

M S : Yes. Based on what he said in the book and based on what [co-writer] Nick [Pileggi] told me. I never spoke to Henry Hill. Towards the end of the film I spoke to him on the phone once. He thanked me about something. It was just less than 30 seconds on the phone.

G S : *You use him as a mirror of American society.*

M S : Yeah, the lifestyle reflects the times. In the early Sixties, the camera comes up on Henry and he's waiting outside the diner and he's got this silk suit on and he hears "Stardust." And he's young and he's looking like all the hope in the world ready for him and he's going to conquer the world. And then you just take it through America—the end of the Sixties, the Seventies, and finally into the end of the Seventies with the disillusionment and the state of the country that we're in now. I think his journey reflects that.

That wasn't planned. But there's something about the moment when his wife says, "Hide that cross," and the next thing you know, he's getting married in a Jewish ceremony, and wearing a Star of David *and* a cross—it doesn't make any difference. Although I didn't want to make it heavy in the picture, the idea is that if you live for a certain kind of value, at a certain point in life you're going to come smack up against a brick wall. Not only Henry living as a gangster: in my feeling, I guess it's the old materialism versus a spiritual life.

G S : GoodFellas *is like a history of postwar American consumer culture, the evolution of cultural style. The naïveté and romanticism of the Fifties.... There's*

*a kind of innocent mischief and charm to the worldliness. But then at a certain
point it becomes corrupt.*

M S : It corrupts and degenerates. Even to the point [that] some of the
music degenerates in itself. You have "Unchained Melody" being sung in a
decadent way, like the ultimate doo-wop—but not black, it's Italian doo-
wop. It's on the soundtrack after Stacks gets killed and Henry comes
running into the bar. Bob tells him, "Come on, let's drink up, it's a celebration," and Tommy says, "Don't worry about anything. Going to make
me." And over that you hear this incredible doo-wop going on, and it's sort
of like even the music becomes decadent in a way from the pure Drifters,
Clyde McPhatter singing "Bells of St. Mary's," to Vito and the Salutations.

And I *like* the Vito and the Salutations version of "Unchained Melody."
Alex North wrote it along with somebody else—it was from this movie
made in the early Fifties called *Unchained.* And it's unrecognizable. It's so
crazy and I enjoy it. I guess I admire the purity of the early times and. . . .
Not that I admire it, but I'm a part of the decadence of what happened in
the Seventies and the Eighties.

G S : *Pop music is usually used in films, at least on one level, to cue the audience to what era it is.*

M S : Oh, no, no, forget that, no.

In *Mean Streets* there's a lot of stuff that comes from the Forties. The
thing is, believe me, a lot of these places you had jukeboxes and, when
The Beatles came in, you [still] had Benny Goodman, some old Italian
stuff, Jerry Vale, Tony Bennett, doo-wop, early rock 'n' roll, black and Italian. . . . There's a guy who comes around and puts the latest hits in. [But]
when you hang out in a place, when you are part of a group, new records
come in but [people] request older ones. And they stay. If one of the guys
leaves or somebody gets killed, some of his favorite music [nobody else]
wants to listen to, they throw it away. But basically there are certain records
that guys like and it's there. Anything goes, anything goes.

G S : *Why Sid Vicious doing "My Way" at the end?*

M S : Oh, it's pretty obvious, it may be even too obvious.

It's period, but also it's Paul Anka and of course Sinatra—although there's
no Sinatra in the film. But "My Way" is an anthem. I like Sid Vicious' version because it twists it, and his whole life and death was a kind of slap in

the face of the whole system, the whole point of existence in a way. And that's what fascinating to me—because eventually, yeah, they all did it their way. [*Laughs*] Because we did it our way, you know.

G S : GoodFellas' *vision of rock 'n' roll style colliding with a fetishized gangster attitude made me think of Nic Roeg's* Performance, *which was about the dark side of the Sixties too.*
M S : Oh I like *Performance,* yeah. I never quite understood it, because I didn't understand any of the drug culture at that time. But I liked the picture. I love the music and I love Jagger in it and James Fox—terrific. That's one of the reasons I used the Ry Cooder [song] "Memo to Turner"—the part where Jimmy says, "Now, stop taking those fucking drugs, they're making your mind into mush." He slams the door. He puts the guns in the trunk and all of a sudden you hear the beginning of this incredible slide guitar coming in. It's Ry Cooder. And I couldn't use the rest of it because the scene goes too quick.

The Seventies drug thing was important because I wanted to get the impression of that craziness. Especially that last day, he starts at six in the morning. The first thing he does is gets the guns, takes a hit of coke, gets in the car. I mean, you're already wired, you're wired for the day. And his day is like crazy. Everything is at the same importance. The sauce is just as important as the guns, is as important as Jimmy, the drugs, the helicopter.

The idea was to stylistically try to give the impression—people watching the film who have taken drugs will recognize it—of the anxiety and the thought processes. And the way the mind races when you're taking drugs, really doing it as a lifestyle.

G S : *The film's first section presents a kind of idealized underworld with its own warmth and honor-among-thieves code. This gradually falls away, reflected in the characters of Tommy and Jimmy.*
M S : True, true. But Jimmy Conway was not Mafia. The idea was, you signed on for that life, you may have to exit that life in an unnatural way, and they knew that. I'm not saying, oh, those were the good old days. In a funny way [*laughs*]—not that funny—but in a way there's a breakdown of discipline, of whatever moral code those guys had in the Fifties and Sixties. I think now with drugs being the big money and gangsters killing people in the government in Colombia, the Mafia is nothing. They'll always be around,

there'll always be the organized-crime idea. But in terms of the old, almost romantic image of it typified by the *Godfather* films, that's gone.

G S : *The Seventies sequence is about losing control, about disintegration.*
M S : Totally. Henry disintegrates with drugs. With Jimmy Conway, the disintegration is on a more lethal level, the elimination of [everybody else]. Earlier there's so many shots of people playing cards and at christenings and weddings, all at the same table. If you look at the wedding, the camera goes around the table and all the people at that table are killed by Jimmy later on.

G S : *Unlike all your other protagonists, Henry seems secure in his identity. What is his journey, from your point of view?*
M S : You know, I don't know. I don't mean to be silly; I guess I should have an answer for that. Maybe in the way he feels through his voiceover in the beginning of the film about being respected. I think it's really more about Henry not having to wait in line to get bread for his mother. It's that simple. And to be a confidante of people so powerful, who, to a child's mind, didn't have to worry about parking by a hydrant. It's the American Dream.

G S : *Once he has this status lifestyle, what's at stake for him?*
M S : Things happen so fast, so quick and heavy in their lifestyle, they don't think of that. Joe Pesci pointed out that you have literally a life expectancy—the idea of a cycle that it takes for a guy to be in the prime of being of wiseguy—the prime period is like maybe eight or nine years, at the end of which, just by the law of averages, you're either going to get killed or most likely go to jail. And then you begin the long thing with going back and forth from jail to home, jail to home. It begins to wear you down until only the strongest survive.

I think Henry realizes the horror he's brought upon himself, how they're all living, and it's way too late. The only thing to do is get out of it. And how can you get out?

G S : *He remains an enigma—untainted by what he's done and at the end achieving a kind of grace as just a regular guy like everybody else. What were you trying to do with the ending?*

M S : It's just very simply that's the way the book ended and I liked what he said, I liked his attitude: "Gee, there's no more fun." [*Laughs*] Now, you can take that any way you want. I think the audience should get angry with him. I would hope they would be. And maybe angry with the system that allows it — this is so complex. Everything is worked out together with these guys and with the law and with the Justice Department. It'll be phony if he felt badly about what he did. The irony of it at the end I kind of think is very funny.

G S : *Why do you have him addressing the camera at the end?*
M S : Couldn't think of any other thing to do, really. Just, you know, got to end the picture. Seriously.

G S : *How did you conceptualize the film stylistically? Did you break the film down into sequences?*
M S : Yeah, as much as possible. Everything was pretty much storyboarded, if not on paper, in notes. These days I don't actually draw each picture. But I usually put notes on the sides of the script, how the camera should move. I wanted lots of movement and I wanted it to be throughout the whole picture, and I wanted the style to kind of break down by the end, so that by his last day as a wiseguy, it's as if the whole picture would be out of control, give the impression he's just going to spin off the edge and fly out. And then stop for the last reel and a half.

The idea was to get as much movement as possible — even more than usual. And a very speeded, frenetic quality to most of it in terms of getting as much information to the audience — overwhelming them, I had hoped — with images and information. There's a lot of stuff in the frames. Because it's so rich. The lifestyle is so rich — I have a love-hate thing with that lifestyle.

G S : *I don't think I've ever seen freezeframes used in such a dramatic way — freezing a moment and bringing the narrative to a halt.*
M S : That comes from documentaries. Images would stop; a point was being made in his life. Everybody has to take a beating sometime, BANG: freeze and then go back with the whipping. What are you dealing with there? Are you dealing with the father abusing Henry — you know, the usual story of, My father beat me, that's why I'm bad. Not necessarily.

You're just saying, "Listen, I take a beating, that's all, fine." The next thing, the explosion and the freezeframe, Henry frozen against it—it's hellish, a person in flames, in hell. And he says, "They did it out of respect." It's very important where the freezeframes are in that opening sequence. Certain things are embedded in the skull when you're a kid.

The freezeframes are basically all Truffaut. [The style] comes from the first two or three minutes of *Jules and Jim*. The Truffaut and Godard techniques from the early Sixties that have stayed in my mind—what I loved about them was that narrative was not that important: "Listen, this is what we're going to do right now and I'll be right back. Oh, that guy, by the way, he got killed. We'll see you later."

Ernie Kovacs was that way in the Fifties in TV. I learned a lot from watching him destroy beautifully the form of what you were used to thinking was the television comedy show. He would stop and talk to the camera and do strange things; it was totally surreal. Maybe if I were of a different generation I would say Keaton. But I didn't grow up with Keaton, I grew up with early TV.

G S :   *Or if you're my generation it would be* Pee Wee's Playhouse.
M S :   Yeah, again, breaking up a narrative—just opens up a refrigerator, there's a whole show inside, and closes the door. That's great. I love Pee Wee Herman. I tape the show. We had them sent to Morocco when we were doing *Last Temptation*; on Sundays we'd watch it on PAL system. Yeah. [*Laughs*]

G S :   GoodFellas *uses time deletions during many scenes: you see someone standing by the door, then they're suddenly in the chair, then—*
M S :   It's the way things go. They've got to move fast. I was interested in breaking up all the traditional ways of shooting the picture. A guy comes in, sits down, exposition is given. So the hell with the exposition—do it on the voiceover, if need be at all. And then just jump the scene together. Not by chance. The shots are designed so that I know where the cut's going to be. The action is pulled out of the middle of the scene, but I know where I'm going to cut it so that it makes an interesting cut. And I always loved those jump cuts in the early French films, in Bertolucci's *Before the Revolution*. Compressing time. I get very bored shooting scenes that are traditional scenes.

In this film, actually the style gave me the sense of going on a ride, some sort of crazed amusement-park ride, going through the Underworld, in a way. Take a look at this, and you pan over real fast and, you know, it kind of lends itself to the impression of it not being perfect—which is really what I wanted.

That scene near the end, Ed McDonald talking to [the Hills]—I like that. [It's as if the movie] kind of stops, it gets cold and they're in this terrifying office. He's wearing a terrifying tie—it's the law and you're stuck. And they're on the couch and he's in a chair and that's the end of the road. That's scary.

G S : *When you're shooting and editing, how do you determine how much the audience can take in terms of information, shot length, number of cuts, etc.? Over the past decade our nervous systems have developed a much greater tolerance of sensory overload.*
M S : I guess the main thing that's happened in the past ten years is that the scenes have to be quicker and shorter. Something like *The Last Emperor*, they accept in terms of an epic style. But this is sort of my version of MTV, this picture. But even that's old-fashioned.

G S : *Is there a line you won't cross in terms of editing speed, how fast to play scenes?*
M S : The last picture I made was "Life Lessons" in *New York Stories*. And that's pretty much the right level. *GoodFellas* lends itself to a very fast-paced treatment. But I think where I'm at is really more the *New York Stories* section. Not *Last Temptation*. *Last Temptation,* things were longer and slower there because, well, of a certain affection for the story and for the things that make up that story. And the sense of being almost stoned by the desert in a way, being there and making things go slower; a whole different, centuries-earlier way of living. *New York Stories* had, I think, maybe a balance between the two. The scenes went pretty crisp, pretty quickly. There were some montage sequences. But still I'd like to sustain [the moments].

In *GoodFellas,* that whole sequence I really developed with the actors, Joe Pesci's story and Ray responding to him, it's a very long sequence. We let everything play out. And I kept adding setups to let the whole moment play out. But if what the actors were doing was truthful or enjoyable enough, you can get away with it.

G S : *The "What's so funny about me?" scene in the restaurant between Liotta and Pesci was improvised?*

M S : Totally improv — yeah. It's based on something that happened to Joe. He got out of it the same way — by taking the chance and saying, "Oh, come on, knock it off." The gentleman who was threatening him was a friend, [but] a dangerous person. And Joe's in a bad state either way. If he doesn't try laughing about it, he's going to be killed; if he tries laughing about it and the guy doesn't think it's funny, he's going to be killed. Either way he's got nothing to lose. You see, things like that, they could turn on a dime, those situations. And it's just really scary.

Joe said, "Could I please do that?" I said, "Absolutely, let's have some fun." And we improvised, wrote it down, and they memorized the lines. But it was really finally done in the cutting with two cameras. Very, very carefully composed. Who's in the frame behind them. To the point where we didn't have to compromise lighting and positions of the other actors, because it's even more important who's around them hearing this.

G S : *What about the continuation of the scene with the restaurant owner asking for the money?*

M S : Oh, that's all playing around, yeah. That kind of dialogue you can't really write. And the addition of breaking the bottle over Tony Darrow's head was thought of by Joe at lunchtime. I got mad at him. I said, "How could you — why now, at lunch? Now we've got to stop the shooting. We've got to go down and get fake bottles." He said, "Well, couldn't we maybe do it with a real bottle?" "No." "Well, maybe we could throw it at him." "No, no, that's not as good." "How about a lamp? Let's hit him with a lamp." So we tried hitting him with different things. It was actually one of the funniest days we ever had. Everybody came to visit that day. And I don't like visitors on the set, but that was a perfect time to have them visit because most of the laughter on the tracks that you hear is people from behind the camera, me and a lot of Warners executives who showed up.

The real improvs were done with Joe and Frank Severa, who played Carbone, who kept mumbling in Sicilian all the time. And they kept arguing with each other. Like the coffee pot: "That's a joke. Put it down. What, are you going to take the pot?" — he was walking out with the pot. It's more like telling him, even as an actor, "Are you out of your mind? Where are you going with the coffee? We don't do that." Another killing, Joe says,

"Come on, we have to go chop him up." And Frank starts to get out of the car. And Joe says, "Where are you going, you dizzy motherfucker? What's the matter with you? We're going to go chop him up here." Frank's impulse was to get out of the car. So Joe just grabbed him and said, "What are you doing?" They improvised.

G S : *Did you ever get feedback from the underworld after* Mean Streets?
M S : From my old friends. A lot of the people that the film is about are not Mafia.

Nick mentioned that the real-life Paulie Cicero never went to the movies, never went out, didn't have telephones, you know. So one night the guys wanted to see this one particular movie, and they just grabbed him and threw him in the car and took him to see the film. It was *Mean Streets*. They loved it. So that was like the highest compliment, because I really try to be accurate about attitude and about way of life.

What the Streets Mean

ANTHONY DECURTIS/1991

MARTIN SCORSESE'S APARTMENT SITS seventy-five
floors above midtown Manhattan and offers an imperial view
that encompasses Central Park and the Upper East Side, extend-
ing out toward the borough of Queens, where Scorsese was born
in 1942. The calming grays and blacks and whites of the living
room's decor combine with the apartment's Olympian height—
so high as to eliminate almost all street noise—to make New
York City seem a distant abstraction, a silent movie playing in
Martin Scorsese's picture window. *Mean Streets* it's not.

For *Mean Streets,* you would have to go to the roof and look
the other way, behind you, down toward Little Italy, the Italian
ghetto on the Lower East Side where Scorsese came of age in the
fifties and sixties. Scorsese returned to that neighborhood—or
at least to a virtually identical neighborhood in the East New
York section of Brooklyn—with *GoodFellas,* which is based on
Nicholas Pileggi's book *Wiseguy,* the story of the middle-level
Irish-Sicilian mobster Henry Hill and his twenty-five-year career
in the criminal underworld.

The movie reunited Scorsese with his homeboy, Robert De
Niro, for the first time since *The King of Comedy,* in 1982, and
assembles a veritable who's who of superb Italian-American film
stars, including Ray Liotta, Joe Pesci, Lorraine Bracco, and Paul

---

From *South Atlantic Quarterly,* Spring 1992. Reprinted by permission of *Rolling Stone.*

Sorvino. Scorsese himself wrote the screenplay with Pileggi. Grisly, funny, violent, and riddled with moral questions posed by matters of loyalty, betrayal, and personal honor, *GoodFellas* also returned Scorsese to the themes that pump at the heart of some of his most urgent films, most notably *Mean Streets* (1973), *Taxi Driver* (1975), and *Raging Bull* (1980).

Though the usually dapper Scorsese is casually dressed in jeans and a faded blue shirt, he is anything but relaxed for the interview. He didn't realize the interview would involve so much time—at least two hours. What about the other things he'd arranged to do? His two daughters, Catherine and Domenica, would soon be coming by the apartment (he had recently separated from his fourth wife, Barbara De Fina). He needs to make some phone calls, change some things around, work some things out. After we start to talk, he moves back and forth between a chair that serves as something of a command center—located, as it is, next to a phone and a movie projector and opposite a wall with a pull-down screen on it—and a place closer to me on the white couch.

Scorsese speaks in the style of a born-and-bred New Yorker. He formulates his thoughts out loud, as if they were terrifically important but continually in flux, in need of constant refinement. Asked a question, he starts talking immediately, stops abruptly, starts and stops again and again until he finds his groove. He gestures for punctuation and emphasis, fires off staccato bursts of insight when he's on a roll, laughs wildly at his own improbable characterizations and verbal excesses. At times, the sheer nervous energy of his intellect propels him out of his seat, and he speaks while standing at his full height—he's quite short—for a minute or two. He walks over to a cabinet several times for nasal and throat sprays to ease the effects of the asthma that has afflicted him since childhood. He alternately concentrates on me with a ferocious intensity and seems to forget I'm there at all.

A filmmaker in a kind of tumultuous internal exile, Scorsese sits edgily poised in splendid isolation over the city that remains one of his most fertile obsessions—and looks to the future with hope and apprehension.

ANTHONY DECURTIS: *I want to start with* GoodFellas. *Obviously you have returned to some familiar terrain. What brought you to that specific project?*
MARTIN SCORSESE: I read a review of *Wiseguy* back when I was directing *The Color of Money* in Chicago, and it said something about this character, Henry Hill, having access to many different levels of organized crime because he was somewhat of an outsider. He looked a little nicer. He was able to be a better front man and speak a little better. I thought that was interesting. You could move in and get a cross section of the layers of organized crime—from his point of view of course. Which could be true—maybe, who knows? It's what he says. You get into two different areas there. What he says the truth is—you have to take his word for it, which is . . . I don't say it's doubtful, but it's like . . .

AD: *It's a version.*
MS: The second element is really the most important one: his perception of the truth. Where, you know, if somebody gets shot in a room and there's five people who witnessed it, you'll probably have five different stories as to how it happened. You know what I'm saying? So you have to take that all into consideration. But that's what fascinated me about the book. So I got the book and I started reading it and I was fascinated by the narrative ability of it, the narrative approach.

AD: *Henry has a real voice.*
MS: He's got a wonderful voice and he has a wonderful way of expressing the life-style. He reminds me of a lot of the people that I grew up around. It had a great sense of humor, too. So I said, "This will make a wonderful film." I figured to do it as if it was one long trailer, where you just propel the action and you get an exhilaration, a rush of the life-style.

AD: *That acceleration at the end of the film is amazing, when Henry is driving around like a madman, blasted on cocaine, trying to deal for guns and drugs while the police helicopter is following him, and, through it all, he keeps calling home to make sure his brother is stirring the sauce properly for dinner that night.*
MS: Yeah. The sauce is as important as the helicopter. That's a whole comment about drugs, too. When I read about that last day in the book, I said I'd like to just take that and make it the climax of the film. Actually, the real climax is him and Jimmy in the diner. A very quiet moment.

AD: *When you talk about the world you grew up in, as it happens, it is virtu-*
ally the same world I grew up in. I went to Our Lady of Pompeii in Greenwich
Village.
MS: Great!

AD: *On Bleecker Street.*
MS: It was the West Side, though. You were on the West Side. That's a
funny thing, on the East Side, we didn't have the influx of other cultures,
that very important bohemian culture.

AD: *My family was Italian and working-class — I wasn't part of that. I grew up*
in a world as enclosed as the one that you describe. But there was always this
sense that there was something else. I mean, when I was a kid, the Village Voice
office was around the corner. So when it got to the point where like, as kids,
everybody was getting in trouble with the police, I had a very clear vision that
there was some way out.
MS: That there was another world. We didn't know that.

AD: *It's a very clear distinction. The bohemian world of the Village was like*
another world, even though you only lived a few blocks from the Village.
MS: I never went to the Village until I enrolled at NYU in 1960. I grew up
on the East Side. From 1950 to 1960, for ten years, I never ventured past
Houston Street, past Broadway and Houston. I think my father took me
on a bus when I was five years old or something. I remember Washington
Square. I was on a double-decker bus. And I remember a friend of mine,
I was about nine years old, his mother took us to the Village on a little tour
to see the little houses and flowers. It was like a wonderland, because they
had flowers. It was a very different culture.

I was used to, you know, wonderful stuff, too, on Elizabeth Street,
which was five grocery stores, three butcher shops all on one block. Two
barbershops. And it was barrels of olives — which was great. Growing up
down there was like being in a Sicilian village culture. It was great. But you
come from there so you know. It's complicated to explain to people who
didn't grow up in it.

AD: *It is. When I'm trying to tell people about it, I refer to your movies. I don't*
know any other representations of it.

M S : A good friend of mine I grew up with just sent me a letter. He just saw *GoodFellas* and he said he had just spent a sleepless night remembering what a great and incredible escape we both made from that area, from that whole life-style.

A D : *I first saw* Mean Streets *after I had left New York to go to graduate school in Indiana. I had never been west of New Jersey, and I saw* Mean Streets . . .
M S : In Indiana!

A D : *And it was like, "Wow, somebody got it. There it is."*
M S : That's the whole story of *Mean Streets.* I mean, I put it on the screen. It took me years to get it going—I never thought the film would be released. I just wanted to make, like, an anthropological study; it was about myself and my friends. And I figured even if it was on a shelf, some years later people would take it and say that's what Italian-Americans on the everyday scale—not the Godfather, not big bosses, but the everyday scale, the everyday level—this is what they really talked like and looked like and what they did in the early seventies and late sixties. Early sixties even. This was the life-style.

A D : *Why was it important to do that? To document that?*
M S : Oh, you know—myself. I mean why does anybody do anything? You know, you think you're important so you do a film about yourself. Or if you're a writer you write a novel about yourself or about your own experiences. I guess it's the old coming-of-age story.

Actually there were two of them for me. *Who's That Knocking on My Door?* and *Mean Streets. Who's That Knocking* I never got right, except for the emotional aspects of it—I got that.

A D : *I watched it recently and was struck by how strong it was. How do you feel about it at this point?*
M S : I dislike it. Only because it took me three years to make. And, you know, we'd make the film and we'd work on a weekend and then for three weeks we wouldn't shoot and then we'd work another weekend. So it wasn't really a professional film to make. It took three years to make. The first year, '65, I cast it. We did all the scenes with the young boys and we had a young lady playing the part of the girl. But later on we came up to about an hour

and ten minutes and there was no confrontation. The young girl was always seen in flashbacks and asides. It was all between the boys. So you never understood what was happening between the Harvey Keitel character and the girl. The conflict was, of course, being in love with a girl who is an outsider, loving her so much that you respect her and you won't make love to her. Then he finds out she's not a virgin and he can't accept that. It's that whole Italian-American way of thinking, of feeling.

Finally we got it released. We got it released by '69, when we were able to put a nude scene in it. In 1968, we shot a nude scene. In '68 there was a new tolerance about nude scenes. Very old, wonderful actors and actresses were playing scenes in the nude—it was very embarrassing. We had to get a nude scene. We shot it in Holland, because I was up in Amsterdam doing some commercials for a friend of mine. We flew Harvey over and we got the young ladies there and we did this nude scene. I came back, kind of smuggled it back into the country in my raincoat, put it in the middle of the film and then the film was released. But it was still a rough sketch to me. I wish . . . ah, it's the old story: if I knew then what I know now it would be different.

A D : *One of the most interesting parts of the movie is the sexual fantasy sequence while the Doors's "The End" is playing.*

M S : Well, that was the scene done in Amsterdam. That was fun.

A D : *The Oedipal drama in the song underscores the Oedipal struggle of the Keitel character. Using that song also captures the way that you were profoundly affected by what was going on culturally in the sixties. But for the characters in your movies, the sixties don't seem to exist. Their world is . . .*

M S : Medieval! Medieval. Well, that's the thing. When I was about to release the film, we were having a problem getting a distributor and my agents at William Morris said to me, "Marty, what do you expect? You have a film here in which the guy loves a young woman so much that he respects her and he won't make love to her. Here we are in the age of the sexual revolution, and you're making a movie about repression! Total sexual repression. Who's going to see it? Nobody."

Yeah, I mean, that was my life. When I went to Woodstock in '69, I mean, it was the first time I started wearing jeans—afterwards. I took cufflinks; I lost one of the cufflinks. Certainly it was having come from that neighborhood and living there completely closed in, like in a ghetto area, not really leaving till the early sixties to go to the West Side. So I had one foot in the university and the other foot in *Mean Streets,* you know, that world, that life-style. I became aware of other people in the world and other life-styles, other views, political and otherwise, much later. But I was quite closed off. It was like somebody coming out of the Middle Ages going to a university.

A D : *In a documentary that was done about you, you said that you would see certain things when you were young and you would say, "Why don't you ever see this in a movie?" I was wondering about what it was you were seeing, or what you felt was missing then in the movies?*
M S : I think it is the way people behaved. I'd be sitting and watching something on television. My uncles would be in the room. My mother would be there. One of my uncles would say, "That wouldn't happen that way. It's a good picture and everything else, I really enjoyed it, but, you know, what would really happen is such and such. He would do this and she would leave him and the guy would kill the other guy." They would work up their own versions of the film noir that we were watching, and they were actually much better. My uncles' and my mother's and father's ideas were much better than what we were watching on TV. And it had to do with what was based in reality. What would really happen.

A D : *That's an interesting aspect about your movies. Obviously you're completely soaked in film history and you've seen a million movies. But your movies never become just movies about movies. There's never anything cute or clever about them. Even when Henry in* GoodFellas *says, when the police are coming for him, that things don't happen the way they do "in the movies," it doesn't seem contrived. Of course, you got that from the book.*
M S : I was going to take that out, but I left it in because I felt it had more of an honesty to it. I hoped it had an honesty to it, if you understand. I always find that sort of thing too cute or too self-conscious or something—though I don't mind being self-conscious at all. I like Joseph Losey's films. You see the camera moving, it's very self-conscious. But it took me years to get to understand the precision of it and the beauty of that, you know? And I don't mind the self-conscious aspect. What I do mind is pretending that you're not watching a movie. That's absurd. You are watching a movie and it is a movie.

But Henry did say, "They don't come to you like you usually see in movies." So he's not talking about this movie. He's talking about other movies that you see. And I was even thinking of saying, "I know you're watching this as a movie now." I was even thinking of putting that in. Then I said, no, it gets too—what's the word for that?—maybe academic to get into that. There's a falseness about that that I wanted to avoid here.

A D : *It seems exactly like what he would say.*
M S : It just sounded right to me, you know what I'm saying? It sounded right in the context of the way he was speaking and all, so I just let it go.

A D : *That approach to things relates well to the subterranean world you deal with in* GoodFellas *and some of your other movies. You depict a real world of consequences, in which people don't get a lot of chances to make mistakes. There is a clear sense that if you step out of line, if you do the wrong thing, you're going to pay for it.*
M S : That's very important. These guys are in business to make money, not to kill people, not to create mayhem. They really want to make money. And if you make a big mistake, you bring down heat on them, you bring attention to them, you cause strife between two crime families, somebody has to be eliminated. It's very simple. Those are the rules. Very, very simple. I mean, you can't make that many big mistakes. You don't rise in the hierarchy if you do. It's very much like a Hollywood situation where, you know, how many pictures could you make that cost $40 million that lose every dime? You can't. It's purely common sense. And so they work out their own little elaborate set of rules and codes.

A D : *It's also a means of working out a certain version of the American dream. In* GoodFellas *Henry says he'd rather be a wise guy than be the president of the United States.*
M S : It's better, because you can do anything you want. And you can take anything you want, because, like Henry says, if they complain, you hit them. It's very simple. It's more exciting, and the opportunity is endless. And this is the great country for it to happen to, because the opportunity here is endless, usually.

However, I always quote Joe Pesci, who pointed out that wise guys have a life cycle—or an enjoyment cycle—of maybe eight or nine years, ten years the most, before they either get killed or go to jail and start that long process of going in and out like a revolving door. I try to give an impression of that in the film when Henry gets to jail and says, "Paulie was there because he was serving time for contempt. Jimmy was in another place. Johnny Dio was there." I mean, this is like home for them. Then the life begins to wear you down. The first few years are the exuberance of youth. They have a great time—until they start to pay for it. Tommy [DeVito, played by Pesci] starts doing things, just unnecessary outbursts. Look why Jimmy [Conway, played by De Niro] goes to jail—because he beats up some guy down in Florida. It's a long story in the book; in the film, it's totally unimportant as to why they're even there. We did it so quickly to show you how, just as fast as it happened, that's as fast as he could go to jail for something he forgot he did.

AD: *Tommy and Jimmy in* GoodFellas *are, like Travis Bickle in* Taxi Driver *and Jake La Motta in* Raging Bull, *walking powder kegs. What interests you about characters like that?*
MS: There are a thousand answers to that. It's interesting. It's good drama. I'm attracted to those kind of characters. And you see part of yourself in that. I like to chart a character like that, see how far they go before they self-destruct. How it starts to turn against them after awhile—whether it's shooting people in the street or arguing in the home, in the kitchen and the bedroom. How soon the breaking point comes when everything just explodes and they're left alone.

AD: *You once said that the La Motta character in* Raging Bull *never really has to face himself until he's alone in his prison cell, hitting his head against the wall.*
MS: Totally. That's the one he's been paranoid about all along. I mean, it gets to be so crazy. If his brother, and if Tommy Como, and if Salvie and if Vicky did everything he thought they did—he can do one of two things: kill them all or let it go. If you let it go, I mean, it's not the end of the world. But, no, no, he's got to battle it out in the ring. He's got to battle it out at home. He's got to battle it everywhere until finally he's got to deal with that point where everybody else has disappeared from him and he's dealing with himself. He didn't let it go. And ultimately, ultimately it's *you.*

A D :   *Is that the source of all that violence, of all that paranoia and anger?*
M S :   Oh, I think it comes from yourself. I mean, obviously it comes from
Jake. It comes from your feelings about yourself. And it comes from what
you do for a living. In his case, he goes out in the morning and he beats
up people. And then they beat him up and then he comes home. It's horrible. It's life on its most primitive level.

A D :   *But that doesn't account for the sexual paranoia.*
M S :   Well, yeah. I don't know if it does. But I really am not a psychiatrist.
It just comes from the fact that the guy is in the ring and you feel a certain
way about yourself. When you're punching it out you feel a certain way
about yourself. You could take anyone, you see; the ring becomes an allegory of whatever you do in life. You make movies, you're in the ring each
time. Writing music—if you perform it, you're in the ring. Or people just
living daily life, when they go to their work—they're in the ring. And, I
think, it's how you feel about yourself that colors your feelings about
everything else around you. If you don't feel good about yourself, it takes
in everything that you're doing—the way your work is, the people who
supposedly love you, your performance with them, your performance in
loving, your performance of lovemaking—everything. You begin to chip
away at yourself and you become like a raw wound. And if a man spits
across the street, you say he spit at you. And then you're finished. Because
then nobody can make a move. You'll think, "Why did you look at me
that way?" Who's going to be with you? Who can stay with you?

A D :   *At the end of* GoodFellas, *you leave Henry in a more problematic spot
than the book itself does. Is there any reason for that?*
M S :   It's not about Henry, really; it's about the life-style. It's about all of
them together. Henry's the one who gives us the in; he opens the door for
us, but basically, it's about all these people. So it's more a comment on the
life-style than it is on Henry. I mean, he's just left out in God knows where,
annoyed because he's not a wise guy anymore. I was more interested in the
irony of that. There wasn't a last paragraph in the book saying, "Now I
know what I did. I was a bad guy, and I'm really sorry for it"—none of
that. Just, "Gee, I can't get the right food here." It's right in line with when
he says as a kid, "I didn't have to wait in line for bread at the bakery." I

mean, it's the American way—getting treated special. It's really a film about that. It's a film about getting to a position where you don't have to wait in line to get served in a store.

A D : *A significant issue in the arts in recent years, and particularly, in your case, with* The Last Temptation of Christ *and* Taxi Driver, *has been various attempts at censorship. What are your feelings about that?*

M S : Obviously, I'm for freedom of expression. I was very glad that *The Last Temptation of Christ* was able to be made by an American company, that I didn't have to go to Europe or to some other country to get the money for it. That's what this country is about, to be able to do something you believe in. I'm for freedom of expression, but in each generation there are threats to it, and you have to keep battling and fighting. I'm concerned about the educational system because it seems to be at a low level at this point in our history and that means that a lot of kids are not learning about this, are not learning that they have to fight for this freedom in this country. I don't necessarily mean going to the Mideast. I'm talking about fighting for it at home, fighting for it in your school, fighting for it in your church. Because they have a low level of education, many people are not going to know that. They're going to take it for granted and it's going to become worse and worse of a problem and there's going to be fewer people to make sure that we secure these rights, to take the right stand.

That's all I'm concerned about. I personally don't like a lot of the stuff I see—it's offensive to me. But that's what it's about. You have to let it go. As far as my personal way of dealing with subject matter, I can't let anybody tell me, "Don't do that, it will offend people." I can't do that.

On one level, when I'm dealing with a Hollywood film, that means I have to do a certain kind of subject matter that will make a certain amount of money. If I decide to make less money, that means I can take a risk on subject matter. So the only criterion on the films I'm willing to take risks on is that it be truthful, that it be honest about your own feelings and truthful to what you know to be the reality around you or the reality of the human condition of the characters. If it's something that's not honest, not truthful, then it's a problem. If you don't believe in it, why are you making it? You're going to offend people to make some money? What for? It doesn't mean anything. The money doesn't mean anything. All that matters is the work, just what's up on the screen. So that's it. I'm not like

some great person who's out there undaunted, fighting off all these people. I didn't think any of this stuff would really cause trouble—let alone
Taxi Driver. The Last Temptation, I knew there would be some problems, but
that's a special area for me. I really demand that I get to speak out the way
I feel about it, even within the Church, the Catholic Church. Some of my
close friends are still priests and we talk about it. I just heard from one
today, and they support me.

A D : *But you must think about the potential impact of your movies. I remember
your saying that you were shocked when audiences responded in an almost vigi-
lante fashion to the end of* Taxi Driver.
M S : To *The Wild Bunch,* too, they reacted that way. I was kind of shocked.

A D : *It would suggest there's some kind of fissure between your moral and spiritual concerns and how the films are perceived.*
M S : No, I went to see the film that night and they were reacting very
strongly to the shoot-out sequence in *Taxi Driver.* And I was disturbed by
that. It wasn't done with that intent. You can't stop people from taking it
that way. What can you do? And you can't stop people from getting an
exhilaration from violence, because that's human, very much the same
way as you get an exhilaration from the violence in *The Wild Bunch.* But
the exhilaration of the violence at the end of *The Wild Bunch* and the violence that's in *Taxi Driver*—because it's shot a certain way, and I know
how it's shot, because I shot it and I designed it—is also in the creation of
that scene in the editing, in the camera moves, in the use of music and the
use of sound effects, and in the movement within the frame of the characters. So it's like . . . *art*—good art, bad art, or indifferent, whatever the hell
you want to say it is, it's still art. And that's where the exhilaration comes
in. The shoot-out at the end of *The Wild Bunch* is still one of the great
exhilarating sequences in all movies, and it's also one of the great dance
sequences in the movies. It's ballet.

Now *Taxi Driver* may be something else, I don't know. It may be something else entirely. The intent was not necessarily the reception I saw. I
know it can't be the reaction of most of the people who have seen the picture. I was in China in '84 and a young man from Mongolia talked to me
at length about *Taxi Driver,* about the loneliness. That's why the film seems
to be something that people keep watching over and over. It's not the

shoot-'em-out at the end. As much as I love the shoot-'em-out at the end of *The Wild Bunch,* I wouldn't put it on for fun. If you put it on for fun, that's something else. That's a whole other morbid area.

There's an interesting situation going on. There's lots of movies that have been cut and movies that appear on video with scenes put back in and you begin to get these esoteric groups in the country, people who become obsessed with getting the complete film. The films can range anywhere from *Lawrence of Arabia* to some very, very shlocky horror film that shows dismembering of bodies and disemboweling of people, so that you can see every frame of disemboweling. That's something else. I can't think about that. I don't know what that is.

A D :   *Living in New York, obviously violence is around you all the time.*
M S :   Oh come on. I just took a cab on 57th Street, we're about to make a turn on Eighth Avenue, and three Puerto Rican guys are beating each other up over the cab. *Over it*—from my side, onto the hood, onto the other side. Now, this is just normal—to the point where the cabbie and myself, not a word. We don't say anything. He just makes his right turn and we move on. It's at least two, three, four times a year that happens. I'm not in the street that much, but it would happen much more if I were.

A D :   *But complaints about violence in your films don't bother you?*
M S :   It's never stopped me. You do the subject matter because you think it's going to make a lot of money—I don't do it. I just don't do it, you know? If I'm making a more commercial venture—I mean a more commercial venture like *The Color of Money*—it's something else. It becomes a different kind of movie and I think you can see the difference. My new film will be something else. It's a more mainstream commercial film for Universal Pictures.

A D :   *What are you doing?*
M S :   It's a remake of *Cape Fear,* the 1962 film directed by J. Lee Thompson, with Robert Mitchum and Gregory Peck. Bob De Niro wants to do it. It's more of a commercial venture. You do have a certain kind of responsibility to the audience on a picture like that because, number one, you have certain expectations from the genre, the thriller genre. You work within that framework and it's like a chess game. You see if you can really be expressive within

it. I don't know if you can, because I always have that problem: loving the old films, I don't know if I can make them. You become more revisionist. I mean *New York, New York* was obviously revisionist. But *The Color of Money* I went half and half, and it should have been one way, I think.

A D : New York, New York *pitted its period style against completely unnerving contemporary emotions in the plot.*
M S : The reality of the story. That was conscious. That was a love of the old stylization, you know, a love of those films, but then showing what it really is like as close as possible in the foreground. That's, I guess, what they call revisionism and that's why the picture—besides being too damn long, it's sprawling—didn't catch on.

A D : *Are there any new directions in which you'd like to move your work?*
M S : I find I have a lot of things in mind and I want to be able to branch out and go into other areas, different types of films, maybe some genre films. But there's no doubt, even if I find something that's dealing with New York society in the eighteenth century, I usually am attracted to characters that have similar attributes to characters in my other films. So I guess I keep going in the same direction. I'm fascinated by history and by anthropology. I'm fascinated by the idea of people in history, and history having been shown to us in such a way that people always come off as fake—not fake but one-dimensional. And I'm interested in exploring what they felt and making them three-dimensional. To show that they're very similar to us. I mean, they're human beings. So just because the society around them and the world around them is very different, it doesn't mean that they didn't have the same feelings and the same desires, the same goals and the same things that haunt us in modern society. And in going into the past, maybe we can feel something about ourselves in the process.

A D : *It seems like that was a lot of the impetus behind* The Last Temptation of Christ, *too, a desire to portray Christ in more three-dimensional terms.*
M S : No doubt. To make him more like a person who would be in this room, who you could talk to.

A D : *There's a genuine concern with spiritual issues in your movies, at the same time that there is also a brutal physicality. How do you square that?*

M S : It's just the struggle, that's all. The struggle to stay alive and to even want to stay alive. Just this corporal thing we're encased in and the limitations of it and how your spirit tries to spring out of it, fly away from it. And you can't. You can try. People say you can do it through poetry, you can do it through the work you do, and things like that. Thought. But you still feel imprisoned. So the body is what you deal with, and it's a struggle to keep that body alive.

A D : *You spend a great deal of time thinking about the world that you grew up in. But you are no longer part of that world. Does that create any complexities for you?*
M S : Oh, because you left it behind doesn't mean that you don't have it. It's what you come from. You have an affinity to it and very often you have a love of it too. I can't exist there now. I don't belong there anymore. But I can damn well try to make sure that when I use it in a film like *Good-Fellas,* I make it as truthfully as possible. What's wrong with that? It's part of your life, and if you try to deny that, what good is it? A lot of what I learned about life came from there. So you go back and you keep unraveling it. For some people it was the family, for other people it's the state. I don't know. Me, it was the subculture.

A D : *What things do you learn there?*
M S : People are usually the product of where they come from, whether you come from a small farm in Iowa and you had your best friend next door and you went swimming in the old swimming hole—in other words, whether you had an idyllic American childhood—or you were a child in Russia or you were a child on the Lower East Side. The bonds you made, the codes that were there, all have a certain influence on you later on in your life. You can reject them. You can say, "Okay, those codes don't exist for me anymore because I'm not of that world anymore," but the reasons for those codes are very strong. The most important reason is survival. True survival. It's very simple. Food, safety, survival. It comes down to that. That struggle of the human form, the corporal, the flesh, to survive—anything to survive. And you learn in each society it's done a different way. In each subculture another way. And all these rules are set up and you learn them and they never really leave you. It's what everybody learns when

you're all kids in the street or in the park. I think those things you carry with you the rest of your life.

And then, of course, it causes problems in that your response to certain stimuli at that time was one way, and when you get the same sort of stimuli now, you've got to be very careful you don't respond in the street fashion. Because they're different people. They don't really mean it. It's something else entirely. It's very funny because, you know, it's like I've seen people do things to other people that I said, "My God, if a guy did that, if that woman did that to me or a friend of mine back in 1960 or in that neighborhood, they wouldn't be *alive*." And you have to realize it's a different world. You just learn your way in and out of it, how to get in and out of the moral inlets of this new world, whatever the hell it is. I don't know what it is. Basically I'm here, in this building. I stay here. Here in this chair. That's it. I answer the phone. They let me out to make a movie. People come over to eat. That's it. I mean, I just do my work and see some very close friends. That's all. So that's what it comes down to. So in a funny way all the trauma of trying to find the new ways to react to the same stimuli in these new societies, it's kind of past me, I guess. I'm past that, which is good.

If you go to a cocktail party, someone comes over to you . . . like, I don't know, some strange *insult* occurs. You know, "How *dare* you!" You know, in the old days, in those neighborhoods, certain people, if you stepped on the guy's *shoe,* you could die, let alone come over and *insult* him. He'd kill you. It's so funny. Oh you'd be surprised how the insults come—it's just wonderful what they do. And people wonder why you don't want to talk to anybody. But it's fascinating. One person in a university, in the academic world, was introduced to me. We were having a few drinks after the David Lean American Film Institute dinner, and the woman said, "I must say I'm an admirer of *some* of your films, because, after all, I am a woman." Who needs it? Who needs it? Who needs it? I mean, look, I make a certain type of film and that does bring out certain things in certain people. What can I say? So you try to avoid it.

A D : *Don't you have a sense of losing touch with things?*
M S : No. I mean, you come from a certain time and place. I can't turn and say, "Well, gee, I'll only listen to rap music now." I can't. I mean, I still lis-

ten to older rock & roll; I listen to the music that I like. You come from a certain time and place and you can't . . . I mean, maybe there are some people who can, some artists, let's say, a painter or a novelist or some filmmakers who can keep up with the times and move along with what audiences expect today. I just think we are of a time, and the generations that come after us, we'll either still speak to them or we won't. We'll maybe miss two or three generations, and then a third or fourth generation will pick up what we did and it will mean something to them. But, I mean, you take a look at, in the early sixties, when you had the French New Wave and the Italian New Wave, with the jump cuts and the freeze frames, the destruction of the narrative form. You had a lot of Hollywood directors trying similar things, and it didn't work. And the guys who remained, the guys whose work stayed strong, are the ones who were not swayed by what was fashionable, who stayed true to themselves. And it's hard because they got rejected. Billy Wilder—everything from the midsixties on was rejected. Especially, I think, one of his greatest pictures: *The Private Life of Sherlock Holmes.* There were a lot of others who tried these flashy techniques and now you look at their films and they don't come out of an honesty, they don't come out of a truthfulness. And I don't say they were phonies. But they were saying, "Hey, that's a new way of doing it, let's try that." But if you can't tell the story that way, tell it the way you know how to.

AD: *What do you think is the flash stuff now?*

MS: I think the formula—what do they call them?—high-concept pictures, probably. A high-concept picture has a basic theme. You can say it in one sentence: "A fish out of water." But you know, high-concept pictures have been around for a long time under different guises. In some cases they were very beautifully made vehicle films for certain kinds of stars. Bette Davis. Clint Eastwood. If you went to see a person, you knew what kind of film you were going to see. Okay, there were a lot of films that were like that, but they had a little more style to them, they had better actors in them, they were better written. But now the more money that's spent on a film, the bigger the audience has to be. Which means it's got to make more money. So you've got to cut it down to the best common denominator that you can get—and probably the lowest—so that it reaches more people.

A lot of it is, I think, the flash kind of cutting that goes on. The man who broke that into films originally was Richard Lester with *A Hard Day's Night*. You really saw the influence of television commercials on the film, and it worked. And now—this is old hat what I'm saying, really, it's really not even very good—the influence of MTV, let's say, over the past eight years on movies, maybe the audience attention span is a bit of a problem now. Things have to move faster. And you feel that. But, I mean, you can be true to yourself. You can really do it in this business, but it has to be for a price. Everything's for a price.

A D : *Your movies have been pioneering in their use of music, but now with MTV, everybody's using music.*

M S : Well, I think they're using it cheaply. I think they're using it unimaginatively. I think they're using it basically to say, "Okay, it's 1956." They're using it to tell you which period you're in.

A D : *In your movies, the relation between the song and the scene takes on so many aspects. I was thinking about the scene in* GoodFellas *where that corpse is rolling around in the garbage and the coda from "Layla" is playing.*

M S : That was shot to "Layla," you know. We played a playback on the set. All the murders were played back on the set to "Layla," to that piece, because it's a tragedy. A lot of those people, they didn't really deserve to die. It's like the unveiling, it's like a parade, it's like a revue, in a way, of the tragedy, the unfolding tragedy. It has a majesty to it, even though they're common people. You may say "common crooks," I still find that they're people. And the tragedy is in the music. The music made me feel a certain way and gave a certain sadness to it, a certain sadness and a certain sympathy.

A D : *One term you've used to describe the making of* Raging Bull *is "kamikaze filmmaking." What did you mean by that?*

M S : What I meant was that I threw everything I knew into it, and if it meant the end of my career, then it would have to be the end of my career.

A D : *Did you honestly feel that?*

M S : Absolutely, yeah. I don't know exactly why, but I did. I just felt it would probably be the end of it, but I might as well throw it all in and see what happened.

A D : *But why, because it might prove too much for people to take?*

M S : Well, I was making a certain kind of film. Films at that time . . . don't forget, it was the beginning of the Reagan era. Sylvester Stallone had created his own new mythology and people were more into that. I mean, after the experience of *New York, New York,* I realized the kind of pictures I was going to make, even if I was dealing with genre . . . this is why I was telling you about the new thriller, *Cape Fear.* It's a very interesting situation, because I don't want it to be necessarily revisionist the way *New York, New York* was. But on the other hand, I want to find my own way in it. Now, does my own way mean, automatically, the undermining of a genre picture in traditional terms, which means that it will not be satisfying to an audience the way the traditional hero films, like all the *Rocky* movies, are?

Anyway, that was the mood of the country. And *Raging Bull* comes out. Who's going to see it? Who cares about this guy? Nobody — that's what I thought. And maybe some people would say, "Well, you were right, because nobody saw it." The film came out a week before *Heaven's Gate* and the whole studio went under. It only made a certain amount of money. The whole mood of the country was different. Big money was being made with pictures like *Rocky* and eventually the Spielberg-Lucas films. I mean, *New York, New York* was a total flop, and it opened the same week as *Star Wars.* We're all close friends, George and Spielberg and myself. But at that time they were the mythmakers, and to a certain extent still continue to be. So at that time I knew which way the wind was blowing and I knew it certainly wasn't in my direction. Therefore I just did the best I could with *Raging Bull,* because I had nothing and everything to lose. I knew that I'd probably get movies to make in Europe or something. But I'm an American. I have to make movies about this country. So what do you do? You just say it's the end of your career, but you don't know any other way to do it, and you do it that way. That's what I meant by kamikaze. You just put everything you know into it. It takes a certain kind of passion to do that. *Taxi Driver* had a kind of kamikaze effect too. Passionate. That's another movie I didn't expect anybody to see. It was done out of real love for the subject matter and for the characters. Or, I should say, out of empathy with the characters in it.

A D : *When you talk about* Cape Fear, *it seems that you want to make a genre film on your own terms without subverting the genre.*

M S : *Subverting* the genre, I think, would be a problem. What I hopefully will do will be to try to blend the genre with me, in a sense, with my expression of it, with the elements that I'm interested in and see if it doesn't derail it too much. If it enhances it, and I get the best of both, that would be great. I don't know if I can. I mean, I still wouldn't be interested in doing — as much as I adore them — the old musicals. As much as I *adore* them. I have no words for them, some of them are so beautiful. I still wouldn't be able to do that. I wouldn't be interested in doing that. I still want to do something with a musical where it's got an edge to it. But I think I would be able to, this time, get a clearer idea of how to approach it.

A D : *What's the difference now?*
M S : *New York, New York,* we made it up as we went along. We had a pretty good script by Earl Mac Rauch and we didn't pay any attention to it. The two methods of filmmaking — the improvisatory style and the old studio style, where you have to build sets — didn't blend. You're wasting money that way, because the set was built and you would improvise yourself into another scene. And then you'd have to *reimprovise* yourself *back* into that set. It was crazy. I think we got some real good stuff out of it — and some real truth about that world and relationships between creative people. But I think it could have been more concise, maybe shorter. Maybe there was too much music. The repetition of scenes between the couple was really more like *life,* where a scene repeats itself and repeats itself and repeats itself until finally . . .

A D : *It becomes tension-producing watching it; it's very unsettling.*
M S : And that's the idea. The way, if you're in a relationship with someone and you've talked it out and talked it out and talked it out and you can't sit, you can't go in the same room! That was the idea. Maybe in that case, it's successful — but I don't know if it's entertainment. I can guarantee you, you're not going to have the head of a studio say, "Marty, let's make a picture where the people get so tense — and it's a musical, okay? And people come out thinking about their own lives, oh my God, and their four marriages, and they get upset — and we'll give you fifty million dollars to make it!" No! They're not going to do it.

A D : *That's like when you told a studio head who asked you why you wanted to make* The Last Temptation of Christ *that you wanted to understand Jesus better.*

MS: I said that to Barry Diller, and he didn't expect that, Barry. It was very funny. He kind of smiled. He didn't really expect that. It was really funny. It's true, though. And I had to learn that that picture had to be made for much less money. You're that interested in something personal—"We'd like to see what happens with it, but here's only seven million. You can do it at seven, not at twenty-four."

AD: *You've said over and over that you don't see yourself as especially literary. But on the other hand you'll talk about* The Gambler *as a model for* Life Lessons, *your contribution to* New York Stories, *and, of course,* The Last Temptation of Christ *was based on the Kazantzakis book. Why do you downplay that aspect of your work and your thinking?*
MS: I guess I'm still cowed a little by the tyranny of art with a capital A. And there has always been the tyranny of the word over the image: anything that's written has got to be better. Most people feel it's more genuine if you express yourself in words than in pictures. And I think that's a problem in our society. And, I've said it many times in interviews, I come from a home where the only things that were read were the *Daily News* and the *Daily Mirror.* Those were the two newspapers, and I brought the first book in. And there were discussions about whether or not I should bring the book in the house, too.

AD: *What do you mean?*
MS: They were worried.

AD: *That you would become . . .*
MS: God knows.

AD: *I mean my parents didn't graduate from high school either, but . . .*
MS: They didn't graduate from grammar school, my parents.

AD: *My parents were obsessed with education and with my going to school.*
MS: Oh, no. Mine, no. Mine wanted me to continue because they understood one thing: you go to school, you make a little more money. It's as simple as that. But what I was doing then was out of the question. First I was going to be a priest and that was one thing. They could take that. To a certain *extent* they could take that. But when I started to have books come

in the house and go to New York University, which was a secular situation, not a parochial, not a church-oriented place, obviously... it was in the sixties, you know? They're not educated people. They said the college is too liberal. It's communist. That sort of thing.

A D : *Were they paying for you to go there?*
M S : My father paid, yeah. They both worked in the garment district. They paid. So having difficulty reading... I mean, I'm not a fast reader, although I'm forcing myself to read as much as possible now. I'm sort of catching up on books that I should have read twenty years ago, forcing myself to read a lot. And usually in certain areas, like ancient history or historical novels, good ones, strong ones. And trying to get to read faster that way.

There are certain kinds of films that are more literary-based. Joseph Mankiewicz's pictures are on a more verbal level—and I love them. *All About Eve, Letter to Three Wives, Barefoot Contessa.* I like those pictures. They had a sense of dignity because of their literary background.

But then what do I make of my attraction to Sam Fuller? People say about Fuller, "Well listen to his dialogue. It's terrible." "Well, yeah, but the visuals and the way he's expressing himself with that move." You don't sit there and say, "Gee, look at that camera move." You get an emotional reaction. And then if it affects you enough and you're interested enough, you go back and you start playing around with it. You see why. "Why was that effective? Oh, gee, that's what he did. He moved that way. And that actor goes flying out of the frame here and the energy of that actor is still felt and you're flying into the wall."

I mean the same kind of visual intelligence you find in Douglas Sirk, and yet I'm not able to enjoy the Douglas Sirk films, maybe because of the genre. At least now in the past ten years I've been able to appreciate them in terms of visuals, in terms of the camera, the lighting, the compositions. The genre just never attracted me when I was young. It was over my head. I didn't know. And I sort of got past the trash level, the lurid quality of *Written on the Wind.* But certainly I didn't miss it in *Duel in the Sun.* I caught it there, and I enjoyed it better in *Duel in the Sun.* The visuals were much stronger for me in *Duel in the Sun.* King Vidor. I thought that was just phenomenal. Granted, it's trash down to the very bone, the very core, the very marrow, but wonderful, just wonderful. I prefer the excess and the hysteria there.

I could talk about this for ages. The literary will always have the upper hand here. It always will.

A D :   *Even though it's become such a visual culture?*
M S :   Oh God yes. I mean look at the things taken seriously. I was just going to point out in 1941—*Citizen Kane* came out that year—if I'm not mistaken the best picture of the year, I think it was *Watch on the Rhine.* [In fact, it was *How Green Was My Valley.*] Now, come on, is that a movie? Is that a movie? A *movie* movie where images were used in a certain way? It did have a certain emotional impact. Look, the war was on, and we were about to be drawn into it. It was very important that that film won at that time. And *Mrs. Miniver* the next year. Very important, you know. But they're not . . . I mean, I like Wyler too but *Mrs. Miniver* is not one of my favorites.

I mean the greatest casualty in terms of being honored is Alfred Hitchcock. And his movies are purely visual. He was never given an academy award. He got the life achievement award but was never singled out for best director. *Rebecca,* I think, won the best picture of the year, but I don't think he won director. Because, again, they said, "Well, he's got clever scriptwriters and he does clever things with the camera."

A D :   *Was there a specific point at which you felt that in terms of your own skill you could say exactly what you wanted to say with film?*
M S :   Oh no. One of the great breakthroughs is to know that you really don't know that much. That gives you a little more to learn. It gives you hope that you always can learn more. And it makes you not arrogant. It makes you get on the set and it makes you realize, "All right, what am I going to do?" Not on the set—that is, in the mind. When I make a picture, in my mind I'm always on the set. I'm on the set right now for my next picture, picking up images. I put myself into a certain mode. I see fewer people and I just try to stay alone. It's a freeing thing to know that you really don't know that much. The best part is the hope to learn. And it keeps you in line with your material. Then there are bursts of inspiration. You do some things and *bang.* You say, "Okay, I'm going to approach that scene." You work it out on the page. You say, "Ah, that happens this way." Bang, you go this way. "And then we're going to move the camera here, and then we are going to shoot this way." And then you wonder how you

thought it up, and you have no idea. You could also devise intellectual approaches, where a character is photographed with certain-size lenses up to a certain point in the film, then the lenses change as the story progresses. That's okay. That will work. I prefer the stuff that just comes out of nowhere. But, you know, you've got to *get* them from out of nowhere. I don't know where that comes from.

A D :   *Well, how do you do it?*

M S :   I lock myself away, usually for about four or five or six days. In the case of *New York Stories* it was two days; I worked on shots. I try to lock myself away and just go to a hotel or stay home and play some music, walk around. Sometimes you do nothing for hours and then suddenly it all comes in a half hour. Sometimes it doesn't come. In some cases you find that for certain scenes you've got to find the location before you can even begin to estimate how you are going to do it. In most of the cases you can say, "No matter what the location is, I know that the camera is going to track, and I know it's going to track from left to right. I know it's going to go from this character to that character and I'm going to go with him." You make certain choices. You either pan them out or you track them out. They are different emotional statements that the audience feels. I can talk about rationalizing it and intellectualizing it for hours, but it is just a process where you have a clear mind and you try to let the story seep in on you and you're taken by it. You really fantasize the movie — practically frame by frame.

A D :   *Which of your movies means the most to you?*

M S :   Well, *Mean Streets* is always a favorite of mine because of the music and because it was the story of myself and my friends. It was the movie that I made that people originally took notice of. But I certainly couldn't watch it. I've watched scenes of it. I could never watch the whole thing. It's too personal. I like certain elements of *Raging Bull.* I like the starkness of it. And the wild fight scenes. The subjective fight scenes, as if you were in the ring yourself, being hit in the ear. Frank Warner's sound effects are just so wonderful. I like the look of a lot of it. And I love Bob and Joe Pesci and Cathy Moriarty. And Frank Vincent. I love the performances. Nick Colasanto. It was just wonderful.

AD: Taxi Driver?

MS: No.

AD: *No?*

MS: I like Bob in it. Oh, I like everybody in it. Cybill Shepherd was wonderful there. Jodie Foster. But *Taxi Driver* is really Paul Schrader's. We interpreted it. Paul Schrader gave the script to me because he saw *Mean Streets* and liked Bob in it and liked me as a director. And we had the same kinds of feelings about Travis, the way he was written, the way Paul had it. It was as if we all felt the same thing. It was like a little club between the three of us. Paul Schrader and myself had a certain affinity, and we still do, about religion and life, death and guilt and sex. Paul and I are very close on that sort of thing. But I must say we merely interpreted it, and the original concept is all his. Now you know another guy can come along and say he merely interpreted it — and *ruin* it. I'm not being falsely modest. But you've got to understand that the original idea came from him. And that's something that I think over the years, when they say, "Martin Scorsese's *Taxi Driver*," that's something that can be very painful to Paul. It's really his.

Raging Bull is something else altogether. It came from Bob, and Paul helped us with it and then we worked it out again. We rewrote it, Bob and I, and the same thing with *The Last Temptation of Christ.* Paul worked on it and then I rewrote it myself with Jay Cocks. But the two that I feel most nostalgic for are *Mean Streets* and *Raging Bull.*

AD: *What about some of the other movies that people don't necessarily put in the first rank of your films?*

MS: Well, on one level they were all hard work, learning experiences. In conjunction with, let's say, Ellen Burstyn in *Alice Doesn't Live Here Any More,* I needed to do something that was a major studio film that was for a certain amount of money and to prove that I can direct women. It was as simple as that. *After Hours* was trying to learn, after *The Last Temptation of Christ* was pulled away, how to make a film quicker. And *The Color of Money* was trying to do a real Hollywood picture, with movie stars like Paul Newman and Tom Cruise. But, you know, each one was a lesson, like going to school. And *Cape Fear* to a certain extent will be that way too. Although in *Cape Fear* — the key there is I got Bob De Niro. And that's like . . . it's fun. It becomes something else.

A D : *How would you describe your working relationship with De Niro?*
M S : We're interested in similar traits of people. Like I said, we felt that we understood certain things about Travis. And it's very rare when three people, the actor, the director, and the writer all feel the same way about it.

A D : *What did you understand?*
M S : You feel you understand the rage; you understand that you have certain feelings yourself. You're not afraid to say to each other, to the people who are seeing the movie, that those are aspects of ourselves. Many people have it under control. This character doesn't. He starts to act out his fantasies. You know, living in this city, at a certain point you may want to kill somebody. You don't do it. This guy does it. It's simple. He crosses over. But we understand those implications. Okay, we're talking violence there. But also the pain of romantic rejection. It doesn't mean that you're always rejected. It means that a couple of times when it happens you feel a certain way and you carry that with you for the rest of your life. And you can pull from it, you know?

Bob is not a guy who knows movies the way I know movies. He can't sit with me and Schrader and talk about *Out of the Past,* Jacques Tourneur's film noir. He doesn't know it. And yet that makes it purer because he's just relating to what's there. It's better. He doesn't have to bring anything to it. He's not taking any baggage with him.

King of Comedy and *Raging Bull* really stem from Bob. *Last Temptation* from me. *Taxi Driver* from Paul. *Mean Streets* came from me. It all kind of shifts and slips and slides around and we always find ourselves coming around. The roulette wheel keeps moving and we stop and we look at each other, and we're all in the same place: "Oh, it's *you* again." It's that kind of thing, where you seem to grow together rather than apart. It's good because there's a trust. And it isn't true where you say, "Oh, it's telepathy." Yes, to a certain extent there is telepathy involved, but not entirely. Once we're in the groove we very rarely have disparate points of view.

A D : *Well, so much experience has gone into making that telepathy real. It's not just something that happened out of thin air.*
M S : No, no. And it doesn't mean it's easier. When there's a collaboration on that level, you expect the best from each other and you won't settle.

A D : *The two of you have created characters that have really entered the culture. How many times have you seen somebody imitate De Niro's scenes from* Raging Bull *or the mirror scene in* Taxi Driver?

M S : We improvised the mirror scene. That's true. I did improvise him talking in the mirror: "Are you talking to me?" It was in the script that he was looking at himself in the mirror, doing this thing with the guns, and I told Bob, "He's got to say something. He's got to talk to himself." We didn't know what. We just started playing with it, and that's what came out.

A D : *You've become synonymous with the notion of a director with integrity. It seems, on the one hand, it must be tremendously gratifying. On the other hand, it seems like maybe it can potentially be paralyzing.*

M S : No, I feel really good about it. I do feel gratified that people feel that the work is—I don't know what words you want to use—personal or un-compromising. No matter what happens, though, there are compromises. You can say, "Yes, I'm going to make *The Last Temptation of Christ* and give me $7 million and I can do it." But it's compromised at seven million. I would have liked certain angles. I would have liked extra days for shooting. But, okay, that's artistic compromise, and what the film has to say is not compromised. But one has to realize it's scary, because you have to keep a balance. You want to get films made that express what you have to say. You try to do that, but it's a very delicate balance.

I'd also like the chance to do exactly what I'm doing now with *Cape Fear,* for example: try to do a great thriller and to give the audience what they expect from a thriller, but also to have those elements which make my pictures somewhat different. I will try. I tried in *The Color of Money.* I don't know if it was totally successful there. Sometimes it's a trade-off. You have to do a certain kind of film in order to get maybe two others of your own that you want. I'm in this period now where I want to start exploring different areas, and you've got to make use of each film you make. You've got to learn from it and you have to utilize it to get your own pictures made—the difficult ones, I should say, because they're all, in a way, your own pictures. And no matter *what* happens, the really hard ones, you're only going to get a certain amount of money for them anyway. So you've also got to think of making money for yourself for the lean years, when you have pictures you're only getting paid a certain amount to make. There are so many different variations. It's playing a game, a line that

you're walking, taking everybody very seriously—the studios and what
they need, what you need. And, see, every now and then you can come
together. Like in *GoodFellas* we all came together. So that was the best of
both worlds: $26 million to make a personal movie. That's very interesting.
The rest, no, there's no guarantee of anything. Each picture you make you
try to learn from, and you try to cover your tracks. I mean, every movie
wastes money to a certain extent, but you don't do it to the point
where...

A D :   *You create problems for yourself.*
M S :   Where you create real problems. But it's not that rational. It's not
"My God how rational he sounds"—God forbid if I do—it's really a matter of being careful and smart. I mean, the artists coming out of America in
film come from Hollywood. The Hollywood film. And I'm proud to be
associated with Hollywood because of that. I mean, I lived in Hollywood
over ten years. Even *then* they thought I was still living in New York. I live
in New York. My parents are here, my kids are here. But I'm still a Hollywood director, and I'm always proud to be considered that by the rest of
the world. To show that America, every now and then, will give me something to do, or give something to other guys—Stanley Kubrick, David
Lynch—who do very specific, very personal pictures. There's so much fun
involved sometimes that it's enjoyable. But it's dangerous.

Slouching Toward Hollywood

PETER BISKIND/1991

MARTIN SCORSESE IS KILLING time. Dressed in a crisp khaki shirt and pressed blue jeans, with a tiny white bichon frise named Zoe tucked under his arm, he is waiting for the sun to go behind a cloud so the next shot will match the last one. He is near the end of the *Cape Fear* shoot in front of a produce stand just outside Fort Lauderdale, Florida. With him are Nick Nolte, Jessica Lange, and Juliette Lewis playing a married couple and their daughter fleeing from a psycho who is stalking them.

While he waits, Scorsese's hand rarely leaves the side pocket of his custom-made jeans, where he works his watch chain like worry beads. He used to have Armani make his jeans, but he felt guilty wearing them. He orders new ones every two years, and since he can't bear to throw away even the most threadbare, his collection goes back fifteen years.

The sun finally goes in. Nolte is on his mark in an instant. Lange is immersed in *The New York Times*. "You can do it, Jessica," Nolte calls. "Just put one foot in front of the other." (They've been ragging each other throughout the shoot—Nolte dropping his pants, Lange refusing to go to the set until "everything is put away.") Lange finally arrives at her position, and they walk through the scene.

"Nah, nah, nah—too long!" snaps Scorsese with his trademark machine-gun delivery. "We've gone through four bars of the theme of *Psycho*. Start them closer to the car."

"I've moved them from pepper to lettuce," says an assistant director.

From *Premiere*, November 1991. Reprinted by permission.

"Start them at the okra."

"You know okra?" the A.D. inquires of Lange.

"Yeah, I know okra."

Starting from the okra, Lange, Nolte, and Lewis walk quickly to their Jeep Cherokee. The scene is wrapped.

For most directors, this shot would be a throwaway. But for Scorsese, there's no such thing as a throwaway. "The hardest thing to do is get people into a car—to make it interesting," he explains. "It's all about the philosophy of the shot. Those people were beaten into the ground. They didn't want to talk to each other." So he decided to start wide. "You have to see the family as a unit, broken up and terrified as it is, and then move into Nick's face, pan to Jessica, and pan back over. Then actually zoom into Jessica looking out, pan across the kid onto Nick's face, so determined to get his family out of there. That's finally the move I used."

Cape Fear is Scorsese's fourteenth feature. With a budget of approximately $34 million, it is the most expensive picture to date from a director who has always pinched pennies. It is the first fruit of a comfortable six-year deal with Universal Pictures for a director who has never had better than a two-picture deal anywhere. The film was initiated by Steven Spielberg and is being coproduced by his company, even though no one could be further from Spielberg's sensibility than Scorsese. And it is a remake of a 1962 studio thriller, from a director who disdains remakes. This project, in other words, is very much a paradox, a bow in the direction of the mainstream from the ultimate outsider.

Shot in CinemaScope, *Cape Fear* is emblematic of Scorsese's love/hate relationship with Hollywood, an ambivalence the industry is more than happy to reciprocate. He is widely considered one of America's most brilliant directors, one of a select circle of contemporaries that includes Stanley Kubrick and Woody Allen, within shouting distance of masters like Akira Kurosawa. His greatest film, *Raging Bull,* was selected as the best film of the '80s by an outstanding array of critics. Yet Scorsese has been mocked and reviled in Hollywood.

Last year, he came back from a ten-year drought with *GoodFellas,* selected as best film of the year by the New York, Los Angeles, and National societies of film critics. Since then, Scorsese has been showered with honorary degrees and has been the subject of books and documentaries too numerous to mention. He has virtually become a national institution. It's a heavy burden to shoulder, and no one is more aware of that than the director himself.

"You have more to lose," says Scorsese, gazing at the view from his apartment window, 75 stories over midtown Manhattan. "Would it be a different risk if every picture I made was about Italian Americans in New York? I don't think so. Because they'd say, 'That's all he can do.' So I'm trying to stretch." His next picture is a good example. *The Age of Innocence* is based on an Edith Wharton novel and set in the very unmean streets of upper-crust New York, circa 1870. It's not the movie of a man content to rest on his laurels.

"I've always said the way I learned how to make movies was by being a wise guy in the theater when I was a kid," says Scorsese, who was raised in Manhattan's Little Italy. He grew up, frail and badly asthmatic, among priests and mobsters—and flickering images on the screen. "We were merciless, my friends and I. You know, picking out clichés, saying the line before the actor said it."

Scorsese had planned to go into the priesthood, but in 1960 he ended up at New York University. There he fell under the spell of a charismatic professor, Haig Manoogian. "When I heard him lecture, all the passion I had for the seminary was somehow transferred over. I said, 'I want to be talked about in that way, because my appreciation of the people he's talking about is so strong.' I knew I was a director. Other people didn't know it, though." He laughs. "What was the matter with them?"

At the time, Scorsese was collaborating with NYU classmate Mardik Martin. "Our wives hated us," Martin remembers. "We couldn't go home, because they would pick on us. We weren't earning a living; they thought we were wasting our time. We'd sit in my Valiant and write *Mean Streets*."

In 1970, Scorsese moved to Los Angeles, where he helped Thelma Schoonmaker edit Michael Wadleigh's *Woodstock*. There, he met a young woman named Sandra Weintraub, whom he lived and worked with for the next four years. His first big break came when Roger Corman hired him to direct Barbara Hershey in *Boxcar Bertha* in 1971.

While he was editing *Bertha,* he resurrected the *Mean Streets* script and showed it to Weintraub. "There was a man talking to God about everything," she remembers. "I said, 'What is this about?' 'It's about growing up.' I said, 'You have the most incredible stories in your head about grow-

ing up. Put them in!'" He did. Jonathan Taplin, an ex-road manager for
Bob Dylan and the Band, arranged the financing.

Scorsese met Robert De Niro at a party and eventually gave him the part
of Johnny Boy. "What they did together, they did in private," says Weintraub. "Definitely no women allowed." One night, after a screening of the
rough cut of *Mean Streets,* Weintraub, Scorsese, De Niro, and a few others
went out to dinner for what Weintraub assumed would be a group dissec-
tion of the film. But De Niro and Scorsese disappeared into the men's
room for two and a half hours and hashed it out between themselves.

After the film was completed, it was shown to the majors, and instantly
turned down by Universal and Paramount Pictures. At Warner Bros., John
Calley, head of production, and two other executives — "all New York
guys" — attended the screening. "After fifteen minutes," says Taplin, "a
waiter comes in, stands right in front of the projector, and yells, 'Who's
got the tuna on rye?' They're not even watching, and Marty is dying.
Finally, they settle in, start to laugh, enjoy the New York humor. Then
Calley gets up. I think we're lost. He says, 'This is the best movie I've seen
all year, but would you mind shutting it off? I've got to take a leak.'"

Calley bought the picture. *Mean Streets* was a critical hit and instantly
established Scorsese as a major talent.

"The period from '71 to '76 was the best time, because we were just beginning," says Scorsese. "We couldn't wait for our friends' next pictures — Brian
De Palma's, Francis Coppola's — to see what they were doing."

Scorsese, Coppola, De Palma, Spielberg, Paul Schrader, George Lucas —
these were the so-called movie brats. The first generation of directors to go
to film school, they took Hollywood by storm, wresting control of the
industry from the old men.

The late '60s and early '70s were the golden age of postwar film in America, a time when directors, newly legitimized by the auteur theory — and
particularly young directors, riding the crest of the countercultural new
wave — were given a degree of power and autonomy unprecedented in the
history of Hollywood. They used their new power to produce a corpus of
startlingly original work that deconstructed traditional genres and by
implication asked troubling questions about American life. This was a film-
intoxicated generation for whom movies were more than escapism, more
than a job or a new Jaguar or a choice table at Spago. Movies were a way of

life, a religion, a means of salvation. As Schrader once put it, "Somehow we knew the world was ours. We were going to go out and make a difference. You know, films of importance had to be brought to the marketplace, and we were going to do it."

In 1973, Warner's asked Scorsese to direct one of these movies, *Alice Doesn't Live Here Anymore,* about an independent woman who must find her way when she loses her husband. It was one of the first films with a whiff of feminism about it. Scorsese was reluctant. "Marty said, 'I don't know anything about women,'" recalls Weintraub. "I said, 'Women are people, too.'"

Alice did well, although the upbeat ending, in which the heroine (Ellen Burstyn) falls for a handsome rancher (Kris Kristofferson), was considered to be politically incorrect. "We tried to work as truthfully as possible within the conventions of the genre," explains Scorsese. "And within the conventions was the studio chief telling me, 'Give it a happy ending!' I said, 'All right.' But the last line is the kid saying, 'Mom, I can't breathe.'"

While he was working on *Alice,* Scorsese read Schrader's screenplay for *Taxi Driver,* the story of a terminally alienated and deranged Vietnam vet who befriends a preteen hooker and then wastes her pimp and his pals in a bloodbath of Peckinpavian dimensions. He loved it, but, says Weintraub, Schrader told him "he was looking for a 'Tiffany director.' [Marty] was really upset by the word 'Tiffany.'" But when Burstyn won an Oscar for *Alice,* Scorsese's stock went up, and producers Michael and Julia Phillips — with financing from Columbia Pictures — were happy to hire him.

Jodie Foster, who played the hooker and was all of twelve at the time, remembers what it was like to be directed by Scorsese: "There's a big difference between somebody who performs with you and somebody who asks you to perform for them. He is there. Marty gets behind your eyes."

Weintraub also recalls Scorsese in those days: "He was tempestuous, volatile. One time I was on the phone, angry with Taplin. Marty grabbed the phone out of my hand, yelled at Taplin, threw the phone and broke it. Then he went down to the street, put a dime in a pay phone, and continued to yell at Taplin." Taplin remembers that "he was always throwing things. For Marty's birthday in 1977, his office gave him ten breakaway glasses and four breakaway chairs. He had a telephone man on constant call because he would regularly rip the phone out of the wall."

"He always had a lot of superstitions that were a melding of Catholicism, general superstition, and some of his own making, forebodings from dreams," Weintraub says. "He had an unlucky number that really bothered him. He wouldn't travel on that date, wouldn't travel on that flight, wouldn't stay on that floor."

It was an exciting but stressful time for Scorsese. His asthma was still a constant problem. "It was the way he manifested his feelings," says Weintraub. "When things would go wrong, he'd reach for the spray. It was a way to get people to feel sorry for him — the man was barely breathing."

Things went wrong a lot. "For me it was just the beginning of going into an abyss for about two years and coming out of it barely alive," says Scorsese. "It was a few weeks after *Taxi Driver* opened that I started playing with drugs." Toward the end of production, he had split up with Weintraub and soon connected with writer Julia Cameron, whom he married.

"It's hard to live with someone when every day people are telling him what a genius he is," says Weintraub, who today is a producer. "If you weren't there for the movie, you couldn't be with him. I would tell him my dream, and he would tell me what movie he had seen on TV the night before." But, she continues, "he gave me a career. If I had fallen in love with a garbageman, I might be collecting trash today. He gave me my love of film."

When *Taxi Driver* was nominated for Best Picture and Best Supporting Actress of 1976, Scorsese got a letter threatening his life. One of his pals unthinkingly called the FBI, creating a sticky situation. "They smuggled the stash out before the FBI got there," says Taplin. "It was that kind of scene." FBI agents disguised as guests attended the awards ceremony that year to protect Scorsese. "Imagine ducking into the bathroom with the FBI all over you," says Taplin, laughing.

Taxi Driver did surprisingly well at the box office and won the Palme d'or at Cannes in 1976. Perhaps it was the success, perhaps it was the drugs, but Scorsese was setting himself up for his first failure. *New York, New York* was a big-budget homage to the old Hollywood musicals, starring De Niro and Liza Minnelli, in which the music overwhelmed the story. "I will always thank the French for giving me that grand prize to allow me to reveal to myself what a total failure I could be," he says now. "You get a big head. You think, 'Oh, I don't have to make up a script, I can work it out on the soundstage when I'm there.' Sure. A lot of guys work that way. Evidently, I couldn't."

Still, the word on the street about *New York, New York*—with its lush sets, big production numbers, and daringly unconventional unhappy ending—was very good. Marcia Lucas edited the film, and every night she would return home to her husband, George, full of the promise of the movie. George, in postproduction on his own movie, was depressed that it was over budget and certain it wasn't going to make any money, according to Weintraub. When *New York, New York* came out, it flopped. Lucas's picture, *Star Wars,* transformed the industry.

The year 1977 was a watershed for American movies. Simply put, it was a moment when the kind of movies Scorsese made were replaced by the kind of movies Lucas and Spielberg made. Scorsese's films came out of the '60s. Despite (or more likely because of) the fact that they were so artfully crafted, they delivered a shock of documentary rawness, energy, and violence that spoke to the Vietnam generation, with its frantic mixture of idealism and destructiveness. But by the mid-'70s, with Jimmy Carter in the White House looking to bind the wounds of Vietnam and Watergate, people were tired of all that. The personal and critical "cinema" of the '60s was dying. Movies like *The Missouri Breaks* and *3 Women* bombed, while directors like Sam Peckinpah retreated to the bottle and Robert Altman eventually stopped trying.

For Scorsese, the consequences of these changes were still to come. While *New York, New York* was in production, he met musician Robbie Robertson, who asked him to shoot a documentary on the Band's last concert, which became *The Last Waltz.* "He was overjoyed," says Taplin—the pressure on *New York, New York* was unbearable. Taplin recalls the day when 150 fully dressed extras stood around while Scorsese spoke to his therapist from his trailer.

Scorsese was spreading himself thin. He had split up with Cameron and was trying to finish two films simultaneously. It was at this point that Robertson moved into Scorsese's Mulholland Drive house. Says Robertson, "We were the odd couple—looking for trouble."

Scorsese, Robertson, and friends like Mardik Martin and actress Genevieve Bujold would sit in Robertson's bedroom, which doubled as a projection room, and watch four or five movies a night. "We had two problems," says Robertson, "the light and the birds. Marty had the house blacked out with shades, and he installed a soundproof air system so you could breathe without opening the windows."

"We were like vampires," recalls Martin. "It was like, 'Oh, no, the sun is coming up.' We never got to sleep before 7, 8 A.M. for six months. We did all kinds of crazy things in those days."

Taplin recalls the first time they projected *Waltz,* and the face of Neil Young, looking wasted and very big, appeared on the screen. "There was a rock of cocaine falling out of his nostril. His manager was freaking out—'I'm refusing to let you put this song in the movie!' I went to an effects house run by these older guys who didn't know cocaine from . . . a booger. I told them, 'This guy has got a booger in his nose. Can you fix it?' They called back in a couple of days and said, 'We've invented a traveling booger matte.'"

"There was a lot of high living," remembers Scorsese. "At first, you felt like you could make five films at once. Then you wound up spending four days in bed every week because you were exhausted, and your body couldn't take it." He was in and out of the hospital with asthma attacks. "The doctor would say, 'Take these pills. You're suffering from exhaustion,'" says Robertson. "But we had places to go, people to see." Martin remembers De Niro, who was not part of this scene, coming over one day and saying, "What's the matter with you boys? Don't you want to live to see if X gets married to Y?"

It all came to a crashing halt on Labor Day 1978, when Scorsese ended up in the hospital with internal bleeding. "Finally," says Robertson, "Marty got a doctor who conveyed the message that either he alter his life or he was going to die. We knew we had to change trains. Our lives were way too rich. The cholesterol level was unimaginable."

During the same period, De Niro and Martin tried to persuade Scorsese to do *Raging Bull.* "I had to find the key for myself," says Scorsese now. "And I wasn't even interested in finding the key, because I'd tried something, *New York, New York,* and it was a failure." He couldn't bring himself to read the script. "I didn't want him to say no," says Martin, "so I catered to his whims and bullshit. This went on for months. It was driving me crazy. But he was not himself." Finally, Schrader did a rewrite, and De Niro, visiting Scorsese in the hospital, made one last stab. "'Are we doing it or not?' Bob asked me," says Scorsese. "I said yes. I finally understood that for me I had found the hook—the self-destructiveness, the destruction of people around you, just for the sake of it. I was Jake La Motta."

As luck would have it, United Artists released *Heaven's Gate* ten days after *Raging Bull,* and the roof fell in. Scorsese's movie bombed. He admits it was a hard picture to sell. "The poster with the picture of Bob's face all beaten and battered—I mean, if you're a young girl, I don't know if you'd say, 'Let's go see this one.'"

The commercial failure of *Raging Bull,* on top of *New York, New York,* was a crushing blow. "Marty wanted the kind of success that Lucas and Coppola had," recalls Weintraub. "He was afraid he would always be the critics' darling but the American public would never love him." He was terrified that he wouldn't be allowed to continue making movies if he didn't make money. "There was nothing in his life besides movies," Weintraub adds. "What would he do?"

Scorsese likes to tell the story about how his first feature, *Who's That Knocking at My Door?,* whose priest-ridden hero couldn't bring himself to sleep with his girlfriend, went against the grain of the sexual revolution of the '60s. Now, again, he was out of step with the public and an industry that was largely given over to the search for blockbusters. He says he made *Raging Bull* with the conviction that it was his last movie. And yet he continued to pursue his personal vision with single-minded persistence.

Somehow, Scorsese got the backing to make *The King of Comedy,* which turned out to be another troubled production. Scorsese had always had difficulty controlling his temper on the set. He did not suffer fools kindly and was easily frustrated. "I'm just an angry guy, anyway. I look out of the window," he gestures to the twinkling lights in the distance, "and I'm angry about the smog. I'm angry about—you name it, I'm angry. You get to a point where the anger in you can explode. You go into little pieces. And then what—you're dead. Finally you realize that it's probably not worth it."

During the editing, Scorsese hit a brick wall. From December 1981 to March 1982, he couldn't work. "I got myself into such a state of anxiety that I just completely crashed," he continues. "I'd come downstairs from the editing room, and I'd see a message from somebody about some problem, and I'd say, 'I can't work today. It's impossible.' My friends said, 'Marty, the negative is sitting there. The studio is going crazy. You've got to finish the film.'"

This episode taught Scorsese a lesson. "It was up to me. Nobody cared, ultimately, even your closest friends. You're gonna act crazy? You're gonna get in a situation where you can't work? Nobody gives a damn. And you wind up alone. You face yourself anyway. It's Jake La Motta looking in the mirror at the end of *Raging Bull*."

The King of Comedy was plagued by negative word of mouth. "A close friend of mine told me, two months before the film was finished, 'The buzz is bad.' I hate that. When the buzz is bad, people don't want to be associated with the picture. You feel totally abandoned. I must say, that was painful. Because the film came out and died in four weeks, and they were right—the picture was a bomb. It's called *The King of Comedy,* it's Jerry Lewis, and it's not a comedy. I mean, already it's a problem."

Scorsese plunged ahead with *The Last Temptation of Christ,* a pet project he had been gestating since Barbara Hershey gave him the Nikos Kazantzakis book in 1971. But it made him an object of ridicule in the Hollywood—New York party axis. "Big people in the business were saying, 'Yeah, I know the pictures you make,'" he recalls. "One guy introduced me to someone who was the head of a company. He says, 'This guy's gonna make *Last Temptation*.' The guy looked at me and laughed in my face. 'Yeah, right. Call me next week.' I mean, I'd come through all those years to get that? It was like a kick in the heart."

Finally, Scorsese set it up at Paramount, only to have the studio pull the plug well into preproduction. "I had to make up my mind whether I really wanted to continue making films. There was such negativity. So what do you do? Stay down dead? No. I realized then, you can't let the system crush your spirit. I'm a director, I'm going to try to be a pro and start all over again. I'll make a low-budget picture, *After Hours*. And then went a couple of notches up the ladder with *The Color of Money,* working with major stars and that sort of thing."

Neither *After Hours* nor *Last Temptation,* when it was finally made in 1988, was successful, critically or commercially. Scorsese, who had feared never being more than the darling of critics, was in danger of losing that slim solace. He had still to learn how to subject his vision to the requirements of the industry. Searching for a new film, he turned down *Sea of Love* and *White Palace* from Universal. It wasn't until 1989, with his episode of *New York Stories,* generally recognized as the best of the three (Woody Allen and Francis Coppola supplied the others), that he regained a piece of critical ground.

Then, in 1990, a decade after his masterpiece, *Raging Bull,* and thirteen years after his last critically acclaimed hit, *Taxi Driver, GoodFellas* proved that he could make art and money at the same time. Martin Scorsese had returned from Gethsemane.

Now the days of drugs and even asthma are behind him. "I haven't had a serious attack in more than a year," he says. With the relative security of his Universal deal and his apparently unassailable critical status, life seems to be looking up. Or does it? He's worried about the perception of him as a film artist—the "*a*-word," as he calls it—and corrects himself when he inadvertently uses the term "cinema" instead of "movies." "I don't want anybody to think we're talking about art," he says. "It's a stigma in the commercial area of movies. A stigma."

He's angry and disappointed that he didn't win an Oscar for *GoodFellas.* "I wish I could be like some of the other guys and say, 'No, I don't care about it.' But for me, a kid growing up on the Lower East Side watching from the first telecast of the Oscars, and being obsessed by movies, there's a certain magic that's there. When I lost for *Raging Bull,* that's when I realized what my place in the system would be, if I did survive at all: on the outside looking in. The Academy sent out a very strong message to the people who made *GoodFellas* and *The Grifters,* no matter how talented they are, that they may get some recognition, but they will not get the award. It just turns out that I produced *The Grifters.* And I certainly got the message."

Scorsese is philosophical about it, sort of. But his friends and collaborators are not. Says Jodie Foster, "When you look at the ten old ladies who put down *Dances With Wolves* instead of *GoodFellas*—I don't know. The Oscars are like bingo. Who cares?" And Paul Sorvino, who played Paul Vario in *GoodFellas,* says, "It's an outrage and a scandal in my mind. What does the man have to do?" Harvey Keitel sums it up: "Maybe he got what he deserves—exclusion from the mediocre."

With his recent success and his virtual canonization, the pressures upon him have, if anything, increased. Bigger budgets, more responsibility (he's producing *Mad Dog and Glory,* from a Richard Price script, starring De Niro and Bill Murray). He's joined forces with Spielberg on *Cape Fear,* and he's moving from his cluttered office in the historic Brill Building on the seedy West Side of New York to MCA's sleek East Coast corporate headquarters on Park Avenue. The move across town is as much symbolic as physical. It could well be the beginning of Marty's Excellent Adventure, his attempt to enter the mainstream on his own terms. The risks are great: commercial failure on the one hand, selling out on the other. "You wanna audience," says Price, who wrote *The Color of Money,* "you gotta play ball. He wants to make big personal movies—the best actors he can get, the biggest audience he can get, to make the smallest films he can make."

Schrader speculates about the direction of Scorsese's career: "*Cape Fear* is the first time he's worked with such a large budget since *New York, New York,* and it demands an audience level and a mainstream sensibility that he's not completely comfortable with. Marty's a conglomerate now. But I think at the end of the day, no matter how hard he tries to sell out, he can't really do it. The thing with Spielberg is a marriage of convenience. We're talking Warren Beatty and Madonna."

Scorsese tried very hard not to get involved with *Cape Fear.* "Bob De Niro and Spielberg asked me to read the script while I was finishing up *GoodFellas,*" he recalls. "And by the end of the editing of the film, I had read *Cape Fear* three times. And three times I hated it. I mean really hated it." The original script took its cues from the 1962 movie, which starred Gregory Peck as an improbably virtuous family man and Robert Mitchum as the psycho, Max Cady, who gets out of jail and goes after Peck for testifying against him. "I thought the family was too clichéd, too happy," says Scorsese. "And then along comes the bogeyman to scare them. They were like Martians to me. I was rooting for Max to get them." But Spielberg and De Niro, who wanted to play Cady, wouldn't take no for an answer. "Finally, Steve says, 'Marty, you dislike this version of the script?' I said 'Yes! Whaddya want from me?' He said, 'Why don't you rewrite it?' And I said, 'Of course!'"

Scorsese Freudianized—or, as he prefers to think of it, Catholicized—the script. It became a drama of sexual guilt and punishment. He shifted the focus to the emotional pathology of the family, with Lange suffering from the aftereffects of Nolte's infidelity and Nolte trying to deal with his daughter's emerging sexuality. "Cady was sort of the malignant spirit of guilt, in a way, of the family—the avenging angel," Scorsese says. "Punishment for everything you ever felt sexually. It is the basic moral battleground of Christian ethics."

Scorsese pauses, laughs. "This sounds like every other picture I've ever made. I could talk this to death. It's ridiculous, but I've got to be careful. Otherwise, people say, 'It's some sort of religious film. I don't want to see it.' Don't listen to any of this! It's a thriller. Go see it! Enjoy yourself!"

When all is said and done, Scorsese has been fortunate. Despite, or rather because of, his failures and struggles, his wanderings on the wild side, he is perhaps the only filmmaker from that enormously hopeful generation of the '70s to have truly fulfilled his promise. Some, like Coppola, have made great movies — *The Godfathers, The Conversation, Apocalypse Now* — but Scorsese has done more than that. He's made a career. He's survived in a business notorious for burning out talent and has arrived at the '90s at the peak of his creative powers. *GoodFellas* was so assured, so perfectly realized, that it is hard to imagine he will stumble as badly as he did in the '80s. "Maybe it was because I fell from grace earlier," he says. "Maybe because other people went through the terror later, so it was harder for them to come back."

The movies have always been Scorsese's life. But along the way he picked up a considerable amount of baggage, including four wives and two daughters. Now approaching 50, he has had to make difficult choices. "I just started divesting myself of all these complications. Your personal life, you know, you deal with as best you can. But you even divest that.

"All the way up until, I'd say, '84, '85, every Sunday my mother and father, my friends would come over. We'd have a big Italian dinner. Whatever different marriages — whatever was going on. It was really good, like the Italian family that I remember growing up. But I don't expect much from people anymore, and I don't really want them to expect much from me. Except when it comes to the work, [where] you're gonna get the best from me. You're alone. That's the way it goes."

The thing that may save Scorsese, finally, from the vertigo of fame is his humility before the shrine of "cinema." As much as he serves as mentor for struggling young directors, as much as he has become a force on the film-preservation scene, as much as he has matured into a disciplined director, he is in many ways still a student. As Barbara Hershey puts it, "His love of film over himself is the great leveler."

"You've gotta be careful," says Scorsese, "because you hear talk: 'Well, Marty, people say in Hollywood, your films are really good and you're one of the best around. . . .' It's an odd thing. You can't believe it, first of all. I think a lot of the pictures I've made are good. But they're not *The Searchers*. They're not *8 1/2*. *The Red Shoes*. *The Leopard*. What I'm saying is I have my own criteria in my head that's private. There's constantly a test. Constantly a final exam every minute of my life. Literally, I have the image of myself always keeping my nose right above the water, the waves always getting to me and about to sink me. . . . I just hope that, you know, *Cape Fear* makes money."

Martin Scorsese Interviewed

GAVIN SMITH/1993

GAVIN SMITH: *Was there a first image that came to you when you were thinking about making* Age of Innocence?

MARTIN SCORSESE: I think the strongest image had something to do with May's face, when she says, "I'm afraid you can't do that, dear." There's something about her face—even before I cast Winona Ryder. It had to do with the eyes and the almost impenetrable framing of her: how wide the shot should be, what should be in the frame with her. Wharton was writing her pretty much through Newland Archer's eyes, so that you go along with him and underestimate her—which I think is wonderful. When the realization hits him in that scene . . . I was interested in the way she presented herself at that moment. Later on I figured out that as she gets up from the chair we should do it in three cuts, three separate close-ups, because I think he'll never forget that moment the rest of his life. He'll play it back many times. When she gets up, I thought we should play it back like a memory. It's a medium shot, then a shot of her coming up in the frame, and then a third one—she almost grows in stature. It's just his perception, his memory of what it's going to be like. I said, If we can get away with that, that'd be great. We shot it very quickly, two takes each, one at 24 frames, one at 36, and one 48.

GS: *Why the different speeds?*

MS: There's something about the way the dress moves. It seemed like a flower opening or something, growing. At 24 frames it was too quick, but

---

From *Film Comment,* November/December 1993. Reprinted by permission.

at 48 it might be better. Not too slow, but a little overcranking. We hardly touched that scene in the cutting.

G S : *There's very little camera movement in that scene; it has a stillness to it, in contrast to the movie up until then.*
M S : The only move is when she gets up and walks towards him; the camera's moving in on him and she enters frame and then it booms down as she kneels, which was a very hard shot to get—one of those strange things, easy to imagine but difficult to operate.

G S : *Were there any other distinct stylistic choices for that scene?*
M S : It's the only time that you see them in a wide, theatrical, almost proscenium frame at the beginning of the scene. He's sitting all the way in the left of the frame and she comes in on the right. It's like they're on stage—and now the final act is gonna be played out. I like that. And the tension of the frames and the cutting, how wide the frame is, how tight it is on him and on her: that to me was fun. It's just a matter of the separateness of the two of them—medium shot of him, medium shot of her, and then she draws it all together, so you see the two-shot looking down at them and then begin the pan around the room. It was kind of difficult to figure out how wide or tight the shots should be. Big closeups there wouldn't have worked.

G S : *I was struck by the undertone of comedy in the scene.*
M S : Yeah. It's very funny, actually. We improvised a little bit, one of the few times we improvised, when he tries to explain to her—"I feel awfully tired and I think I'd like to make a break," and she says, "From the law," which is right from the book, and he says "That too...yes." So that it might be easier if he says, "I want to give up everything," if he bunches it all together, it gives him a way out to talk to her about it.

G S : *I thought there was a certain comic edge to Newland's key reaction shot.*
M S : It's the checkmate. He's caught. That was it. "You see I was right." Suddenly after all that time underestimating the person and everybody around him: that was fascinating. Just the overwhelming realization is funny. It's not at his expense, it's just the humor that I see, a certain kind of horror humor. That scene was the key scene that made me say I have to make this picture.

Also the preceding scene at the dinner. Rather than playing it out in normal dramaturgy in terms of him at the head of the table talking to Ellen and everybody smiling, I decided to use mainly voiceover, literally from the book. The gracefulness of the prose has a kind of scathing, ironic violence to it: the shot begins high looking over the table and you hear, "It was considered the most important thing for a young couple to give their first proper dinner." She describes everybody at the table, gilt-edged menus, Roman punch, etc., and then the camera comes up on his face for the words "farewell dinner for the Countess Olenska." It also has a kind of funny horror to it. And then the camera booms all the way back. I just imagined the camera went up and you'd have the table; that [would be] enough. But when we got the camera up there and I realized we had the footmen there, too, all around the room like guards, I said, This is wonderful—the armed camp! [*Laughs.*] So much fun!

And then Newland out of sorts in the library when the men are having cigars and brandy, and Michael Gough takes him over to the fireplace, he's talking about cooking, nonsense really, and the camera moves in on the back of Newland's head, music comes up, and the wall goes red, like a blush. And as that dissolves into the image of him walking into the other drawing room, the red goes out over the dissolve and the camera pans off his face and you hear bits and pieces of people conversing, either cutting people up hypocritically or talking about trivial things—like May talking about getting a bronze reduction of the Venus de Milo, which I love.... It's all right, I have silly things around my rooms, too, but: it's just that if you have to live with that level of conversation for the rest of your life, it's very very disturbing, to say the least.

G S : *When the wall blushes red, was that done with light or did you also have to do something in the processing lab?*
M S : We did the wall turning red on the set, but the image we dissolve to was normal color and the red went away too quickly; it was like a jump in color. The only way to do it was to smooth out the red optically over the dissolve, and as the full image comes in and the other image is fading out, gradually lose the red also.

G S : *What were you trying to evoke in those "color-outs" that ended certain scenes?*

M S :   The fades to red and yellow. I was interested in the use of color like brushstrokes throughout the film, the sensuality of painting, how the characters expressed themselves by sending each other flowers. The flowers could be sensual, but they couldn't allow *themselves* to be overtly sensual, so it just didn't seem right to fade to black; it had to be something rich in color and texture. Sometimes the colors were darker images. When the voiceover says, "The refusals were more than a simple snubbing. They were an eradication," Ellen looks towards the camera and it goes a rust color, rather than a bright color like red. The yellow bursts open when she gets the yellow flowers, but I was stuck. We couldn't go from yellow to another color, so we went to white in the aviary.

We spent a long time on exactly how long the bursts of color should be on the screen. In [Michael Powell's] *Black Narcissus* there's a use of orange when Kathleen Byron faints. Later on, in *Rear Window,* [Hitchcock does it,] too, with the flashbulbs.

G S :   *Your handling of time transitions is interesting—you seem to draw time out using dissolves. For instance, the establishing shots of the Beaufort ball....*
M S :   I just didn't want to take shots of people arriving. It gets to be kind of boring. We do have the arrival and entry of Newland. But it was also like opening up an old music box and seeing all the people appear and dance to the music; all these ghosts, the past, comes alive in a way and takes you into another time and place.

G S :   *What about much later, when you dissolve Ellen and Newland's respective exits from the veranda in Boston?*
M S :   There, it's that he never wants to take his eyes off her and she fades away. He puts his head down and he fades away, like his soul goes with her. It's very romantic, I guess, but I felt they just had to fade away. I even added this voiceover that's not in the book, about how he might see her at a party, he might be seated next to her at a dinner; when you're carrying that kind of torch, just that idea alone keeps you living for a while. The fact that she fades away makes it more poignant to me.

G S :   *You knew you'd use dissolves before you shot it?*
M S :   Yeah, I imagined it that way.

GS: *When you shoot each scene, do you have a tentpole image around which the rest of the coverage falls into place that you make sure to get during that day's shooting?*

MS: Yes. Absolutely. Practically every scene. Usually it's the first image. Sometimes I live a little dangerously and figure it out when I get there.

GS: *At what point did you realize you could previsualize and precut scenes shot by shot in your head from text?*

MS: In school. NYU film school was not what it is now. There were very few film classes. The majority of classes were required courses: liberal arts, English, classics. I didn't do much reading when I was a kid because we didn't have any books in the house; my mother and father were garment-district workers who never read. So I grew up watching movies on TV. When I did start to read, it was in high school. I still have a problem reading; I do more these days but not as much as I'd like to.

Images would come to me as I was reading books or listening to music. It started when I was putting together my first short film. It was all precut in my head. It was an easy film to do because it was based on kind of an Ernie Kovacs/Steve Allen sense of humor—anything happens. Truffaut's cut in *Shoot the Piano Player* where the crook says "May my mother drop dead" and the mother drops dead. All that mixed together, plus a couple of short films directed by Ernie Pintoff; a Mel Brooks sense of humor. And it used narration, which meant you could cut any which way you wanted.

GS: *Any film where you didn't previsualize?*

MS: Yes, *New York, New York*. However, not the "Happy Endings" sequence; that was shot first, and all the musical sequences with Tommy Dorsey and his band, the jazz sequences with De Niro playing the saxophone—all worked out in advance. Everything else was pretty much improvised. I wasn't very happy with the improvising. You have to fail in order to know where you're gonna go. The trick of failing is that with smaller films it's easier. But with studio money it's a real problem. We took all those chances on that film.

These days, however, I come up with one or two shots that have to be in the scene that involve camera movement or cutting or some device, some visual vocabulary, and then fit that to wherever I shoot it. I visualize, but at the same time you open it up a bit. There's a way to keep that balance. I don't know how you keep it, I can't say that if you keep the balance you get 20 percent as opposed to 80 percent—you don't know. That's part of the tension of making the picture, a tension you can't avoid. When I get there I say, Oh, I wonder where I'm gonna open it up today, where's it gonna go another way? You're aware that anything can happen and you want to keep the life of the scene and keep breathing, and yet: You need two tracks at the same time.

When May says, "I showed Ellen my ring," in the aviary, we move from her face to see his face on the words "Ellen" and "ring." And what I did then for coverage was a mirror image shot the opposite way, same movement. Who knows? Maybe you intercut the two.

G S : *You can't cut from moving to static shots and back.*

M S : You could cut from movement to nonmovement in certain cases, but in that kind of move you can't; it just doesn't look right, it's too jarring. I'm interested more in the dancelike effect of it. Especially when the camera dances around to see his face with no expression at all as he takes the news that she showed Ellen the ring.

If you go back and look at the picture, you notice how if you look at May earlier in the film you can see her looking at Ellen at the moment where they go to Mrs. Mingott's right after the ball and her mother's helping her with her coat; she glances over at Ellen. That's the first time. And you can watch every scene with her, like the aviary scene: the dialogue is "I sent roses to your cousin Ellen, was that right?" and she says, "Oh *very* right." Then she lets him know that Mr. van der Luyden sent a hamper of flowers and Mr. Beaufort sent flowers too. Oh! [*Gesturing to indicate a knife twisted in his stomach.*] She's so good.

G S : *Just the fact that you reveal his face at that moment is enough to make the point.*

M S : Exactly.

G S : *It's a good example of the camera indicating that something's going on in a character without the actor having to indicate.*

M S : Exactly. A cut can do that.

G S : *That's the definition of a reaction shot—not that the actor reacts but that the cut implies a reaction.*

M S : And sometimes the problem is when to cut. One of the hardest scenes to cut was when he goes to Mrs. Mingott to talk about moving up the wedding and she tells him about Ellen's past life in Europe. We had a little problem with who to be on. Basically, Mrs. Mingott is giving us exposition but we need to see the effect on him. It looks so simple, but it wasn't.

G S : *Her line about being surprised Newland wasn't interested in Ellen is the perfect moment for a cut to him.*
M S : We had to cut to him to see his reaction. If you look at it, though, he waits a beat, then he reacts, like he can't believe she said that.

I guess it's a cliché, but even though my taste in movies are all kinds — from Stan Brakhage to Bresson, Russian, Japanese and Chinese films, Maya Deren — over the years I'm pretty much stuck in narrative cinema, and I'm stuck with certain forms, and I'm playing around with those forms. Especially in a picture like this, where I didn't want to develop the film to a climactic sequence and handle that sequence in a normal narrative dramatic style. The dinner party could have been done very straight — and could have been just as effective with everybody smiling and looking at him and next thing you know he says goodbye to Ellen. . . . We could have played it out dramatically, but I wanted to display it, like he's in a display case, and have the prose add that extra dramatic punch.

G S : *The use of dissolves in the film is very unusual.*
M S : It's like painting. I stumbled onto it. A lot of them were scripted. However, again, unintelligently, designing certain shots — for example, in the conservatory scene at the ball: Newland says he wants to kiss May, it dissolves and he kisses her and they start to move, and it dissolves and they're sitting down. It was all shot as one take, and it just took ages to get them to sit down.

G S : *So it's time deletion.*
M S : Yes, it's really just pragmatic. But what was happening was that besides the dissolves that were indicated in the script, I stumbled upon the idea of shortening many of the shots that I took, sort of like a brush coming through and painting bits and pieces of color, swishing by. Texture, it's all about texture. The one I like the most is a very simple one: the dinner scene in France during the honeymoon montage. It's a high angle of the table,

and the camera booms down and dissolves as the camera's going over the table and the food, and then it tilts up and you see Jonathan Pryce and Daniel Day-Lewis talking. That was all one shot, and as I was doing this I thought, This is impossible, how many more tracks along the table are we going to stand in this picture? And I said, Let's pull the middle out of the shot. And that is one of the best ones of all because it looks like an Impressionist painting.

G S : *So there is a whole dimension of the visual style that you didn't conceive of until after you finished shooting.*
M S : Right. But I did know if anything it was gonna be dissolves. I knew going in that we were going to use more dissolves than usual, as opposed to *GoodFellas* where it was mainly cutting.

G S : *The dissolves also reinforce the impression of seamless, continuous surface.*
M S : I didn't want it broken up. I liked it to be smoother.

G S : *Is it fair to say you're torn between strict narrative and more digressive impulses?*
M S : Absolutely. This is the gamble I took with this picture. There's no doubt. I've been lucky enough in the past few months to talk to Elia Kazan a lot about some of this, and he also has been interested over the years in trying to tell a narrative story differently rather than be stagebound, let's say to three acts. Again, the last sequence, the most important sequence in the film, the farewell dinner for the Countess: the narration is restating the obvious, very often. In a funny way it has an almost distancing effect. It's kind of interesting.

G S : *Another divided aspect of your approach to the film is that you want both an intensely involving emotional texture and a distanced, standing-back from the action. The film shifts between these two perspectives.*
M S : Yeah. That's the feeling living in a society like that, or if you've ever experienced anything like what's happening in the story. Myself, I've found that's what happens. Incredibly subjective passion, and then finding a way to distance yourself because something just isn't right to be done at the moment, isn't right to be acted upon or just doesn't work out, and therefore, in public or in other situations, you have to find a distancing effect,

to keep your emotions distant. There's a kind of humor and understanding that comes with the phrase "It just isn't done." Okay, it isn't done. Meantime, it's happening. Meantime, the feelings are going on. But they just aren't acted upon. I find that to be very funny, and also to be very telling of society and the way people act.

G S : *You've used first-person voiceover in a number of your films but never third-person, which is more unusual. Did you see the narrator (Joanne Woodward) as an autonomous character?*
M S : I wanted to give the audience the impression of the feelings I had when I read the book. Literally as is, Edith Wharton. It's a narrator who's very tricky, who's presenting the story in this way to teach you a lesson.

G S : *Did you have a discussion about how you conceived the narrator?*
M S : Never did. The first time that came up was from the studio. Columbia Pictures asked, "Who's the narrator?" I said, "Who cares?" The narrator's telling the story.

G S : *Is the camera in complicity with the narrator?*
M S : I think in certain scenes, like the dinner scene, absolutely. Using what may seem to be obvious voiceover narration with the imagery — people said, "You don't need the voiceover." Well, maybe not, but I preferred it. Yeah, you could take the voiceover out and just have music there.

G S : *You never considered making it without a voiceover?*
M S : Oh, never. I love that idea of a female voice, taking us through, very nicely, and setting us up for the fall. That's the whole thing. You get to trust the voice and then she does you in [*laughs*], like he gets done in. I thought that was so wonderful, I can't lose that aspect of it.

G S : *Is it that the narrator withholds what she knows about May or doesn't realize it at first?*
M S : I think she withholds. Maybe. It's part of the lesson that's to be learned.

G S : *At many other times the camera seems tied to Newland's subjectivity. For instance, when he imagines Ellen coming up behind and embracing him at the*

cottage, the composition is identical to the opening shot of the two actors in the
play that moved him so much a few scenes earlier.
M S : Very much — he talks about taking the image away with him.

G S : *So at such moments, the film's images seem to originate in Newland's*
subjectivity.
M S : Maybe it's a mixture. To mix all this together may not be the right
thing to do, but I don't know what's right and what's wrong, really, when
I'm making a movie. I think you make your own set of rules for each one
in terms of the subjectivity of the piece. In fact, the ball sequence begins
with the narrator explaining who people are, but ends subjectively: May
looks up into the camera and who's standing there? It's Archer. But you
could look back at it and it could be Archer's point of view looking at
everyone at the ball.

G S : *That is similar to a device you use throughout the film exemplified in the*
shot where the camera moves back with Ellen as she crosses the drawing room,
then pans 180 degrees to Newland and continues, now moving in on him as her
POV and then she enters her own POV shot and sits.
M S : Yeah, right. I started playing around with that idea when I did that
"Mirror, Mirror" episode of *Amazing Stories*. Actually I did some of that in
Taxi Driver, too, where it's Travis' POV and he steps into it. Here it's more
fun because not only was the camera tracking back with her, it also slowed
down speed, overcranking, and then as we pan to him we go back to normal
speed. There's this new device that allows you to do it almost imperceptibly.

G S : *In camera rather than optically.*
M S : Right, so you get the beautiful image with no grain. The new Arriflex
camera does that. Later we use it when he sees her on Boston Common
and she's sitting there reading. The camera swish-pans, and that swish-pan
was done undercranked, and when we landed on her we got back to normal. Skip Livesy put sound effects of fluttering wings of a bird over it.

G S : *Is the use of a sound effect like that to reinforce the subjectivity of the shot?*
M S : Yeah, like a piece of music. Sometimes it's just the nature of the sensuality and texture of it. It's hard for me to describe how I feel when I listen

to a piece of music, so it's hard for me to describe. It's the experience of it. I told Skip in certain places this film is a little hard because it's not a modern world and you can't play with sounds like screeches of cars, sirens, telephones ringing, and jet plane noises, that I usually like to play with. Here it was a little difficult to figure out how the natural sounds that occur could be distorted or have them blend in with other things. Very often I think of sound effects in a piece, but later on. If you look at those three cuts that I like, where she stands up and she tells him in the last scene that he can't go, we have a sound effect of the fire crumbling.

G S : *Why did you cut in those inserts of the fireplace embers in several scenes? Are they punctuation?*

M S : Yeah—I had to be very careful with that because it was too obvious. It's in the book in the middle of the scene where he goes to her house at night to explain that she shouldn't divorce her husband; the embers fall. I kind of toyed with it, but I didn't want it to become such punctuation . . . and yet I became very interested. . . .

Sometimes I sit here in this chair [*the interview took place in the living-room of Scorsese's house on the Upper East Side*] and about one o'clock in the morning a horse and carriage goes by, and there are no cars on the street. This place was built around the 1860s. I'm transported to another century. I think about, for example, we're talking now . . . it's the 20th century. . . . If I'm sitting where you're sitting, maybe while we're talking I might be looking out the window and notice a certain red truck that goes by. I may, in the middle of a scene, cut to that and then cut back. What's happening is that the elements of their life . . . when she remembers what he told her that night, she'll always remember the sound of that fire. She'll remember what the embers looked like. It's what you focus on in important moments in important conversations. If I'm talking on the phone to somebody, looking this way at the Japanese dolls, if I look at the Japanese dolls now I'll remember that part of the conversation. I found it interesting to put myself into that time and place where during conversations they avert their eyes and look at something else. What would you listen to? The clock ticking, of course; the fireplace; and at the end of the film, after all the credits have rolled, we do a little trick, the horse and carriage goes by. That's the sound I hear at night sometimes. That's for the purists.

G S : *It's a refinement of the freezeframes in* GoodFellas.

M S : Yes, but it's very dangerous because I didn't want them to be exclamation points. In *GoodFellas* it could be an explanation point: BANG, they freeze. "Now let me tell you what's happening here. They've just told me to go down south to kill somebody. I know exactly what he means, he wants me killed. This is my closest friend and mentor—and now how am I going to behave?" And BANG, back into normal speed. It's almost like an aside to the audience; it's kind of funny, it comes right out of Truffaut and Ernie Kovacs. [In *Age of Innocence*] it's not emphatic. I'm trying to make it that sense of memory and loss, déjà vu almost.

G S : *So it captures the phenomenon of nostalgia for the present as it unfolds—memories of things as they occur in the present tense.*

M S : Right. As you get older—I'll be 51 soon—you're nostalgic for certain relationships, people, events, right when they begin. When you say hello, you have that moment of, Oh, it's over already. The story's so emotionally powerful that I wanted all the characters to remember everything that was happening at the moment when all those conversations were taking place. The clock ticking. The fireplace. The horse and carriage going by. The flutter of birds wings. Kids playing in the park. When they see a kid walking a dog, they'll remember the time on Boston Common.

G S : *How does that relate to the emphasis on the details and trappings of their lives, which aren't essential information but don't seem incidental, either?*

M S : What I thought was interesting about that was all these details are presented in the book. In that society, they mean something to these people—each plate, each piece of china. It was almost like having a High Mass.

G S : *You're trying to break down the traditional schism between filmic and novelistic detail.*

M S : It really doesn't get done right in movies, and I wanted to do it like a novel—you're right about that. For the first 40 minutes of the picture you have a lot of that, up until the point when Ellen crosses the room and sits down with Newland. Then the picture proper begins, in a way. Up to that point it's setting the scene and going off to what may seem like extraneous detail. In actuality the details give you the impression of what he has to cut through in order to break away from that society. If you don't show it, I think you'd have a sense of why doesn't he just leave? But if you keep adding and keep adding imagery of details, and keep explaining what these details mean, that there is nothing casual about anything, then you begin to realize how difficult it is for him to make a move. Because he's been bred that way. If he came in from the outside, it wouldn't mean anything. He can't make a move.

Very often I just like the idea of ritualistic use of objects. Table manners: Americans cut their meat and then put the knife down and take the fork in our right hand and eat a piece of meat. The British cut the meat and then use the fork with the left hand and bring it up to their mouth upside down. Now which is right and which is wrong? It doesn't matter. But in the society you're in, it matters. I find that fascinating, the arbitrariness of it and what it signifies.

G S : *Tell me about the way information is presented in the opening sequence by combination of camera movement and editing. You make them function together.*
M S : I was more interested in what I normally did with the music in *New York, New York* and *The Last Waltz* and all the fight scenes in *Raging Bull*, which were constructed like music. I just wanted to get the impression of the richness of the texture of a night at the opera and the audience almost being more interesting to look at than what was going on on stage. I wanted to get a visual counterpart to the power of the music, again by listening to the music and envisioning the camera moves.

G S : *What about the flickering, strobe editing effect where you pan across the audience?*
M S : I couldn't bring myself to take a shot and put the usual mask over it that shows that he's looking through opera glasses. You put a little black mask over it and then you just pan around the audience. It's very boring, and I know you don't do that; it doesn't look that way if you do it with opera glasses. I was almost literalizing the effect of what it looks like when you look through binoculars and try to pick up certain details. Stumbling through that, we fell upon the idea of exposing one frame at a time, stop action, and then printing that frame three times and then dissolving

between each shot so that each three frames was a dissolve. That took about a year to figure out. It was so complicated that it was the last thing I finished in the film.

G S : *That was the moment when I realized this was not going to be like any other film I'd seen before.*

M S : Good. That's great. When you look through binoculars in a place like that, it's almost a kaleidoscope of images; you see so many things on the periphery of your eyes. I just wanted to create a sense of that, not literally a re-creation—because I don't believe in literal effects that way. I remember in *Odd Man Out,* a film I love, there's a device that's used in the bar where people start speaking through the beer bubbles on the table. It was a little too literal; the tortured poetry of the film didn't even need that. It was okay, it was really not destructive, [but] I didn't want to be that literal.

G S : *You must think very carefully about what will be the first image in a film.*

M S : Absolutely, yeah.

G S : *So what's the significance of opening on the flowers and then the camera moves up to the opera singer's face and then pulls all the way back?*

M S : Well, it was the flowers. He loves me, he loves me not. I knew that the first image had to be flowers, that's for sure.

G S : *Why isn't the flower motif resolved at the end of the film?*

M S : Well, times change. Sometimes it's beyond resolution, it's been used up, like a good luck charm that maybe you've used up all the good luck from.

G S : *In terms of how it moves and cuts, the film seems to slow down as it progresses, until it's almost still at the end. Was that a conscious stylistic arc?*

M S : Oh yeah. It seems to slow down, and at the same time, in the last 15 minutes a lot happens, it speeds up. Slowing down in the last part has to do with the older age. You just take a little extra time to do things when you're older. The melancholy of him sitting there in the Paris hotel room, the look on his face standing outside Madame Olenska's apartment—it just takes longer.

G S :   *Throughout the film you frequently pan from Daniel Day-Lewis to what he's looking at, from subject to object. In that last scene, when he looks up at Michelle Pfeiffer's apartment, you use cuts instead of pans. Why?*

M S :   You better cut because the audience is ahead of you. Why do you need to pan? And even if you pan and skip frames to make it quick, it's overstating the case. The other point is you're always tying the two together when you're panning. Here, you can't do that. Not anymore. They can't be together the way they were before. They'll always be together in their hearts. But one cannot ignore the complete separateness of the jump. It's got to be a brutal cut straight to the window. Can't pan it.

G S :   *My impression is that the pan has fallen into disuse in recent years. You seem to be working hard to revive it as a useful piece of filmic vocabulary.*

M S :   I'm trying, but what's happened is that, because of the ability of audiences to accept more information, a film has to move faster and quicker, and very often panning, if you don't want it to strobe [*i.e., cause a flickering effect in the image*], has to be slow and slows down a picture. So if you can find a way to make it quicker and unite the two people without overstating it, that's great. Panning works in location-type situations, a desert or a jungle or a city, where you can pan straight across — start with two characters, pan them out of the frame, and you pan across and see other things going by, and you see the entire world and you pan over to something that's going on across the street. You can utilize that in the narrative and then you don't have to swish it over. Very often, in the old days, you watch a pan across a desert, showing you the desert — okay, come on! It worked then, but now people don't seem to want to go for it. People are ahead of you all the time, so you have to find real uses for it.

G S :   *Do you try to break a film down into acts stylistically as well as in terms of narrative?*

M S :   Practically every film I do. *Raging Bull* a lot. I remember being affected by Carl Dreyer's *Gertrud*. He alternated very static scenes between Gertrud and her ex-lovers with flashbacks that were overexposed, and used a very fast-moving camera. Here's a guy in his seventies when he made the film, still had a lot of energy and incredible visual poetry. I was very affected by such a free use of imagery, somebody breaking this very static scene. I felt the fight scenes in *Raging Bull* should be like those flashbacks in *Gertrud*; they should open up and the camera should just fly, it should have that kind of breaking of the narrative. Anything could happen.

G S :   *Why did you shoot* Age of Innocence *in widescreen?*
M S :   Actually it's arbitrary. Ever since I saw my first widescreen movie, *The Robe,* at the Roxy Theater, I've wanted to use widescreen. I was II at the time, I think; I went home and did my drawings in widescreen. I never used widescreen until now because of the panning and scanning problems on TV. But I've always wanted to do everything in widescreen.

G S :   *So by shooting in nonanamorphic Super 35 you get around the pan-and-scan drawback.*
M S :   Yes. But also, the more restricted they are as characters, the more locked in to this prison of a world, it almost makes them more lonely. On TV it should be very interesting because it's full frame and I love the way it looks full frame also.

G S :   *Why was* Cape Fear *shot in Panavision rather than Super 35?*
M S :   That was very tricky because of the thriller aspect. I wanted to see if we could create a psychological thriller for the widescreen. It was the first time I used anamorphic lenses, and I wanted to learn. I thought it was time to start using widescreen because purists who were interested to see the composition of the films invariably would look at it on TV with a laserdisc. That's happening now, and American Movie Classics often shows widescreen films letterboxed; in about five years the TV screen's gonna get wider anyway.

G S :   *Some DPs really don't like Super 35. They don't think it has the resolution of anamorphic.*
M S :   I'll tell you why I chose it here. I think DePalma had a hard time with it on *Bonfire of the Vanities* because you can't make a print from your original negative; you always use your dupe because you can squeeze the image and go on to an internegative. But the lenses that do the squeez-ing—I believe Technicolor's bought some new ones and they did a beautiful job on *Age of Innocence,* and we were very concerned about it. You do give up a certain amount of quality. Not a lot, but enough. The problem with anamorphic for me was that I discovered I only had the use

of maybe five lenses, and so when I was doing *Cape Fear* there were certain shots I designed that took me a very long time to get, because of the lenses I was using. Michael Ballhaus pointed out to me that in Super 35 you can use any size lens and we could shoot faster and get exactly the shots I wanted, so you could use a 10mm lens—which we did at times—for the overhead shots of the table.

G S : *You use long lenses in only a couple of places in* Age of Innocence.
M S : I really dislike long lenses. . . . I was gonna say intensely, but I should-n't, because Kurosawa's use of long lenses is just extraordinary. In *Raging Bull* I shot one fight, the first Sugar Ray fight, with long lenses, designed it to have that one look, put some flames in the foreground to mirage the image. That worked for me there. When long lenses came into use in the Sixties, I thought they were so overused; and the image seems amorphous to me, it doesn't have a direction. I'm not talking about the use of long lenses by, say, Peckinpah, where he shot action pieces with maybe six cam-eras and intercut it all. The actual power of the piece is in the cutting; it's all choreography and music, in a way—his films are like music. So you can't say, "Oh there's one long-lens shot, I don't like it." No, it all blends together, and he shoots so many different angles. But I'm talking about people standing on a street corner and picking up some shots of people in the distance—there's nothing to it.

G S : *It's always struck me as bad grammar—say, in a dialogue scene—to cut from a long-lens shot of one actor to a prime-lens reverse angle of the other.*
M S : Oh, it's ridiculous. It's happened a few times to me. In *New York, New York* we shot only with a 32mm lens, the whole movie. We tried to equate the old style of framing, the old style meaning 1946–53. But I use long lenses every now and then.

G S : *In* Age of Innocence *there's the shot of the crowd coming up Fifth Avenue, a sea of faces.*
M S : I should have used a longer lens. I got there and realized it should have been longer, or maybe the camera should have been angled down further. I just saw the image in my head that way. I found that image while I was looking at some films saved from Otoscope rolls. Otoscope, you used to put a nickel or a dime in whatever it was at the turn of the

century; [It was like] a flipbook of pictures. You used a crank, and as you cranked the images would flip by and they would move, but they were on paper. The Library of Congress has been able to save a whole bunch of those and put them onto a negative. One was a wideshot of Broadway, the camera looking sort of down, you see the whole street and the sidewalks. The street was as it is today—a mess. Horsedrawn carriages, horsedrawn trolleys, nobody could walk in the street, horse manure all over the place. So everybody's packed on the sidewalk on the right of the frame, all wearing the same bowler hat, all going to work. I also noticed from those Library of Congress films that before the high buildings were built in New York, it was very windy because of the two rivers. Hats were flying. All packed on the sidewalk. Today people could cross the street a little easier than they could in those days, because of the horses—anything could happen; if you look in the old newspapers, there were lots of accidents every week with animals in the street.... And so I imagined all those people walking together, looking the same, as being a predominant image of that period.

G S : *What exact function does that image have?*
M S : Well, it comes off the fading out of her out on the veranda; then he fades away, and rather than go straight to him meeting the secretary, Monsieur Rivière, there should have been this transition of the next stage of their lives, how they're gonna conduct themselves.

G S : *Obviously in this film, opera, theater, and painting perform a similar function as going to the movies does in all your films from* Mean Streets *to* Cape Fear*—as a combined narrative comment and psychological index. But this film perhaps has a far greater investment than your others in spectatorship and the interpretation of the visible. And exposure to art is often a pivotal experience for the characters.*
M S : Absolutely. To hear an opera, to hear a part you liked, you either had to learn to play it on the piano yourself or view it every time it came to town. The same with the plays. He would leave before the play was over so that was the last image in his mind. You had to make a *real effort* to appreciate and relish certain works of art. Go to a museum and stand there and look at a painting, not just buy a book with reproductions. That's your only chance. That's it.

GS: *What purpose do the various paintings serve within the film?*
MS: Paintings were so important; like movies to us today. Mrs. Mingott had many genre paintings with dogs. Mrs. Archer has genre paintings of Italian peasants and that sort of thing. I studied a lot of the genre paintings of the time, and they always had little elements that, if you keep looking at the painting, you notice more things and it tells a story, it tells a way of life. And you lived with that painting, and so I found that to be almost like theatrical experience.

Dante Ferretti had a good idea with Mrs. Mingott's house, for example. I had the idea of putting the painting of the Louvre there, so that you dissolve into the painting within the painting. When I said, "We'll go up the paintings along the wall up the stairs," Dante said, "Why don't we have a trip up the Hudson River?" Which is what it is — all Thomas Cole and other painters from the Hudson River Valley School.

GS: *What about the "widescreen" painting Newland looks at?*
MS: That's very important. We had to show the difference between the paintings in everybody's houses. Mr. Beaufort, for example, has more decadent paintings. Mrs. Archer has bucolic ones — cows, farmland. Mrs. Mingott, quite eccentric, puts whatever she wants on the walls. But how are we to show that Ellen was a different person with a different perspective? And how to show that to a modern audience? In other words, the paintings in her house were very different, and they were striking in their difference to Archer. My researcher, Robin Standofer, found a school of Italian painters, the Macchiaioli School, who were before the French Impressionists, and we reproduced two of those paintings — one with the woman with no face, which would certainly be shocking to the audience because it's different from what we've seen so far in the film, and another one that was painted on a long plank of wood.

GS: *Certain scenes employ striking compositional devices: for instance, the candlesticks symmetrically framing all the single shots of the Archer family in an early dinner scene. What were you trying to convey?*
MS: Simply a sense of order and propriety. Every place I turned, candles were there, so I utilized it that way to lock them in and break the frame up. I like breaking up the frames in widescreen the way Max Ophuls did in *Lola Montès,* so there's a little picture within the picture between the candles.

G S : *It makes the cuts from one person to another feel like jump cuts.*
M S : Uh huh, I know. We took that chance. I thought that would be inter-esting.

G S : *Did you shoot any other coverage for that scene?*
M S : No. Later on I do it again in the Thanksgiving dinner, where Sillerton Jackson is talking about Beaufort's financial crisis and the center of the frame is the centerpiece. You can barely figure out who's sitting where. I didn't care about that.

G S : *The first dialogue between Newland and Ellen at the van der Luydens' din-ner is covered with matching images that are a fusion of over-the-shoulder and two-shot.*
M S : They had to be in each other's frame. They couldn't be singles. I thought to do that was pretty conventional, and I was a little disturbed by it, but it was the best I could do. At a certain point I decided we should move the camera in very slowly on both angles—but again, that's pretty obvious, I think.

G S : *I didn't think the images were conventional. There's a certain dynamic in the frame.*
M S : Well, the flowers are in the frame on her angle and also the bottom half of a Joshua Reynolds. That was interesting: the flowers, the painting, her, him, all pulled together, rather than just her and him. That's what saved it for me.

G S : *In general, do you ever just feel like shooting something in a fixed master-shot, just stand back from things?*
M S : Often. I've done it a few times. Not the whole scene, but the begin-ning of the scene in the library with the proscenium business. I didn't take any coverage of that. It's just perfect. If by that time the audience isn't with the picture.... The slowness of the pace in the scene that's gonna fol-low, the excruciatingly painful pace of it hopefully, they wouldn't be with you anyway. So forget it. You might as well take a chance.

Martin Scorsese's Testament

IAN CHRISTIE/1996

WHAT DO WE EXPECT of a Scorsese film? We know what the young
Scorsese learned to expect of a Powell and Pressburger or a King Vidor—
intensity and rapture. But what do we expect when a new Scorsese is
unveiled, as *Casino* was on the final night of the London Film Festival?
Passionate commitment to a subject, consummate technical mastery, a
masterpiece amid the mediocrity of routine Hollywood.

It's a tall order, like asking an athlete to break a record on every outing.
Scorsese's films rarely earn big money, but they're as expensive to make as
those that do. So reviews and reputation are vital. His acknowledged
artistry helps the studios feel like occasional patrons of the art they daily
prostitute. But the equation is fragile, combining as it does studio pride,
critical and industry respect, and audience response to bewilderingly intense films in a bland era.

Intense like a Jacobean tragedy, in the case of *Casino*. Except this blood-
spattered triangle of love and revenge isn't set in some renaissance court,
but in a modern equivalent—the neon and rhinestone baroque of a Vegas
casino. The film opens with Sam 'Ace' Rothstein (Robert De Niro), a gifted
gambler and bookie, being blown up by a car-bomb. Ace's voiceover narration, seemingly from beyond the grave, explains how years ago he was given
Paradise-on-Earth by a murky cabal of Mafioso kingmakers, in the shape of
a new casino, the Tangiers. While Ace is the *de facto* boss at the Tangiers,
overseeing day-to-day operations and ensuring no one is swindling the

From *Sight & Sound,* January 1996. Reprinted by permission.

house, the front man is Phillip Green (Kevin Pollak). Green is a seemingly unimpeachable casino president, who has a clean record but also a secret partner, Anna Scott. The money starts to flow, and soon attracts Nicky Santoro (Joe Pesci), a violent desperado from Ace's past, who offers him his muscle; he takes charge of the bosses' skimmed share of the profits, sending them back east, a task overseen by whingeing underworld middle-manager Artie Piscano (Vinny Vella). Violently impulsive though Nicky is (at one point, to extract information, he puts a man's head in a vice), he is the kind of meticulous killer who ensures a hole in the desert sand is dug before he shows up with a 'package' in the trunk.

All goes well until Ace self-destructively chooses Ginger McKenna (Sharon Stone), a former prostitute and consummate hustler at the gaming tables, as his wife, and as the only person whom he will trust. Ace and Ginger have a child, Amy, but Ginger feels herself trapped within the marriage; turning to drink and drugs, she becomes dangerously unstable, and badly neglects Amy. Wanting to leave Ace yet determined to get what she feels her due, Ginger plots to retrieve money and jewels from a safe-deposit box and entices Nicky with sexual favours to help her. As the triangle locks into place, the authorities exploit the situation to bring down both Ace and Nicky. Worried about securing his permanent gaming licence, and to distance himself from Nicky's worsening reputation, Ace has him banned from the Tangiers. The court refuses to grant him a gaming licence anyway and, to the embarrassment of the mob, Ace starts his own television chat show to maintain his visibility. Nicky, running a lucrative set of rackets of his own, comes under surveillance while the tribute he sends back east diminishes. Finally, the godlike crime bosses demand retribution for transgressions against the established order of things.

The stuff of legend and archetype, the story of Ace, Nicky and Ginger could be told any number of ways. Co-screenwriter Nick Pileggi has told it once already in his book *Casino*: the true account of Frank 'Lefty' Rosenthal, Anthony 'Tony the Ant' Spilotro and Geri McGee (the real-life counterparts of Ace, Nicky and Ginger respectively), and how they rode the roller-coaster of mob influence in Las Vegas during the 70s. Or the story could be told as a Western, somewhere between John Sturges' *The Law and Jack Wade* and Brando's brooding *One-Eyed Jacks,* with Ace as a bad man who strikes lucky in the West and marries a saloon girl, before his past catches up with him, and unwanted acquaintances come calling.

But isn't it also *GoodFellas* 2? Yes, in that it deals with the 70s after the 60s of *GoodFellas,* finding Las Vegas an ideal microcosm of that decade's false glamour. Yes also, insofar as Scorsese and Pileggi have mined another rich vein of America's grim history of organised crime and revel insolently in their findings. But it's also darker, more complex and more ambitious. It shows with pseudo-documentary precision how Vegas ruthlessly preys on gamblers large and small to feed the insatiable appetite of the crime bosses. It shows a glittering, festering latterday Babylon surrounded by desert, in which appearance is everything, and nothing is what it seems.

Most daring of all, in the midst of this decadence, shot through with the horrors of men clubbed to death, tortured and blown up, we're invited to laugh at its rulers' foibles, admire their wit and enterprise, and finally grieve over their destruction. The Rolling Stones and Bach's *St Matthew Passion* are juxtaposed on the soundtrack, as if *GoodFellas* was erupting into the drawing rooms of *The Age of Innocence.* When the real Frank Rosenthal launched a self-advertising television show from his casino, the opening edition was hit by technical faults and the station transmitted instead, with an irony entirely appropriate to *Casino, The Fall of the Roman Empire.* Like Syberberg 'tempting' us with the seductive appeal of the Führer in *Hitler, A Film From Germany,* or Eisenstein lavishing his montage magic on the luxury of the Romanov dynasty in *October,* Scorsese in *Casino* challenges us to face up to the lure of evil, the deep fascination of Lucifer and the fallen angels that Milton understood.

Eisenstein? Milton? Come on—surely it's only rock'n'roll? Yet Scorsese's films have a habit of ageing into classic status. Again and again, his precarious miracles have been found wanting at first sight, only to reappear as milestones. Only time will tell whether *Casino* has truly done it again for him.

IAN CHRISTIE: *What was the hook that persuaded you to tackle another mafia subject after* GoodFellas?
MARTIN SCORSESE: The first newspaper article Nick Pileggi showed me was about the police covering a domestic fight on a lawn in Las Vegas one Sunday morning. And in that article it slowly began to unravel, this incredible ten-year adventure that all these people were having, culminating in this husband and wife arguing on their lawn, with her smashing his car, the police arriving, and the FBI taking pictures. As you work back to the beginning, you find this incredible story with so many tangents, and

each is one more nail in their coffin. It could be the underboss of Kansas City, Artie Piscano, constantly complaining that he always had to spend his own money on trips to Las Vegas and never got reimbursed. Or it could be the unrelated homicide that made the police put a bug in the produce market that Piscano kept in Kansas City. Even they've forgotten about it, but it picks up all his complaining and alerts FBI men round the country to all these names. They're surprised to hear the names of the Vegas casinos being mentioned in a Kansas City produce market. What's the connection?

Then, quite separately, a court decrees that Anna Scott should have her share of the money as a partner of the president of the Tangiers. But instead of settling with her, the mob shoot her, which also really happened. This then brings police attention to their frontman, the president, although he was in no way involved in the decision to kill her, and he begins to realise what's going on, although there's nothing much he can do about it. And then you have Ace Rothstein and Ginger and Nicky Santoro, all very volatile characters. I just thought it would be a terrific story.

I C : *How much is based on real characters and events?*
M S : Pretty much everything. Piscano is Carl DeLuna, who kept all those records. Mr Nance, who brings the money from the casino to Kansas City, is based on a man named Carl Thomas, who was recently killed in a car-crash. Mr Green, the Tangiers president, Rothstein, Ginger, Nicky Santoro and his brother—these are all based on real people. Sometimes things that happened in Chicago are placed in Vegas. We did have some problems about being specific, which meant saying "back home" instead of Chicago, and having to say "adapted from a true story" instead of "this film is based on a true story," which was the lawyers' language.

I C : *Was Las Vegas unfamiliar territory for you?*
M S : I'm pretty familiar with the characters around the tables and in the offices, but the actual place, and the gaming, were new to me. What interested me was the idea of excess, no limits. People become successful like in no other city.

I C : *It gives Ace a chance to create something, rather like an oldtime prospector going west, who lands in a small town and by sheer hard work makes his fortune. But because he makes the classic mistake of loving without being loved, he falls.*

M S : Well, it's his own fault. He says, "I know all the stories about her, but I don't care, I'm Ace Rothstein and I can change her." But he couldn't change her. And he couldn't control the muscle — Nicky — because if you try to control someone like that you'll be dead. When his car was blown up it was pretty obvious who gave the order for that. But as Nicky says at one point in the film, so long as they're earning with the prick *they'll* never OK anything — the gods, that is — meaning they'll never authorise killing him. But Nicky likes to be prepared, so he orders two holes to be dug in the desert. That's the way they talk. This is the actual dialogue from a witness protection programme source that we had.

I C : *It's really Sodom or Gomorrah, surrounded by the desert, isn't it?*
M S : Yes it is. We don't want to lay it on too heavily, but that was the idea. Gaining Paradise and losing it, through pride and through greed — it's the old-fashioned Old Testament story. Ace is given Paradise on Earth. In fact, he's there to keep everybody happy and keep everything in order, and to make as much money as possible so they can take more on the skim. But the problem is that he has to give way at times to certain people and certain pressures, which he won't do because of who he is.

I C : *What about the whole country-club strand? Is this because he's Jewish and wants to be accepted socially?*
M S : He says when he accepts that plaque, "Anywhere else I'd be arrested for what I'm doing. Here they're giving me awards." This is the only place he can use his expertise in a legitimate way, and so become a part of the American WASP community. That's why Nicky tells him in the desert, "I'm what's real out here. Not your country clubs and your TV show. I'm what's real: the dirt, the gutter, and the blood. That's what it's all about."

I C : *It's a great scene in a classic Western setting.*
M S : That's where they had to go to talk — in the middle of this desert. And Nicky had to change cars six times. I always imagined that the Joe Pesci character must be so angry, and getting angrier as he changes each car, until he gets out of the last one and De Niro can't say a word when he lashes right into him. But you know in this case I'm on Nicky's side. The rest *is* artifice, and if you buy into it it's hypocrisy. Know where it's coming

from and know what the reality is. Don't think you're better than me, or than the people you grew up with.

ıc : *This creates the same moral dissonance that was so powerful in* Good-Fellas, *where you want to see someone succeed, but it's the wrong business!*
ms : Very often the people I portray can't help but be in that way of life. Yes, they're bad, they're doing bad things. And we condemn those aspects of them. But they're also human beings. And I find that often the people passing moral judgment on them may ultimately be worse. I know that here in England there were film-makers and critics who felt I was morally irresponsible to make a film like *GoodFellas*. Well, I'll make more of them if I can. Remember what happens at the end of the movie, where you see Nicky and his brother beaten and buried. That's all based on fact—I saw the pictures of the real bodies when they dug up the grave. Now it's shot in a certain way, very straight. And I happen to like those people. Nicky is horrible. He's a terrible man. But there's something that happens for me in watching them get beaten with the bats and then put into the hole. Ultimately it's a tragedy. It's the frailty of being human. I want to push audiences' emotional empathy with certain types of characters who are normally considered villains.

ıc : *You go to considerable lengths to make Nicky an attractive figure. He even comes home every morning and cooks breakfast for his son . . .*
ms : Based on the real man, who did that. It's an interesting dilemma for both of them. They both buy into a situation and both overstep the line so badly that they destroy everything for everybody. A new city comes rising out of the ashes. Who knows what the realities are there now, where you've gone from a Nicky Santoro to a Donald Trump? Who knows where the money's going? But I'm sure it's got to be very, very good somehow for those entrepreneurs coming in with the money. You'll probably see a film in 15 years exposing what they're doing now. What we show in this film is the end of the old way and how it ended. They got too full of pride, they wanted more. If you're gambling you want more, like the Japanese gambler Ichikawa, who bets less money than he normally would bet when he's tricked into coming back. But for him it isn't winning 10,000, it's losing 90,000, because normally he bets 100,000.

ıc: *It's a neat little parable about gambling.*

ms: We always had problems with where it was going to be placed in the structure. But I said it's very important to keep the move into Bob's face when he says, "In the end we get it all." They do, they really do. What an interesting place, because they're a bunch of cheats, watching cheats, watching cheats. Ace Rothstein and those guys know how to cheat, with handicapping and basketball games. They make it so natural that you wouldn't be able to tell whether the game is fixed. I'm sure he has that ability.

ıc: *There's a fantastic symphony of looks in the film, with everyone watching everyone, and you push it and push it until we reach—*

ms: —the all-seeing eye. That's when he sees her for the first time. Before they had the video eye-in-the-sky, they had men with binoculars who had been cheaters up on the catwalks, trying to find other cheaters. I just thought it was really wonderful, with nobody trusting anybody.

ıc: *There's another documentary thrust in the film: how money gets skimmed and multiplied and diffused, and then distributed in equally bizarre ways.*

ms: That was 20 years ago, before the old mob lost their control. At that time every casino was 'owned' by some mob from a different part of the country. The Tangiers is fictional, but there were four—the Stardust, the Fremont, the Frontier and the Marina—which the Rothstein character controlled. So we just made them one giant hotel and combined all the elements. Where else could a great handicapper become the most impor- tant man in the city, with total control? We tried to show how far his control ran, even over the kitchen and the food. Insisting on an equal number of blueberries in each muffin may seem funny, but it's important because if the muffins and the steaks are good the people who are playing there will go and tell others. It's not just paranoia and obsessive behav- iour—there's a reason: to make the Tangiers the best place on the Strip.

ıc: *And his TV show really existed?*

ms: Totally real. When everybody wants him to quieten down, he goes on television. He forgets why he's been put there, and he gets overblown, with the clothes he wears and everything, and the old guys "back home," those guys said, "What's he doing, going on television?" The real show wasn't very good, as I think you can tell . . .

I C :   *Shades of Rupert Pupkin in* The King of Comedy.
M S :   Exactly. But he thought of it as a place to be heard, which is what it became.

I C :   *The bosses are seen in some highly stylised ways. When we see them round a table, they're like a group painted by Frans Hals.*
M S :   Yeah, they're definitely old-world.

I C :   *Then we see them in another mysterious nowhere place, with stark almost silhouette lighting like a scene from Fritz Lang.*
M S :   That's the back of the garage, and Bob Richardson lit it like that. It's where Remo says, "Go get them," and they put the guy's head in a vice — not that they intended to do that. But after two days and nights of questioning they didn't know what else to do.

I C :   *This is so excessive that we know it's got to be real, because you wouldn't invent it. But it also seems to belong to a Jacobean horror tragedy.*
M S :   It really does. The incident actually occurred in Chicago in the 60s. There was a Young-Turk argument which ended with guns and two brothers and a waitress were killed. It caused such outrage that they wanted the men who were with him also, and they finally got them and killed them all. But Joe found the human way of playing the scene: "Please don't make me do this." But he's a soldier and he has to take these orders, and he has to get that name, otherwise his head is in the vice.

I C :   *Although Ginger is as important a character as Ace and Nicky, we really only see her through their eyes and so she remains more of a mystery. Is she hustling him from the start, or does he kill whatever chance they had?*
M S :   She tells him exactly how things are in that scene where he proposes. Reaching the age of 40, if you find someone maybe you try to make it work in a reasonable way. I think they may have had a chance, if it wasn't for that city and what they were doing in it. Although I think there's something in Ace's character that ultimately destroys everything.

I C : *Does it get worse, as he gets more and more wrapped up in his role as casino boss?*

M S : I think he's responsible for the emotional alienation. You get it when she goes to the restaurant and she says, "I'm Mrs Rothstein" and the other lady says, "Well, you might as well get something out of it." It's how he treats her. He won't let her go. If he lets her go, he believes he'll just never see her again. He'll hear from her through a lawyer, but he'll never see her again.

Their daughter Amy is unfortunately just a pawn to be used. By the last third of the film, Ginger is definitely disturbed, she's no longer in her right mind. Whether it's from drugs or drink doesn't matter, she's completely gone. It doesn't excuse anything she does, but it does heighten the horror of what's going on—like tying the child up.

I C : *That really happened too?*

M S : Yes, only I think the child was younger (the real couple had two children). It's not something you'd invent; nor her reaction to Ace in the restaurant when she says, "Oh for God's sake, the babysitter wasn't there, and it was only for a little while, I was going to come right back."

I C : *Sharon Stone gives a very committed performance which shows she's got a range which hasn't always been called upon.*

M S : I agree. De Niro really helped her through those scenes. He's very generous with her and you can see how he's always helping. It's a scary role, a tough one—like when she takes cocaine in front of the child: that was her choice.

I C : *She has to spend nearly a third of the movie in a state of falling apart.*

M S : Yes, and she did that with her whole body and with the clothes. She worked with the clothes, like that David Bowie-type gold *lamé* outfit she's wearing for the last third of the picture. It's a little baggy in places, because she tried to make herself look as bad, or as wasted, as she could. You could make ten films about each of those characters, all different, and I don't know if I did justice to any of them. I just wanted to get as much in as possible, plus I wanted to get all of Vegas in there as well. And also the whole climate of the time, the 70s.

I C : *You shot the whole film in Las Vegas. Did you shoot in a real casino?*

M S : Oh yes. And we shot during working hours. Barbara De Fina figured out that the extra time it could cost would probably be the same as to build one. And you won't have the electricity and the life around you, which is what we got. We would fill the foreground with extras dressed in 70s costumes, and the background would sort of fall off. Sometimes we shot at four in the morning. I really love the scene when Joe comes in with Frank Vincent and they're playing blackjack, even though he's banned from the place, and he's abusing the dealers. That was four o'clock in the morning, and you hear someone yelling in the background because he's winning at craps. The dealer went through the whole scene with Joe, who was improvising, throwing cards back at him and saying the worst possible things. Halfway through the scene, the dealer leaned over to me, and said, "You know, the real guy was much tougher with me—he really was uncontrollable."

I C : *Why does the film have to be so long?*

M S : You have to work through the whole process of these three people who can't get away from each other. Every way they turn they're with each other. It's not even a story about infidelity. It's bad enough that they both were unfaithful to each other—the marriage was in terrible shape as it was—but worse that she starts with Nicky, because Nicky is the muscle. If anybody can get her the money and jewels it's Nicky.

I C : *The most remarkable thing about the film's structure is that you start with Ace being blown up.*

M S : In the very first script we started with the scene of them fighting on the lawn. Then we realised that it's too detailed and didn't create enough dramatic satisfaction at the end of the picture. So Nick and I figured we would start with the car exploding, and he goes up into the air and you see him in slow motion, flying over the flames—like a soul about to take a dive into hell.

I C : *It's like one's whole life passing before you in an extended moment. But you show the explosion three times.*

M S : That's right. I show it three times, in different ways. Finally, the third time, we see it the real way. That is how he remembered it. The actual fellow this is based on told me he saw the flames coming out of the air conditioning unit first, and he didn't know what it could be. Then he looked down and saw his arm on fire and he thought of his kids. The door wasn't properly locked, so he rolled out and was grabbed by two Secret Service men who happened to be casing the joint because of Ronald Reagan's visit the following week. They pulled him aside and it was only when the car went up that he realised it was intentional—at first he'd thought it was an accident. That's why I did all the details. Once you realise you could have been killed, then you never forget those moments.

I C :   *Did the internal structure of the film change a lot as you worked on it?*
M S :   Yes, it did, a lot. And that's where Thelma Schoonmaker came in very strongly, because she hadn't read the script, but just watched the footage come in and was able to take charge of elements that were in the middle, like the documentary aspects. Thelma and I used to edit documentaries 25 years ago, so she's very, very good at that. It is the most harrowing kind of editing you can do because you're never sure of the structure and you're not following a dramatic thread. There's story, but no plot. So what you're following is the beginnings of Ace coming to Vegas, then the beginnings of Nicky in Vegas and the beginning of Nicky and his wife in Vegas and their child. Then Ace is succeeding in Vegas, and what's Nicky doing? He's sandbagging guys. Ace's rise culminates with Nicky being banned. Then that takes us to Nicky rising, which is his montage of robbery—"I'm staying here, you're not getting rid of me." He creates his alternative empire. Then you start to bring the two tracks together. But up to the point at which Nicky builds his own empire we had a lot of reshuffling of scenes and rewriting of voiceover. Finally, we put all the exposition at the beginning. At first we had split it up throughout the film, but it was too little too late, although on the page it looked all right. So in the end we took the explanation of the skim and moved it up front.

I C :   *You've become really interested in voiceover. What does it do for the spectator?*
M S :   There's something interesting about voiceover: it lets you in on the secret thoughts of the characters, or secret observations by an omniscient viewer. And for me it has a wonderful comforting tone of someone telling you a story. And then it has a kind of irony much of the time. Sup-

pose you see two people saying goodnight, and the voiceover says, "They had a wonderful time that evening, but that was the last time before so-and-so died." You're still seeing the person, but the voiceover is telling you they died a week later, and it takes on a resonance, and for me a depth and a sadness, when used at moments like that. The voiceover in this particular film is also open to tirades by Nicky. If you listen to him complaining—about the bosses back home, how he's the one out here, the one in the trenches—then you begin to understand his point of view. Why should I have to work for somebody? Why don't I go into business for myself? You can see the kind of person he is from these tirades in voiceover.

I C : *Did the change in visual style come from working with a new cinematographer, Bob Richardson, or from the subject's needs?*
M S : Well, there are a lot of tracks and zooms; as well as pans and zip-pans. There are also more static angles, cut together very quickly, because of all the information being crammed into the frame. If you did too much moving you wouldn't be able to see what we're trying to show. So that became the style—a kind of documentary.

I C : *You talked about excess as the keynote of Las Vegas, but the most excessive thing is De Niro's wardrobe.*
M S : That was Rita Ryack, who's done a number of films with me, and John Dunn also worked with her. We had 52 changes for Bob, a lot, but in reality the person he's based on had many more.

I C : *It becomes a visible sign of him going off the rails.*
M S : Absolutely. The mustard-yellow suit, the dark navy-blue silk shirt with navy-blue tie, with crimson jacket. We chose the colours very carefully. Our rituals in the morning, once we narrowed down the idea of which outfit, were to choose which shirt, then which tie, then which jewellery. If you look closely, the watch-faces usually match the clothes—even the watch he wears when he turns the ignition on. We were always rushed—I just needed a close-up of him turning on the ignition. Then we look at it through the camera, and we think, oh yes—the wristwatch. So we set the angle to show the watch as well as possible, for the short amount of time it's on. And if you look at the film again, or on laserdisc, you can see a lot

of detail in the frames that we put there. Nicky didn't have that many changes, maybe 20 or 25. And Ginger had about 40 I think.

IC: *You've worked with Dante Ferretti on a number of films. What kind of relationship do you have in terms of planning the overall look of a film?*
MS: The casino we used, the Riviera, looked like the 70s, although it was only built in the late 70s. That was the centrepiece. Then we were trying to find houses that were built in the late 50s or early 60s, which are very rare. There was one house which we finally got, and I laid all my shots there, rehearsed, and then about two weeks later we lost it. Then we had to find another house, and finally it all worked out for the best, because that's the best one we found. It was an era of glitz—a word I heard for the first time in the 70s—and I think you can tell what Dante brings to a film when you just look at the bedroom. Especially in the wide shots, in the scene where she's taken too many pills and she's crying, and he's trying to help her. There's something about the way the bed is elevated and it looks like an imperial bed, a king's or a queen's bed. There's something about the wallpaper—everything, the dishes on the walls—that says a great deal about character. Dante made it regal, not just in bad taste—even though some of it is bad taste—but the quality is good, and that moiré silk headboard is a backdrop for a battleground, a silk battleground.

IC: *I'm interested you say "regal," because I also found myself thinking the film is about a court, with a king who chooses a consort, and what we see is the rise and fall of a little dynasty.*
MS: Exactly. They're on display all the time. Appearance *is* everything, to the point where he didn't want people to smile at him or say hello. You can see it in how he stands and looks around.

IC: *The music for* Casino *uses the same general approach as* GoodFellas, *but the range is broader—like starting with the 'St. Matthew Passion.'*
MS: I guess for me it's the sense of something grand that's been lost. Whether we agree with the morality of it is another matter—I'm not asking you to agree with the morality—but there was the sense of an empire that had been lost, and it needed music worthy of that. The destruction of that city has to have the grandeur of Lucifer being expelled from heaven

for being too proud. Those are all pretty obvious biblical references. But the viewer of the film should be moved by the music. Even though you may not like the people and what they did, they're still human beings and it's a tragedy as far as I'm concerned.

I C : *In* GoodFellas *and again in* Casino *the music becomes another way to direct the viewer, like the voiceover. Each piece of music brings its own associations.*
M S : That's right. There's Brenda Lee singing 'Hurt'; the Velvetones doing "The Glory of Love'—there's a lot, over 55 pieces I think. Then there's the breakdown of style in 'Satisfaction,' from the Stones to Devo. I was very lucky to be able to choose from over 40 years of music and in most cases to be able to get it into the film.

I C : *Is this all coming from you, this setting the musical agenda of the film?*
M S : Very much, yes. We did have one piece planned, but I decided to use it at the end instead of the beginning. Why waste it, because it has an almost religious quality.

I C : *In fact "The House of the Rising Sun" encapsulates the moral of the film.*
M S : Yes, it's a warning: "Oh mother, tell your children not to do what I have done." We kept that for the end. And then lots of early Stones.

I C : *Which you had wanted to use more in* GoodFellas*?*
M S : I did, but I just couldn't fit in any more. It wasn't that we didn't have any room, but certain songs and pieces of music, when you play them against picture, change everything. So it's very, very delicate. In *GoodFellas* the sound is more Phil Spector, while in this picture it's more the Stones, especially 'Can't You Hear Me Knocking?,' which is a key song in the film.

I C : *You follow the same rule as in* GoodFellas *of keeping the music strictly in period?*
M S : Yes, as far as possible. When Ace and Nicky need to talk, after the argument in the desert, they get into a car in the garage to have a private conversation. What would happen? They'd sit in the car and keep the radio on. And what's playing is 'Go Your Own Way' by Fleetwood Mac, which is a key song of the mid-late 70s. No matter what the mood of the

conversation, that music is playing. So we were able to use music at that point that would take you further into the time. The sounds change from the beginning of the film from Louis Prima to Fleetwood Mac. You see, it's not so much the Bach that begins the film as the Louis Prima that cuts it off, creating a strong shock effect. I knew Louis Prima had to be in there, but we came to that later, and I remember the Bach was the first thing I had in mind.

I C : *The Bach comes back at the end, followed by Hoagy Carmichael.*
M S : For the splendour of the destruction of this sin city it has to be Bach. Because the old Vegas is being replaced by something that looks seductive, kiddie-friendly, but it's there to work on the very core of America, the family. Not just the gamblers and the hustlers and the relatively few gangsters who were around, but now it's Ma and Pa Kettle. While the kids watch the Pirate ride, we'll lose your money.

I C : *Why did you quote Delerue's music from Godard's* Contempt?
M S : I liked the sadness of it. And there are other movie themes in the film, like the theme from *Picnic,* over Mr Nance sashaying into the count room — the implication being that it was so easy you could waltz in and waltz right out with the money. The theme from *Picnic* was such a beautiful piece of music that it was played on jukeboxes and Top 40 all the time, so you would always hear it and you still do in Vegas. The other one was 'Walk on the Wild Side,' by Elmer Bernstein and Jimmy Smith. That has a nervous energy that's good, especially in that sequence where we use it, the killing of Anna Scott. Again, it was a very famous piece of music that was taken out of context from the film, and became a part of life in America at the time. Along with these, it seemed interesting to try the *Contempt* music and see what we could do.

I C : *That's also a movie about a man who has a problem in his relationship with his wife.*
M S : He certainly does! After the Bach you can't do anything. The only thing would be *Contempt,* to wipe the slate clean. And then after that the only possible thing is one of the greatest songs ever written, 'Stardust' — the only piece that could sum up the emotions and thoughts about what you've seen.

I C : *What will your next film be?*

M S :   The new film, *Kundun,* is basically written by Melissa Mathison, and it's a very straightforward story of the finding of the Dalai Lama as a young child, in Amdo province of Tibet. It takes you through the maturing of the boy until he was a young man of 18, when he had to make a decision which he knew would be dealing with—literally—the life or death of his own country. What interested me was the story of a man, or a boy, who lives in a society which is totally based on the spirit, and finally, crashing into the twentieth century, they find themselves face to face with a society which is one of the most anti-spiritual ever formed, the Marxist government of the Chinese communists. Mao finally leans over at one point during the Dalai Lama's visit to Beijing and says to him: "You do know that religion is poison, don't you?" At this point he realises that they're all finished. And the only way to save Tibet was for him to leave, and take it with him. What interests me is how a man of non-violence deals with these people—that's ultimately the story. I don't know if we'll be able to pull it all together.

I C : *Where will you shoot it?*

M S :   In Northern India. And after that, I hope to make *Gershwin,* a musical. After spending so much time with those people in Vegas I've got to try something radically different. I can't go back, it's just too much. This was a very consuming film, and the negativity of the people was very difficult. But I'm sure the next one will be difficult for other reasons.

The Art of Vision: Martin Scorsese's *Kundun*

GAVIN SMITH/1998

THE ELUSIVE SEARCH FOR peace, for equilibrium, has always
been latent in the films of Martin Scorsese. But still, what does it mean for
American cinema's undisputed poet laureate of the street to make an "historical epic" about the spiritual coming of age and flight into exile of the
young Dalai Lama after the invasion of feudal Tibet by communist China?
Kundun, which takes its name from the Dalai Lama's formal title, surely
originates in an impulse to get closer to the transcendental source, which
in turn demands the embracing of an Otherness seemingly antithetical to
the milieux and manners of urban America. In those terms *Kundun* is a
worthy soulmate to Jean Renoir's *The River,* which also begins with a
painted image from a tradition that offers a gateway to ancient religious
wisdom. But while Scorsese's film has the same spirit of humanist grace
and the same profoundly moving cumulative power as Renoir's, its extraordinary visualization and mesmerizing textures and patterns carry it into
another realm of formal wonder—a uniquely metaphysical spectacle.

In some ways *Kundun* seems a companion piece to *The Last Temptation
of Christ*: both films begin with the image of a sleeper awakening, both are
about the emergence of dormant divinity in human guise, the protagonists
of both films embark on transformative voyages of discovery. But where the
Christ of *Last Temptation* trades in his low self-esteem for an exultant sense
of revolutionary mission, the Buddha-child Dalai Lama of *Kundun* follows
a reverse trajectory: from egocentric infant to selfless religious statesman.

From *Film Comment*, January/February 1998. Reprinted by permission.

Scorsese's films are almost always constructed around narcissistic protagonists who typically deny or defy reality in order to inhabit increasingly lonely, paranoid fantasies of supremacy and control, sustained by forces of both repression and anarchic violence. Either cut off from redeeming connection to community or oppressed by it, their self-defeat, breakdown, and entropy seem preordained. The disruptive, anguished Christ of *Last Temptation* descends remotely from this tradition. By contrast, *Kundun*'s Dalai Lama is not so much outside this pattern as its benign negative or mirror image. In his splendid isolation, he's the very foundation of the world of the film, but his selfhood is the calm at the eye of the hurricane, propelled by curiosity and the getting of wisdom rather than some compulsive need for gratification and oblivion. What previous Scorsese protagonist has even had the option to follow the path to spiritual enlightenment?

And enlightenment for Scorsese is envisioned, among other things, as Cinema itself: The Dalai Lama's visionary dream states, which manifest themselves with beguiling seamlessness within the action, and his eerie consultations with a hissing Oracle, are supplemented by recourse to a telescope (a surrogate movie camera), and a flickering movie projector that yields glimpses of the Pathé silent *The Hen That Laid the Golden Egg*, a newsreel of the destruction of Hiroshima, and the geopolitically apposite *Henry V*. Through these and other devices, *Kundun* systematically works through a series of plays on vision—both spiritual and sensory—and viewpoint that in some ways represent a culmination of Scorsese's formal inquiries. If all his films are ultimately, inescapably interiorized, their momentum always spiraling relentlessly inward, *Kundun* is the first that exists in the mind's eye from the beginning, that locates the art of vision in a realm where exterior landscape (Tibet, history) and interior landscape (a sand-painting mandala, an infinite capacity for compassion) unite in an epic of the psyche and the spirit.

Sure, it's only a movie. And *Kundun* isn't naïve about its own position in the marketplace. Scorsese is careful to pull the curtain back to sneak a peek at what goes on behind closed doors when powerful men gather to take care of business. And it's certainly business as usual in China, where Mickey Mouse and McDonald's are finishing what Kissinger and Nixon started: after all, the visionary chairman of Disney recently pronounced with characteristic soullessness, "The Chinese don't understand that films are often gone in three weeks." The ephemeral and the enduring—nothing could be more germane to the concerns of *Kundun*. You decide: who'll be lucky to be even a footnote in movie history. Eisner or Scorsese?—G.S.

GAVIN SMITH: *How did this project come to you?*

MARTIN SCORSESE: Jay Maloney, at the time my agent at CAA, sent me Melissa Mathison's script. Usually I have my own projects lined up. I like to do the films I want to do, but then again, the way this business has been going I have to slip in a *Cape Fear* or even a *Casino* to a certain extent—because that wasn't on my agenda, it was on Hollywood's agenda for me. So to bring in a script from outside is almost unheard of. I had known about Melissa though *E.T.* and another project I was involved with very briefly in the late Eighties, something that we talked about but which she didn't have time to write—*Winter's Tale,* from a Mark Helprin book. And she reminded me that I knew her twenty years ago in Los Angeles in the mid-Seventies.

I read the script and liked its simplicity, the childlike nature of it, that it wasn't a treatise on Buddhism or a historical epic in the usual sense. It's just too much to know about Tibet and China and their relationship over the past fifteen hundred years. That was all incidental. What you really dealt with was the child and the child becoming a young boy and the boy becoming a young man—his spiritual upbringing, and this incredible responsibility which he inherits and how he deals with it on the basis of nonviolence. And the concept of him escaping and taking Tibetan culture and religion with him to the rest of the world.

GS: *The journey* Kundun *takes the viewer on is unlike anything you've under-taken previously, and it brings you ultimately to a more emotional place than any of your other films except perhaps* The Age of Innocence.

MS: It is about where you arrive. I must say that we had to go from the end back to the beginning, and it was quite a journey for us, too. First of all, Melissa Mathison's writing: we went through fourteen drafts, and we knew we were on the right track when our last draft resembled the first and second drafts more.

We had a leisurely time rewriting the script, and different concepts came up during our working together. I tried to get more historical detail in; for instance, the 13th Dalai Lama was the first to be photographed, so we began with him, showed the photography session. I was getting into the cultural aspects of it. Finally I realized that scaling down everything and keeping it personal would cut away a lot of the unnecessary political intrigues and, much as I admire them, typical elements of historical epics. And so it made it something very simple.

Something similar happened in the editing. I delineated the sections by the different ages of the Dalai Lama. The first section with the 2-year-old was pretty much straight narrative. In the section with the 5-year-old, who goes to the Potala for the first time and meets the Lord Chamberlain, scenes began to be shuffled around. And the 12-year-old section, same thing. And then in the section with the 18-year-old Dalai Lama, scenes were shuffled more. So we wound up cutting the picture purely on an emotional level, almost like a documentary, so that we shuffled around scenes that were shot for other sections of the picture and also in different locations. And what worked more for us were the dreamlike states rather than narrative scenes.

G S : *Working on these drafts, was there a point when you felt sure this was a film you could make?*
M S : I think the only real concrete thing was when I realized that I should probably try to do everything from the child's point of view. Not just low-angled shots or camera movement that's low-angle, but that as the child is growing, everything around him is seen by him, so the audience shouldn't be privy to a lot of information that the boy is not privy to. And when the Dalai Lama is privy to it, it's incomprehensible to him. Like in a family, if the adults are talking and there's a problem, a child can tell. And there's the fear and uncertainty, the parental figures coming and going—for example, Reting.

I wasn't interested in the romantic, emotional view of Tibet, crystallized over the years in *Lost Horizon*. On "Frontline" last week there was a snide reference to emptyheaded, well-meaning people in Hollywood making films about Tibet, and I really didn't like that. I needed to show that it wasn't Shangri-La, that there were political problems, that monks had guns, there were dungeons and an army. How do you show that without explaining all that was going on between Reting and Taktra, the older teacher? The only way I could do it was to do it through the child's eyes—at least to infer, by the child witnessing these things, and asking, "Where's Reting?" "Well, he's away." "How long's he going to be gone?" "Oh, about three or four years." And then he asks later, "Why do monks have guns?" "Yes, in this case they have guns." In this case they have guns. I liked very much playing on the Kashag wideshot, where they're a little uncomfortable in answering all these questions. There are all kinds of hints in the picture, all the way through. His father was very friendly with Reting.

G S : *Yes, you get these glimpses of the father and you're wondering, Well what's going on here?*

M S : [*Laughs.*] He's having a great time. He prospered well, but he died suddenly. Reting is said to have been very close with the Chinese; that's maybe one of the reasons for finding the boy in Amdo Province, which is practically a Chinese province. They had to make a deal with a Chinese warlord, it cost them a lot of money and took three years to get the kid out of Amdo. There's a lot going on there, and we just wanted to imply it, so that those who know the story can say, Fine, it's accurate, and those who don't know could ask questions, and if they're interested, there's a lot of books on it.

G S : *Did you meet the Dalai Lama?*

M S : I first met with him through Melissa, a brief meeting in Washington, and last year we wound up going to India for final meetings. The week *Age of Innocence* opened, I went to visit Melissa and Harrison Ford at their house in Wyoming with Barbara De Fina and some other associates of mine. The Dalai Lama was also there with his retinue, and we talked for two days. Melissa really had the relationship with him, and what she did was question him about certain specifics, and if something was dreadfully wrong he would say, "Oh, it wasn't that way." Or he would say, "I don't really agree with that so much, but it's totally up to you — that's your prerogative to use if you want." But there were some key political things, like the use of the state seal, which had to be made very clear.

G S : *Had he seen any of your films?*

M S : No. That's why Melissa and everybody were giggling: they wondered which one of my films they should show him. I don't think they came up with anything. But some of the people around him had seen *Last Temptation.*

G S : *To what degree was going into this completely unfamiliar milieu a source of difficulty?*
M S : It was freeing in a way. Once we got to shoot and had those nonactors in the scenes, something about their faces and presence took over. Often the emotional impact goes through them.

G S : *Well, you've said before that films like* GoodFellas *have an almost documentary or anthropological aspect.*
M S : Yes, absolutely. I remember Pauline Kael saying that *GoodFellas* was like *Scarface* without the lead [role]. Well, yeah. That was a criticism, but . . . why should we have a lead? How about the lead being the lifestyle? Well, then you can't identify with anybody. Well, I think you could; there were enough people in that film that you could identify with.

G S : *By structuring the film around one character's point of view, was there a sense of putting on a formal straitjacket, and was that part of the challenge?*
M S : Yes, I think so. To do that, and also imply the culture and imply the spirituality. And enough shots that imply it are layered one to the other, one over the other, that ultimately I was gambling on the emotional impact.

G S : *It's a strange process, making a film and it all being a gamble, having no guarantee that it will culminate in the emotion you're looking for.*
M S : Can't guarantee. No. Thelma [Schoonmaker Powell, Scorsese's editor] was a big help in pulling together certain scenes, giving me ideas and playing around with certain things. We knew that we were out on a limb. It was a process filled with anxiety, to say the least.

G S : *When you live with a film every day for two years, do you go through many stages in terms of your emotional connection to it?*
M S : [*Laughs.*] Yeah. With *King of Comedy*, I wasn't in very good physical shape at the time and I had very great difficulty shooting every day. I've always felt badly over the years that I tried Jerry Lewis's and Robert De Niro's patience a lot by not being physically well enough to pull myself together in the mornings to really know what I was shooting. [*Laughs.*] It was just a bad period in my life. . . .

G S : *When you come to editing, is there a danger of becoming deadened or desensitized?*
M S : No, I don't become dead to it. I get jaded to certain sequences and certain cuts, but if you become dead to it, then the picture's just not working, which means I'm not working. That means I can't make a movie. I get angry, frustrated, excited, very happy, then totally depressed, and anxiety-ridden constantly. It's a situation where you can't sleep well and the process is on your mind constantly. I had a similar thing happen in *Casino.* The writing with Nicholas Pileggi was fraught with anxiety and difficulties, because I tried to create sort of an epic out of America and Hollywood in a way. And it's not tried and true; even though we were still dealing with narrative, we were trying to venture out into a different kind of storytelling, so you don't know where the pitfalls are going to be. Yeah, you take a gamble and say, It's going to be wall-to-wall narration, and the narration's going to be layered this way and that—okay. In *Kundun,* no narration. Simple shots. Not simple in execution, but simply done, where the lighting takes over.

G S : *Can you imagine making a film at this point where there is no gamble?*
M S : No, I'm afraid not. There's got to be a challenge to the storytelling. As far as a straight narrative story, I came close to that in *Cape Fear,* and I really tried, and I found that I don't really have the talent for it. I mean, I don't know where to aim the camera to tell the audience what the plot is, what they should be looking at. I get hung up on something else.

I watch Hitchcock films constantly. I was watching the famous murder scene in *Torn Curtain* the other night. They've stabbed him, they've done all kinds of things, and he's still not going down. It cuts to the woman, a medium shot, and she looks camera left, and it cuts to: the stove. Cuts back to her—it's not a closeup of her face looking. Something abstract happens with the way he's photographing the stove, the angle he takes. It's a subliminal thing. When I direct, a person's looking, I take a closeup of them looking, or a medium shot, and we move in, or a medium closeup and just hold and then we see what they see. Usually you have to get it from their point of view, because I like an angle, I don't shoot head-on. Every time Hitchcock does it, it has a purity.

G S : *In* Kundun, *when they show the young Dalai Lama the painting of the 5th Dalai Lama, you swish pan to the painting and then jump cut in closer. That's your equivalent of that.*

M S : Yeah. A lot of that comes from Kurosawa. In *Yojimbo,* when [Mifune]'s asked "What's your name?," he looks out to the fields and you see a wide-shot of the fields and then a tighter shot of the fields, and he says, "Green Fields."

It's an interesting point—here they are in the Potala. Buddhists. Should the camera be that frenetic? Well, for a child, why not? He may be precocious but he's not into a state of meditation yet. He looks at the 5th Dalai Lama and he's thinking, Where am I? And he's looking at that statue of the 7th Dalai Lama and that's kind of scary.

In *Age of Innocence,* the dissolves as we tracked along tables with all the colors and food became, to me, like little impressionist paintings, very sensuous. It's a dilemma—if you do something like *Age of Innocence,* and the people are so repressed and you're so sensuous in the way that you move the camera or the way you create the images or the impression of the film, maybe that isn't right. Maybe it should be more formal, colder, more objective, I don't know. At the time I thought that was the way to go because he was dying inside and so was she, they had this incredible passion that was coming out in every other way. There's another style of making films like that where everything is rather objective, very simple, very good acting, good scripts, good sets—but there's something missing. There wasn't much missing when William Wyler did it in *The Heiress,* there was something about the way his objective lens had a power, but those were studio sets and he had designed it like a piece of theater almost.

G S : *Did you set out to oppose* Kundun's *form to its spiritual, meditative context?*

M S : We tried to. It depends, scene by scene. When the Dalai Lama is being taught and Taktra says, "Lower your head, you're exhibiting too much pride," each frame is very formal and it's cut in a very straight narrative way. What we found interesting there were things that I didn't know until I got on the set—the way the robes that they were wearing were draped, the kind of mountains or triangles they formed in the frame. When you intercut these shots, it's like an abstract chessgame: three forms, two forms, a single form, always with these robes. And the fact that he's in front of the teachers and they're on either side of him just afforded you an interesting way of presenting things, the formality and the precision of the teaching. It kind of dictated itself.

At the Kalachakra ceremony at the end he says some lines I picked from a book of verses Melissa gave me, *Shanti Deva*: "Just like a dream experience, all that has gone before will not happen again, all that's to come will not happen again." I tried to visually create this kind of thinking—thinking that [says that] right now is not real, you're with me but the past has already happened, as I'm speaking it's the past already. So there are the camera moves that kind of caress the boy, sweeping around. And once again we used a lot of dissolves, which increase the idea of the dream for me, they make it softer. Also, as with *Age of Innocence*, there's the idea to wash the picture with images.

G S : *Did you try to place* Kundun *in relation to any cinematic tradition or genre?*
M S : Oddly enough, I felt comfortable thinking of the picture in terms of Italian neorealism. I don't need to look at a De Sica picture again, or the Rossellinis, but I did, just to put me in a frame of mind. And I looked at a lot of Satyajit Ray, *Pather Panchali,* and *The Music Room* I looked at several times—one of the greatest musicals ever made, a miracle. I looked at the New Chinese films a lot—Zhang, Chen, and particularly Tian Zhuangzhuang's *The Horse Thief,* which was shot in Tibet. If anything, *The Horse Thief* reminded me of what I could not get, but it had a good mood and a very interesting way of approaching the people, I like the spirit of it, so it stayed with me. It was simple, but not objective—it was very emotional.

G S : *On the other hand, were you trying to do without familiar reference points, to take the viewer outside of the kind of realms they've encountered in cinema?*
M S : Exactly: to put a Western audience in the middle of a farmhouse in Amdo in the middle of nowhere in Tibet, and then in the middle of this palace, and not explain any of it. Not to condescend, but to throw you into the middle of a culture and let you sink or swim. If it's alien, if you've never seen anything quite like it, you don't know what they're doing or even what the ceremony is sometimes—whether it's religious, political, or

just eating breakfast—what do you get, how do you hook on to the people? There's only one thing—you hook on to the people, which is what it
should be. That was the other big challenge.

G S :   *There are a lot of links in terms of narrative strategies to* The Last Temptation of Christ—*for instance, the emphasis on the political background and
intrigue. But how would you say the approaches to spirituality differ in each film?*
M S :   Oh God yes, you're right, there's a political story going on there for
hundreds of years before he's thrown in the middle of it. I'm not that
knowledgeable about Buddhism. I'm interested in it because of the way
people behave; I'm interested in people who behave with kindness and
tolerance. I felt more free to explore the idea of kindness, tolerance, and
compassion. In *Last Temptation of Christ* I was bogged down in my own
convolutions of the practical application of Christianity to everyday life.
It's a generality, because there are Christian mystics and Catholic philoso-
phers who have a much cleaner, clearer view of what it is, but it seems like
Christianity is such a worldly religion in a way. Part of what attracted me
to Catholicism was the magical or supernatural aspect of it, which, in a
bad way, could partake of superstition. I think Buddhism has a purer,
clearer approach to living. I may be wrong, but maybe the allure for me to
do the film was to try and find a place in this world where one can live
that way, through tolerance and compassion. And judging by behavior
and those who have studied the religion, there must be something that
gives them more peace of mind than the Western religions. I'm not saying
Western religions are inferior, I'm just saying that the Western world is a
certain way. Here we are sitting here [*indicating his apartment and the video
projector, currently running a film*], there are projected images on the screen,
out there it's *Rear Window,* there are a thousand people, outside I've got to
go to the mix, I've got to fly on a plane to go release the film in Europe—
where does one deal with peace of mind? Are there ways to achieve it?

G S :   *If creativity is a means of achieving deeper understanding of life, did making* Kundun *bring you to a new understanding of your own spiritual life?*
M S :   I think there was a change. Part of it, too, is that my life changed a
great deal during the making of the film: my mother died, other things
happened in my life that were major changes, even to the point that the
dog we had died. And there are certain things you've got to take in life

and . . . it's life. A cycle. That doesn't mean I don't get angry from time to time. I got a little angry during the editing because of the oppression of the film; there it was coming down on me like a train, and it wouldn't stay in line. It wasn't a narrative. Now, I'm telling you how much I don't like to do a narrative, but you know, it does help sometimes! So I was getting very angry, and my editor and my producer bear the brunt of that sometimes— I'll go in and complain and yell and scream. But out of that frustration comes radical thinking: What is wrong? Here there's weakness, here there's weakness, and I'm pointing to the boards above the editing machines that have the names of each scene. Rip this over here, move this over here. Thelma will suggest, "Do this," and I'll say, "Yeah, and if we do that, you can do this, this, and this"—BANG, and it opens up a whole new way of thinking about how to do the picture. Because of the world around me, being a New Yorker, being American, being Western, there's a certain pressure that builds and pushes me to force the picture another way. It comes out of frustration and sometimes it comes out of anger.

G S :   *Was making* Kundun *a kind of purging of the negativity of the subject matter of* Casino?
M S :   Yes, absolutely. I like *Casino* a lot, but the world that it was in was not the healthiest. It's about greed, and there's nothing there anymore, no morality, no spiritual backbone, not even a code. The older Italian guys had a code, but when the money kept coming in, that went out the window. It's a spiritual wasteland. And the architecture of Vegas reflects that—it's very depressing. So there was no doubt that I wanted to get as far away from that as possible.

G S :   *Is artistic creativity in any way a spiritual process for you?*
M S :   There's no doubt. I thought about this for years. I wanted to be a priest for a long time, and then I realized I would be a terrible priest. I think I wanted to be a priest out of ego rather than understanding of what a priest is supposed to be. When I complain on the set or I'm in the editing room and I can't get something to work, when you're traveling so much you don't know where you're going, and every day is a performance in a way, it's true: assuming one believes there's a God, I was meant to do this. I don't know how to say this without sounding silly, but in doing this, it's like an act of faith, or an act of worship. I get angry but I have to think,

What are you doing? This is what you're made for. Why do I have to be there at 11 o'clock? You better be there at 11 o'clock, that's what you do. You have to do this—that's all you do. Necessarily you say, Well you should have a family, you should be able to raise children. Yeah, to a certain extent—I tried that, I wasn't so great at it, and I continue to try to do it now. Both my children are young adults now, so it's a little different.... There's no doubt about it. In fact, at the production meeting in Morocco I explained to everybody that the people in the film are nonactors, but they're Tibetans, and for them, as for us, I must say, the whole picture is a religious act. Remember that on the set, treat these people with respect. They're not real actors—sometimes with an actor, if they're complaining or there are tensions... it's a different way of approaching things, very different than on *Casino,* where it's more comfortable in a way, because Joe Pesci's in his trailer smoking cigars and playing cards in between takes with three or four of his friends—I've seen that image since I was a kid. I know what it is. I know that I can't go there, it's his way of keeping me out of his trailer, because he's smoking, see? I have to yell from across the way. So already you're family, it's a whole other thing. For me, even *Casino*'s a religious act. I can't do anything else. This must be the reason why I'm still breathing. Otherwise, why do it? It's too much trouble, believe me. Go into teaching, whatever. I made enough movies. Why go on? Because apparently that's what I do [*laughs*]. Some may say, I do well or not well at all, or I've gotten better or gotten worse over the years, but even if I get worse, I can't do otherwise, I've got to try and do it. So that's the only thing to keep me going—to know that it's work equaling prayer. That comes from a very basic religious upbringing, it had more to do with the Church and with my parents. So this picture was overtly this way and *Last Temptation* was that way, there's no doubt. It was interdenominational or interfaith. And on this film, it was wonderful: Tibetan film, Catholic making it, written by a Buddhist, shot in a Moslem country, with the call to prayer every day.

G S : *Do certain images evoke or embody the film's spiritual concerns in specific terms, such as the helicopter shot approaching the mountain ridge and the lake below, then the closeups of the lake surface?*
M S : You know what the lake is? There's another way of layering in the story. When they go to receive the vision to find the new Dalai Lama, they do it at a certain lake, surrounded by mountains, a beautiful ice blue color.

Reting and his group would go and sit there and look in the water for days until they saw a vision. That's why when he closes his eyes we go to the lake and see the water rippling and when it dissolves he sees the vision—in a sense it's almost a literalization of seeing the vision. But the audience should not have to know that to be taken there. It's a spiritual experience.

With *Last Temptation* I wasn't totally satisfied. We never quite finished the picture because we had to release it so fast—though that's no excuse. Thelma was saying last night that it would be nice to have another two months of editing. But here I wasn't bogged down by my own Christian concepts—Heaven and Hell, Sin, Redemption—so I was able to feel freer with trying to reconstruct situations or visualize and cut directly to the heart of what I thought were spiritual matters. Because I wasn't encumbered by iconography, maybe the accumulation of scenes, behavior, the people, the way they moved and spoke, all of this along with very often the verses he recites, could get into something that was more pure. Not that one [film] is better than the other, but I felt freer; there's an innocence to it. There's too much guilt in Christianity for me [*laughs*]. How do you show spirituality on film? I don't know, but I do know one thing. You do it with people. And if it's a shot of a face, it's a shot of a face. And those Tibetans moved and thought a certain way—they absorb the spirituality, and they project it. So it was really to get them in the right frame, to compose them as well as I could—that's what I think it is, I think it's them, their reaction, their dignity. Not that they're the only ones in the world who have that, but they behave in a certain way and they know exactly what they're doing, and that's very interesting to me. The spirituality emanates from their belief—they are doing it for real. The ceremonies are real. Whether you believe in religion or not, there's something special about it, it's genuine.

GS: *There's a recurring camera movement in the film in which it seems to turn a corner or pivots around—is that another way of evoking some kind of metaphysical experience?*
MS: Part of that came out of the idea of enclosing the Dalai Lama. When he closes his eyes and envisions the four walls of Norbulinka in the daytime, he says, "I see a safe journey," then he closes his eyes again and sees the mountains and then says, "I see a safe return." The walls of Norbulinka literally enclose him. That's what he has to leave and what he has to return

to. And the mountains enclose the country of Tibet. The idea of being closed off and special, a special place. . . .

GS: *So the camera is tracing the outline of that enclosure?*
MS: Literally, yes, it's a metaphor. That's the impression of Tibet, and really, he is Tibet. If he doesn't return physically to that country, he's still there as far as I'm concerned, because he has taken the country and the culture and the religion and brought it out to the West. So inside of him are the mountains and the walls.

GS: *The film's other characteristic camera movement is the 180-degree pan from subject to object, from viewer to point of view, or vice versa. Why that emphasis?*
MS: Well, it's tying them together, literally in the same frame. I tried to have more of that, but it didn't wind up in the final cut. Rather than straight cuts, I thought it would be more organic if the two were in the same shot ideally. In some cases we cheat, we pan the camera and dissolve in the middle. I remember something Melissa said when were talking about Buddhism and listening to Joseph Campbell talking about the idea of My Brother's Keeper and the idea of being made up of molecules and atoms—where do mine really end and yours begin? We're all really part of each other, and when there's an action there's a reaction, whether that's physical or moral. That's what I became very much aware of, dealing with this subject matter. And I tried to link everything together if I could. Basically we're all one, that's the idea.

GS: *Why is one of the first moments of the film—the 2-year-old Dalai Lama waking up and then a horizontal POV showing his parents' legs walking through the frame, then the POV righting itself vertically—reprised near the end?*
MS: That was in Melissa's original script. She has the boy sleeping, and I imagined starting on the closed eye of the boy, not both eyes, and then coming up and twirling the camera so that his face is then full frame and vertical, but: it would look slightly different because actually he's lying down. This is the face of the Buddha who's been reborn. Originally in her script there were some shots of mountains in the beginning; I said, "I don't want that because everybody would expect that," so she thought of sand paintings. And in order to make that just a little more interesting we took one shot of a mountain which becomes a sand painting, and then we

go into a mandala—but the mandala's inside him in a way, in his eye, in his head. He's the center of the mandala—and you twirl out from the mandala, from his eye, and we see his point of view of his mother and father in the morning, and basically a humble farmhouse. I thought it would be interesting to do it literally from his point of view; I always remember that shot in Nicholas Ray's *Rebel Without a Cause,* where James Dean is lying on the couch and he sees his father approaching him. A lot of people have done it, but it's interesting, it immediately puts you right inside the kid's point of view. Then Melissa had at the end that he's sick and he's sleeping, and he has a waking dream in which he thinks he's back in the farmhouse and he sees himself asleep. Basically what she meant to point up was that his last night in Tibet was spent in a farmhouse that was very similar to the one he was born in, so he went full circle, and the humble origins are always there.

G S : *Is there an attempt to link the notion of spiritual vision to vision in the everyday sense—in other words, eyesight, looking, point of view? For instance, all the moments where the Dalai Lama's point of view is filtered through curtains, robes, or fabric, or the way the telescope becomes a central object in his world.*

M S : Basically, it's about the boy becoming cognizant of the world around him, and that means people's behavior, politics, how people live daily life in the city of Lhasa—and he can only see that through the telescope. He's only given a glimpse of the everyday life of his people through fractured viewing. It's not complete. He's not allowed out, it's just not done. Dying to get out. Again, this played right into what I wanted to do with how much he could see. If it's one-third of a CinemaScope frame, that's what he can see and he's removed from that—and yet he's the spiritual leader of the country.

G S : *Does his telescope represent to him what the movie camera represents to you, in terms of connection to the world?*

M S : I had to understand, in a way, to find a common thread between myself and the boy so that I could explore what his perception was. But in my world, the movie camera moves me away from . . . my movie camera really goes right back to when I was raised on the Lower East Side. Because

of asthma and other reasons, in some ways to stay alive on all levels—
there are many different ways, you don't have to be killed to be dead—I
had to sometimes distance myself. The objectivity was almost like using a
movie camera. I would hear my father or my uncles and aunts talking
about movies, they loved movies, but in discussing the plot of a film, even
liking it very much, they would always say, "Well, of course, in real life
this would have happened and that would have happened—but they can't
show that in the movies." And I never forgot those discussions at night
around the dinner table or during the holidays, and I always thought, Gee,
it would be great to show what they said couldn't be shown [*laughs*]. And
that's what happened. "Ah, they can't show that, they would never do
that. . . ." Well, yeah—but why not?

They appreciate it so much, they loved it so much. It was my own link,
being loved by my mother and father, because they took me to the movies
all the time. So the movies I make now are mainly for them. Both of them
would have liked this one. It's too bad they couldn't see it this time.

G S : *Where did the inspiration come from for one of the film's most extraordinary dream images—the long crane up from the Dalai Lama standing in
a sea of dead monks?*
M S : When I got the script it was pretty much there. This is a good example of the Dalai Lama's input into the picture through Melissa. He had
nightmares, and this was a vivid nightmare of his. The other was the
blood in the fish pool. This was a way of showing the violence. This is
what it's really about.

G S : *That image reminded me that you were originally going to direct*
Schindler's List.
M S : Yes, that's right. I had an interest in that because of the amazing
amount of anti-Semitism and hatred that showed itself when *Last Temptation of Christ* was about to come out, where the right-wing Christian
groups immediately attacked Jews. It was a total shock to me. I grew up
with Jews; I understood the Holocaust, but I didn't fully understand the
depth of such hatred. I know about it other ways in America, I know about
Gentleman's Agreement and street stuff, and there's a lot of it in *Casino*. So
my involvement in that project in a way was to give a little back.

G S : *So you sort of gave the film its first push.*

M S : It really started with Sydney Pollack, who was involved with Steven [Spielberg] and another writer. And then I got Steve Zaillian. Ultimately it was a project close to Steven's heart the way *Last Temptation* was to mine, and finally he's the one who should have done it. I'm a history buff and I know it goes back to the Crusades and 132 A.D. when Jerusalem was destroyed again, I know all that, you can see documentaries and read books, but you have to experience it a little, I think. And also the idea that the guy was considered by everybody else to be a total bum and a lowlife and he's a great hero—so what makes a man? What makes him good and decent? Could a decent man behave in an uncouth manner?

G S : Kundun, *just like* Casino, Taxi Driver, *and* Raging Bull, *ends with the main character alone with himself, sealed off from the world.*

M S : Yeah, he's gone through something and he's achieved something. He's achieved becoming. He's become truly the spiritual leader of his country.

G S : *Where do you find yourself in that image?*

M S : I tried to when I did *Raging Bull,* when he's looking in the mirror and reciting the speech from *On the Waterfront.* I knew that I had to get to his place. Knowing Jake personally at that time, he was a very interesting man, he was very subdued. It's an odd thing. Sometimes I'll look at an animal and the animal is at peace. Sometimes fighters are like that, real fighters who get in the ring every day. Part of the brutality, part of being human, I don't know what it is, but Jake had gone through a terrible journey and come out the other side alive and reached some kind of understanding of himself. That's what I saw in him and that's what ultimately made me make the picture.

I got into that character ultimately and it was really myself when I made the movie and realized what the hell I was doing and stopped fooling around and trying to kill myself and make the movie. Because I was interested in dying basically, that's all. I was having a good time doing it, until it got really serious—then I got scared [*laughs*]. So it's a miracle I'm sitting here now talking to you. That's what the quote at the end of *Raging Bull* means—it's about myself, not Jake. Apparently it's been misunderstood, I didn't think anyone was going to see the movie, so I put this quote up there to remind myself that people judge people a certain way, particularly Jake La Motta, they say this and they say that, but all I know is that I found myself through him. I found an understanding and I got a little more tolerant with myself. Not a lot.

He was a major factor in that. Bob De Niro did his thing in the film, and so of course Bob had a lot to do with it because he had to be him. And so it became part of myself and part of De Niro and part of Jake, and a certain kind of man.

G S : *You make it sound like a mystical experience.*
M S : There's no doubt something odd happened to me when I was doing it. Not odd . . . but something happened, yeah, I died and I came back to life. I really thought I wasn't going to make many more movies, just something from time to time. I also didn't know the way the world was going with cinema, too, how it was going to change. I knew *Star Wars* had changed things, but *E.T.* hadn't happened yet. . . . So we have Jake with himself in the room at the end, and that's where I really wanted to be, but I really couldn't get there. I was on the first step making that film. With *King of Comedy* I felt I'd slipped again. It went back and forth until finally I was able to get back on track with *Last Temptation of Christ.* Then it became a joke because nobody really looked at the picture, except Vincent Canby, who said it was the longest picture ever made, which was really sweet.

G S : *Are you near that point now with* Kundun?
M S : Yes I am.

G S : *And now you're going to plunge back into the inferno.*
M S : Yes, I know. It's a little scary, but the trick is, when you're back in the inferno, what is it about? What's the other angle you're going to take on it? I'm working on a film about Dean Martin with Nick Pileggi now, which deals with American show business from the Forties to Seventies, a long picture. Hollywood, nightclubs, that sort of thing—a world that always allures me. It deals with Martin and Lewis, Martin's participation in the Rat Pack, and then finally his coming to terms with himself, just basically going home and sitting in front of the TV. There's something very interesting about him. I'm always interested in doing something with music, with Hollywood—but without the narration style that we had before. There we know: epic style. Lots of detail, money, popularity, celebrity—really about

celebrity. I'll always be excited by that, like with *King of Comedy.* Maybe it's part of why I make movies: one of the first things that you learn as a moviegoer is that an actor up on a screen is a celebrity — that's the venue that takes you into that world. I didn't know there was a director when I was 7, that there was somebody behind the camera doing those things. It was just up there on the screen. So show business is a world I know very well and I always feel comfortable there. If there's another way to tell a story in that world, I'll try to do that. There's a way to do it. Quite honestly I'm not that interested in doing another gangster picture, in terms of violence and that sort of thing.

G S : *But show business in that period is a gangster business.*
M S : It really is. But it works a little differently. Very often performers are court jesters or troubadours for the gangsters, whether they like it or not, because the gangsters own the places. That's part of the world they're in. If you really spell out what a person is and this is why they did this and why they did that, I don't think it's very interesting. But there's this guy up there and he represents something and he went through a lot, and touched upon a lot of different areas of American life, right in the center of the century. I love him, I love Sinatra, and that's my period, that's when I was coming of age. Basically, even though *Mean Streets* pretends to be the Seventies, it's really 1963, before The Beatles. And so it's America, the Fifties, when things change, right up to 1963 with the assassination. . . . America changes, they represent a certain thing. A lot of people in show business behave in a way that others might perceive as bad, but these are performers, and I have a lot of respect for them. They've got to go out on a stage, they're not acting. If you're a singer or, particularly, a comic, the audience responds to you personally, not you as a character. If they don't like you, they don't like you. So you have to have a lot of guts. People say, "Oh they want applause, they want to be loved" — yeah, they want to be loved, most people do. This is their way of getting it, but they give back a lot. Okay, Jerry Lewis was a certain way, Dean Martin was a certain way, but they all have the same need.

G S : *Which they deny.*
M S : Oh yeah. Not Lewis so much, Lewis was honest about it. Dean Martin loved to give the impression that it was so easy — it wasn't. Especially

this extraordinary relationship with Jerry Lewis. But he wanted to be cool. These men were our gods at the time.

G S : *So it's another religious epic.*
M S : I'm afraid so. I hope the boys don't mind [*laughs*]. Even when things are tight—you could do a picture about me in the Seventies, throwing things through windows, I won't like it, or even now to a certain extent, but I understand being judged by people.

G S : *Did you know Martin?*
M S : No. Sammy Davis I actually did know. He was very nice to me in the mid-Seventies in L.A.; he gave me a lot of advice.

G S : *Sinatra?*
M S : No. I spoke to him once on the phone and saw him once at an event for a friend and said hello, that was it. We're also working on one about George Gershwin, which John Guare has written. Again, the idea of American show business, the whole idea of music coming out of Tin Pan Alley and the Brill Building area is just amazing to me, the Jewish immigrant creating American popular music, and how that came out of a need to belong, to assimilate—writing songs about Swanee, what is this? Creating the illusion of the South! It was fantastic. Thank God I was born at a time when I could appreciate that and also get the full impact of the beginning of rock and roll. Now I don't listen to much popular or rock music— although some of it's pretty good, I was there already. The last thing I got really excited about was punk rock; I thought that was interesting because it was still angry. I liked that. *Gangs of New York* [an as yet unrealized period epic written by Jay Cocks about street gangs] was going to be set in the 1840s and I was going to use The Clash on the soundtrack. They were concerned that it would be anachronistic—I said, "No, that's the point [*laughs*]!" But the picture was too big. I still may do it one of these days. It would be interesting to have that beat.

G S : *It's striking how many of your films are about people who create these illusions and then inhabit them and get consumed by them. Even in* GoodFellas—
M S : Oh yeah, the Copacabana club is a total fantasy. I'd been on the streetcorner a lot when I was young. I love monologists, people telling sto-

ries, comics, because I lived in an area where I saw men hold sway over groups of people by telling them stories, like a storyteller in front of a campfire in prehistoric times. With great design and rhythm, real stories, somewhat embellished. Literally, *GoodFellas* is the way I heard stories told on the streetcorner, totally, with the asides and everything. *Casino* takes that one further, now you're in a bank where deals are being made. You realize that a lot of the guys I'd be with—I'm not talking about a person becoming used to themselves in a positive way, accepting a certain spiritual nature, but I find in every culture the same people on the corner. The same way as with Archer in *Age of Innocence*—there's no street corner, but there are these place settings, this dinnerware and these special ceremonies. That's his streetcorner. And he makes the decision to stay there. I think all my life has been wanting to get out. And I'm interested in a lot of the people who "got out" and what they took with them. Because without that streetcorner, I have nothing. I may have the Church, but the Church was also the streetcorner. I don't go down there very often now that my parents are gone, but that's what I am. For some reason I make these movies, something happened, I went another way—but I'm still there.

Everything Is Form

AMY TAUBIN/1998

AMY TAUBIN: *I remember talking to you a few years ago, just before you started* Casino *(1995). You were already committed to* Kundun, *and I was trying to figure out why you wanted to make it. I had the impression then that your commitment was to the Dalai Lama, that he had had an extraordinarily seductive effect on you.*

MARTIN SCORSESE: I started getting interested in him in 1989, when he won the Nobel Peace Prize. Before that I didn't hear anything about Tibet. Tibet isn't interesting to us, they aren't bombing anyone. But then I began seeing him on television a little bit. And I was beginning to understand the scope of the situation, and the way he was behaving fascinated me. Meaning that I think he was doing the right thing. I think he behaves the way we all should behave. And then I met him with Melissa, and what happens is that you want to be like him. And I don't find that with many clerics in my own religion. I always wanted to make a film about priests and nuns who've had to overcome their own pride in order to deal with people, to have true compassion. In the modern world, they're bogged down a lot of the time. Because the social problems, the emotional problems, the psychological problems are so rampant in our society now, particularly after the breakdown of the two superpowers, and with the world getting smaller. It's a kind of spiritual and moral anarchy. So they're just trying to hold everything together. Between baptising a baby and performing last rites on a homeless man cut in half by a train when he fell on the tracks—I mean,

From *Sight & Sound,* February 1998. Reprinted by permission.

how much can you take? So when I see anybody who really practises compassion, kindness and tolerance, which most of our religions preach but don't practise, and who practises the most revolutionary concept—nonviolence—that's extraordinary. So that's what attracted me to him.

The Dalai Lama is in the process of handling one of the greatest catastrophes and tragedies, and he's handling it in an extraordinary way. And I think anyone like that should be supported. I grew up in an area where the people, even though they try their best, are prone to the other way, which is destruction. So whenever I see anyone constructive—I mean basically the whole country has been smashed and all these pieces have splattered out into the diaspora, but they're still alive. The younger generation is having problems continuing the culture, but it's still alive, and who said Tibetan Buddhism was going to continue to exist the way it existed for 1,400 years? It changes. But that's what I saw in him. I'm still Catholic, I'm not a Buddhist.

AT: *Did you ever try to meditate?*
MS: I find it very hard to meditate. But even though I got angry a lot doing the film—because of the weather, because the horses weren't hitting their marks, I make a lot of jokes about it but the horses were a problem, they don't care, they're not interested—I found that there was a way you could tap into this meditation, to puncture this incredible package that you carry around of anger and semimadness, and let it seep out, and just remain calm. There's ways of doing it, and I used it a lot. The actual meditation is very hard for me. I even had that problem when I was an altar boy—you have to meditate. I didn't know what to think about. Well, the idea is not to think about anything. I didn't know that. Bertolucci called me when I was about to start shooting, and he said, "Have you learned that everything is form and form is emptiness?" No, I'm always the last to know. But thank God, I've got this information now [*laughs*].

AT: Kundun *is one of the rare films where the meaning is embodied in the form. When the Dalai Lama says that line about past, present and future being one—it's Buddhism, but it's also about editing. It sounds like Dziga Vertov: "The Kino-eye is a victory over time."*
MS: We shot the film according to the script, but then in the editing Thelma [Schoonmaker] and I really shuffled things around. I worked on

the script with Melissa for a couple of years. At the fourteenth draft, we realised we were back in drafts one and two. I had tried to bring in some historical aspects and then realised we didn't need that. It would only clutter it up and make it conventional: even though some masterpieces, such as *Lawrence of Arabia,* have been made as historical epics, it's still a conventional form. I wanted to capture the essence of their spirit: who are they, their culture and their religion? So we went back to the early drafts, but made it even more from the Dalai Lama's point of view. The only way I could do the film — because I'm not a Buddhist and I'm not an authority on Tibetan history — was to stay with the people. Stay with the kid [who ages from two to 24 in the film] and literally see things from his point of view.

And then Thelma and I looked at the first cut, and I said, "We have to shuffle scenes." We started shuffling scenes around without worrying about what monastery they were in and, to a certain extent, what part of the world they were in. And we turned certain scenes into dreams without marking where the dream started and ended. We just went with the emotion of the thing. There was a storyline but we just kept the basics of it. And as I did that, I realised that that's the way to go in order to create a sense of Tibet — and not as a Shangri-La. I don't know, I may be naïve, but there are some Tibetan mystics who push the limits of the spiritual and go further. That doesn't mean there aren't Catholics or Christians or Jews or Muslims who do that. But Tibet was closed in by these mountains and they couldn't go outside, so they went inside. And there's got to be something we can learn from that. So Thelma and I kept playing around with the picture, but it was very anxiety-provoking because you don't know how it's going to turn out. You're flying without a net.

AT: *How long did it take you to edit?*
MS: The real heavy work was done from January to August last year, but we worked into October. The excruciating part was from August to October. Because it's not traditional drama, we worried about how long will an audience hold. Will it hold till after he gets back from Peking [about two-thirds of the way through the movie], because all the violence comes after he gets back from Peking? And there's no conflict until the Chinese invade [about half-way through] and then the conflict is so overwhelming that you can only deal with it on a personal or spiritual level. We could have

shown conflicts within the Dalai Lama's family or political conflicts with Retin Rinpoche [the Lama who discovers the Dalai Lama] who actually tried a *coup d'état*. That guy had a racket going. Human beings, there's always corruption. But we wanted to take the audience and immerse them in this very serene world, and then disrupt it. But you've got to be immersed first.

I don't want to make movies anymore like *Cape Fear* (1991) that stick to a conventional plot. I'm getting bored, I don't like working for someone else. Doing someone else's movie is a hard job. But *Cape Fear* turned out to make the most money, so it gave me *The Age of Innocence,* it gave me this picture, it did a lot. But working for other people—I was talking to Brian De Palma over the holidays. And he said, "Do you find you're getting a little bored with the entire process?" At our age, sometimes, yeah. That's why each project has to be special for me. This one was very special. Even though the form itself was more created in the editing and in the writing rather than the shooting. But I had nonactors which was a very different thing for me. And that kept my interest.

A T : *They're all amazing. The young man who plays the oldest Dalai Lama gives one of the best performances of the year. And it's not that he's doing an impersonation.*

M S : I went with what was genuine in that young man, Thuthob [Tenzin Thuthob Tsarong]. And I couldn't do Mao [Robert Lin] as an impersonation either. The only thing I could do with Mao was to do what the Dalai Lama told me about him—that Mao spoke very slowly, as if every word was of great import. And he moved slowly, I think because of the medication he took, because his lungs had been ruined before the Long March. And that moment where he says, "Religion is poison." That's exactly what the Dalai Lama told us he said, and how Mao moved closer to him on the couch. And that the Dalai Lama couldn't look at him any more, he just looked at Mao's shiny shoes and knew that that man is just going to wipe everything away.

A T : *At that moment, Mao could have been a Hollywood mogul saying, "Art is poison."*

M S : I wasn't thinking of that. It was more that he was an incredible gangster. I always had a morbid fascination with gangsters. Some of them were my role models despite what my father told me. Obviously, I'm interested

in the consolidation of power. But the Chinese never expected that the
Dalai Lama would do so much after he got out.

A T : *Did you rehearse the cast as if they were actors?*
M S :   Yeah. Two weeks before we started shooting, we did readings. The
Tibetans also worked on the lines themselves, and they'd even drilled the
kids. They had a lot at stake, they represented their whole culture. Some
only had a few lines and that's all they could do because they were very
self-conscious. I thought of Robert Flaherty—*Elephant Boy* (1937), or
Louisiana Story (1948)—or Rossellini's *Flowers of Saint Francis* (1950) where
he actually put strings on the non-actors. And he'd pull a string and the
person would say a line. To a certain extent, there's an awkwardness about
them that I really like. What was very good was that in the first week-and-
a-half the ice was broken, because we had to deal with the two-year-old in
the breakfast scene. So we rehearsed and rehearsed and by the end of five
days they understood about hitting marks, about repeating lines, about
making sure the light was hitting them in a certain way. The idea was
making them as comfortable as possible and not treating them like props.
They aren't actors, they're not even a group of people who said it might be
fun to make a movie for five months. No, they are really living it, they are
it, their very being is there in the frame. They directed the picture, in a
sense. They forced me to see things in a certain way—framing, camera
movements, and when not to move but to hold on those faces and the
incredible turmoil and emotion that's going on beneath the surface. They
grounded me. There were little things I didn't know they were going to do.
Like the throwing of the scarves at the end. I thought they were meditat-
ing but then they said, "And now we throw scarves." Great, but let's get a
close-up of the mother throwing the scarf, and let's do it in three different
speeds, and let's track on it. It was that kind of fun. It was so enjoyable to
do. And that kid Kunga [Tulku Jamyang Kunga Tenzin, who plays the
five-year-old Dalai Lama] was amazing. He was taking over the production.
He was doing me. I'd see him walking with his hands in his pockets, and
I'd say that kid is doing me. And then the 12-year-old [Gyurme Tethong]
had a different presence. And the 18-year-old [Tsarong]. But we'd have to
watch him; sometimes he'd walk and he'd shuffle because he's an 18-year-
old kid. And we'd say no, the Dalai Lama doesn't shuffle. But what a
presence.

AT: *And the beautiful stuff he does with his glasses. Because his near-sighted-ness becomes part of the character, but it's also a metaphor, it relates to the way you use the telescope. How when he's inside Tibet, he's trying to see out past the mountains, and then in the very last shot, when he's exiled, how he tries to see back in.*

MS: Exactly, that thing with the eye and the lens.

AT: *What has the response from the Tibetans been?*

MS: So far, very positive. They were very moved. Maybe it is the kind of film that's made more for people who already agree with the subject. I wanted to make a film for everybody to see, but also for them, something that they could feel was an expression of their culture, as if they made it themselves. It wasn't a matter of going in and getting the real lowdown on the sociological set-up, on the real politics of Tibet. That's another movie. And there are lots of movies you could make. You could make a movie on just the fall of Lhasa day by day. There's a wonderful book on that and I've read all that stuff, but I wasn't interested in that.

AT: *It seems as if there are more dissolves in this film than in any of your oth-ers. Those fast dissolves are what makes it seem like memory.*

MS: I knew from the beginning that some shots were going to wind up supering or dissolving. I knew it when I was shooting. Otherwise, it would have to be too concrete. We tried to think of the whole picture as memory. For example, Dante [Ferretti, the production designer] built a lot of the rooms as accurately as possible. But one of them—the room that has the giant Buddha, the room where he's enthroned—that was part imagina-tion. It's the impression of a child. Last night I was in Corona, Queens, that's where I was born. We lived there from 1942 to 1950. And I've never been back there since. So we drove around to the little two-family house that I grew up in. And it was dark, so it was very strange. And yet I imme-diately said, "That's the house." It's still there. It came out of the darkness but I knew the look of the brick. It was amazing. So we tried to give the impression of the child's memory through the whole look of the film.

AT: *There's always a lot of music in your films, but this one is almost an opera.*

MS: I don't really know much about modern music. But after I saw Paul Schrader's *Mishima: A Life in Four Chapters* (1985) and then Godfrey Reggio's

Koyaanisqatsi (1983), I said that one day I would love to be able to make a film that would cry out for a score by Philip Glass. And then I went to a few Tibetan benefits in New York and he was always performing. I like the emotional power of his music, and yet the music is intellectually disciplined. Before I went to shoot the film, I sat down with him and I said I'm thinking of music here, here and here. He sent me about ten cues. I called him up and told him this is perfect, just keep going in that direction. And he finally admitted that he had waited 20 years to do this. I knew that the last 30 minutes of the picture had to build emotionally with the music. It's got to go. But then we had some real problems. Because we had to build there and then build again in the last shot when he looks through the telescope. While we were editing, he kept writing to our rough cut. We kept telling him not to because we're going to change things. And he said it didn't matter. So every time we changed it, he changed it. And it went back and forth until we came up with what we have in the film.

A T :   *It's all of a piece—you're a westerner and you've directed this film from a western point of view, and Philip's music is a western version of the Tibetan music that has always been important to him. But still, I could have used less of his arpeggio noodling.*
M S :   We put that in. He felt it was boring, but Thelma and I felt it gave a certain emotional drive to those sections of the film. Sometimes it may be too much music, sometimes not enough, I don't know. But that's what we finally, how shall I put it, we didn't finish the picture, we kind of abandoned it. That's it, I'm not touching another frame. Although I just looked at a new print of the dupe negative yesterday and I'm still perfecting some of the colour, in the last reel particularly.

A T :   *Tell me technically about what everyone refers to as the* Gone with the Wind *shot—the nightmare image of the Dalai Lama surrounded by thousands of slain monks. Is it digital? Because the camera doesn't only seem to pull up and out, it seems also to go more wide angle—like a combination of Renaissance perspective and a flat Tibetan art perspective.*
M S :   It gets wider, but that's the actual shot. We didn't go wider digitally; we digitally duplicated groups of monks. The actual shot is just a circle of monks around him, and a lot of empty ground around them. So we digitally rephotographed the monks and put them in. To start with, there were

200 monks. That dream and the dream of the blood in the fishpond were nightmares the Dalai Lama actually had at that time, and he told them to Melissa. And I said, that's enough, we don't need armies coming in. And of course, the puff of blood coming into the fishpond is this incredible moment in Mario Bava's *Blood and Black Lace* (1964) [*laughs fiendishly*], when the woman is in the bathtub and she's dead and she's got black hair, a white face, and bright red lips, and it's a white bathtub and this blood pumps up.

A T :   *The response to the film is very peculiar.*
M S :   Totally odd. Melissa and myself, Barbara [DeFina, the producer] and Thelma, we're all very, what can I say, "This is what life is and it's the business" — it's very interesting. God. I think that for some of the critics, the film isn't pure enough. It isn't *Flowers of Saint Francis*. It doesn't feel like you're on the edge of documentary. One is aware of the big machine that made this film; it couldn't be other than an American movie. So that makes the purists crazy. And on the other hand, it's not dramatic enough to satisfy the ones who eat up big studio pictures. But what interests me about it is that it's such a hybrid, and if you can't have hybrids, then nothing will develop. By not letting in the influence of other cultures, of foreign films, we're now feeding off our own entrails in this country. We have to have hybrids, to attempt to go somewhere else, maybe make some mistakes or maybe not, and we'll see later on. And also we got thrown in with what the press calls 'Tibetan chic.' Hollywood goes Tibet. Which is so cynical. It's a disgrace. Because some people have a heart big enough to want to help out, the press makes fun of them. An absolute disgrace.

A T :   *And the other stupid line is that* Kundun *isn't critical enough of Tibet, as if the fact that Tibet was a theocracy excused that China marched in and murdered over a million people.*
M S :   Apparently that's the case. The Tibetans had a bad system of government and it had to be changed. In changing it, did you have to wipe out so many people and destroy almost every monastery? Is that necessary? Well look, we have a lot of business to do with China so we have to be careful. If we weren't doing business with China, they'd be the worst — Mao would be like the Ayatollah. It's a farce, in a country that seven years ago went to war for oil, blood for oil, so we could take an extra few flights to LA, or basically, for the Texas oil machine. It's a total disgrace. But what's

MANY FILM fans,
fraid of sentiment, make fun
f old bad movies (*Mystery*
cience Theatre, etc.) rather
17) the g... *Journey with Martinnes*. As
Through American Movies, a
poetic, uncynical, four-hour
tour of films that Scorsese
adores, and of the directors
behind them. "Conductors of
visual symphonies," he calls his
beloved "auteurs."

I talked to Scorsese once
when, a long time ago, we met
after he liked something I'd
written. We conversed excited-
y about old movies we both
oved, with John Ford's *The
Searchers* at the center of our
enthusiasm. A *Personal Journey*
eels like a second private chat.
t's extraordinary how many
odd films he champions that I
lso swear by: *The Cat People,
The Land of the Pharaohs,
Gun Crazy.*

But anyone seeing this film
vill feel Scorsese is talking
ntimately to him or her. The
ommentary is so contagious,
he choice of clips so mar-
elous. Watching almost
traight through, I kept mur-
muring, "God, I *love* movies!"
Thanks, Marty.

ism of the press about people getting involved with
isney stood up to the Chinese and said, "Yes, we are
king the film," there was this piece in *Time*. It said
the life story of the Dalai Lama, and then, in dashes,
ckbuster." Who are these people? Show me a face. To
blockbuster"! But Richard Corliss gave us a good
ne through for us on *Last Temptation* too. But the
o wrote for *Time* on *Last Temptation*—that was dis-
ed on my wall, it's so appalling—and I know for a
rite it without seeing the film. Then he saw it and
ughing because it is what it is. I'm just getting this
ic off my chest and how it's grist for the mill. But
hat's a blockbuster," well it's *not* a blockbuster, OK.
different from other pictures, we're trying other
ockbuster, it's not *Lawrence of Arabia*. It's something
e of Arabia when he gets up on top of the train and
d silhouettes against the sun. Maybe it's that part
m not saying it's as good, but you know, maybe it's
But this cynicism about Tibet, you wouldn't do it
ch, you wouldn't do it with Judaism, you wouldn't
, not in the press. It's very bad attitude. And it's like,
everybody's heard about Tibet now for four months, it's enough. It's like we
have blinkers on, and when it's Asians, you can't take them that seriously.

AT: *And David Denby's review in* New York Magazine, *saying that maybe you
just can't make a movie about Buddhism because it's too passive. What is he
saying? That you're only allowed to make action movies?*
MS: It's like this conversation I had with Elia Kazan a few years ago. He
said, "Yes, I can make pictures with plots and the normal traditional
action. But what if you do something that's passive? Can you make a film
about passive characters, where inaction is action? Then you really see if
you can go inside the mind and the heart." Maybe we didn't do it in this
picture completely. I know for some people, we did. How many years more
must we just do act one, act two, act three? Polish cinema has done something else. Kieslowski has. And Russian cinema. There's a new Sokurov film
that Paul Schrader told me about [*Mother and Son*]. This is also cinema.
Why can't America make cinema like that? And I know we're also dealing

with the marketplace, with LA. It's a hard town. There was a time when we were worried that Disney wouldn't stay with the picture. But they have and they've been very supportive. They even showed up at the premiere in LA. I turned around, and there was studio head Joe Roth, and he took pictures with us.

AT: *Given what's happened, if you had it to do again, would you?*
MS: Absolutely. This is what you live for. I wish I could find another project like this one day.